MVFOL

THE HUNT FOR MARTIN BORMANN

THE TRUTH

By the same author:

Bloody Aachen
Patton
Death of a Division
Bounce the Rhine
First Blood
The March on London
Slaughter over Sicily
The Last Assault
Kommando
Werewolf
Death on a Distant Frontier

THE HUNT FOR MARTIN BORMANN
THE TRUTH

by

Charles Whiting

LEO COOPER
LONDON

First published in the United States of America by
Ballantine Books Inc. in 1973.

First published in Great Britain in this revised edition
in 1996 by LEO COOPER
190 Shaftesbury Avenue, London WC2H 8JL
an imprint of
Pen & Sword Books Ltd
47 Church Street, Barnsley, South Yorkshire S70 2AS

ISBN 0 85052 527 6

Contents

ACKNOWLEDGEMENTS

My own hunt for Martin Bormann, some twenty-odd years ago now, took me to two continents and six countries. In the end I discovered what really happened to the 'Brown Eminence', the power behind Hitler's throne. But all my personal efforts to discover the truth would have been of little avail without the help and co-operation of many men and women (some of whom had no reason to help me) of several different nationalities. In particular, I would like to thank the following. In the United Kingdom, Professor Hugh Trevor-Roper (now Lord Dacre) of Oxford University, Anthony Terry, formerly foreign correspondent of the London *Sunday Times,* and my good friend and fellow author, Mr Eric Taylor. In the United States Mr James McGovern, formerly of the CIA, and Mr Tom Stubbs of the US Air Force. In Germany the former Grand Admiral Karl Doenitz, Herr Jochen von Lang, once of *Stern* magazine, Herr Heinz Hoehne, formerly of *Der Spiegel*, Messrs Heim and Zander, both ex-members of Bormann's staff, Dr Ernst Hanfstaengl, who had once been Hitler's press spokesman, Frau Lina Heydrich, the widow of Reinhard Heydrich, the man with the 'iron heart', as Hitler described him, Bormann's brother, Albert, Herr and Frau Herman Buch, brother and sister-in-law of Gerda Bormann, the former editor of the Nazi paper *Westfaelischer Beobachter*, Herr Schwaeber, and the ex-Gauleiters of Düsseldorf and Augsburg, Herren Florian and Wahl. In Spain the man who had once rescued Mussolini and whom Eisenhower called in 1945, 'The most wanted man in Europe' – Otto Skorzeny.

And in other countries a few more, who'd better not be named.

CHRONOLOGY:
THE HUNT FOR MARTIN BORMANN
(1945–1973)

May–October 1945: Rügen, Denmark; Flensburg, northern Germany.

July 1946: House-to-house search in Munich.

1947: Bormann in Sydney.

1947: Bormann in Egypt.

March 1947: American intelligence looks for Bormann in Spain.

April 1947: British intelligence looks for Bormann in Egypt.

July 1947: Rumors reach Europe that Bormann is living at the foot of the Andes.

1948: SS Obergruppenführer Berger states Bormann is a Russian agent and has fled to Russia.

March 1949: Frankfurter Allgemeine Zeitung reports a Russian officer saw Bormann in Soviet hospital in May 1945.

August 1949: Bormann reported to be farmhand in southern Tyrol (Italy).

November 1949: Bormann "seen" in Munich.

April 1950: Danish newspaper reports Bormann is in South Africa.

October 1950: The German emigrant Hesslein reports Bormann is in Chile.

1952: Bormann reportedly seen in Bolzano, Italy, in May 1945.

July 1952: Reported in Tangiers.

February 1953: Again stories that Bormann is in Roman monastery.

October 1955: Heinz Linge, Hitler's valet, returned from Soviet POW camp, states Bormann is dead.

April 1956: Otto Günsche, also from Hitler's staff, returns to report Bormann dead.

1958: Bormann "seen" in Ecuador.

1960: "Seen" in Argentina.

1960: Bormann reported sought by Israeli secret service since 1952 in South America.

January 1961: Reported in Spain.

April 1961: Senior District Attorney Fritz Bauer, Frankfurt, states "Bormann is still alive!"

May 1961: Bormann lives in Brazil.

November 1961: Bormann now in Chile?

1962: Erich Steinhauer (a fake Bormann) arrested in Berlin.

1962: Juan Keller (a supposed Bormann) arrested in Spain.

June 1962: Bormann reportedly escaped from Germany by U-boat. Went to Argentina. Visits Germany once every year.

1964: Israeli secret service reportedly hunting Bormann in Peru.

March 1964: "Richard Bormann" arrested in Brazil.

March 1964: Bormann's "grave", discovered in Paraguay (died February 1959).

March 1964: Simon Wiesenthal: "Bormann is alive in South America!"

April 1964: Czech Jaroslav Dedic states: "I buried Bormann in Berlin in 1945."

July 1964: The "Bormann grave" in East Berlin empty.

November 1964: German government offers 100,000 marks reward for the apprehension of Martin Bormann.

May 1965: Bormann reported in South America again.

July 1965: Fresh attempts fail to find Bormann's grave in the Invaliden Strasse, Berlin.

October 1965: Ex-Israeli secret agent Friedmann offers to "deliver" Bormann for $50,000.

1966: Bormann living in an Indian tribe in South American Mato Grosso jungle.

1967: Bormann reported in Kolonie Waldner 555 in South America.

1968: Ex-CIA agent James McGovern: "Bormann is dead."

1971: Ex-Chief of German Intelligence Gen. Reinhard Gehlen reports Bormann was living in southern Russia until 1967.

December 13, 1971: German government gives up search for Martin Bormann.

1972: East German police authorities order another search for Bormann's grave. It ends in failure.

December 7/8th, 1972: Two skeletons found by builders excavating near original search area. One fits Bormann's physical characteristics including a healed collar bone break.

September 24, 1973: German authorities officially announce that Bormann is dead.

PROLOGUE

The facts are now clear, and if myths, like the truth, depend on evidence, we are safe. But myths are not like truth; they are the triumph of credulity over evidence. The form of a myth is indeed externally conditioned by facts; there is a minimum of evidence with which it must comply, if it is to live; but once lip-service has been paid to that undeniable minimum, the human mind is free to indulge in its infinite capacity for self-deception.

HUGH TREVOR-ROPER, 1947

INTRODUCTION
TO THE 1996 EDITION

On the night of 1/2 May, 1945, a fat man began to run. That terrifying night the undersized 45-year-old Nazi, with the pugnacious chin of a run-to-seed boxer started the greatest adventure of his long career. Against the blood-red backdrop of a dying Berlin, he and other Nazi *Prominenz* ran for their lives. One by one they were killed or apprehended by the victorious Russians. But Bormann and his little group still kept on. They knew the terrible revenge the "Ivans" would take on them if they were captured.

Then it happened. They fell into the hands of a Russian patrol, which had built a huge bonfire in the middle of one of the ruined streets. Most of the *Prominenz* and the SS troopers with them surrendered. They had no choice. But Bormann and Hitler's doctor, Ludwig Stumpfegger, sidled out of the glare of the flames. Like Bormann, Stumpfegger, who had conducted terrible "experiments" in the concentration camps, knew surrender meant death. They started to run once more. Perhaps there was still a chance for them. Thus Martin Bormann, the power behind Hitler's throne, disappeared from history.

But in death – and he was soon to die – he became famous. Before that May of 1945, when Hitler's vaunted Thousand Year Reich died violently, the German public had known nothing of him. Indeed, when Allied Intelligence started to look for him so that he could be brought to trial at Nuremburg (just in case he *was* still alive), they possessed only one photograph of him. For if Martin Bormann loved power, he also cherished his anonymity. The Roman poet Juvenal has described his type well: "He could cut a throat with a whisper". That was the way Martin Bormann worked. He remained in the background, working his way up the ladder until he became Hitler's right-hand man by blackening the reputations of those who stood in his way through innuendo and suggestion.

Once the Third Reich had collapsed after only twelve years, the hunt for the surviving leaders began. One by one they were captured. It wasn't difficult to recognize them. Every ordinary Tommy and GI knew what they looked like. They had watched them strutting and threatening on the newsreels for years. Some committed suicide. Others ended their lives on the gallows after the Nuremburg Trials or spent the rest of their days in Spandau.

But the "man in the shadows", Hitler's brown eminence*, the man Hitler himself called "my eyes and ears", could not be found. Had he died in Berlin that night or was he still running? The Allies had to be sure. After all Bormann, who was sentenced to death *in absentia* at Nuremburg, was the last of the *Prominenz* not to be accounted for. The great hunt was on!

The British started it. They were followed by the Americans. The Russians also took a hand. In time the case, still unsolved, was passed over to the Germans. In the end private individuals, journalists, policemen, professional Nazi hunters, writers, intelligence agents from half a score of nations sought the missing Nazi.

The search for Martin Bormann became the biggest manhunt the world has ever known with all the elements of a real-life detective story. It was a story of treachery, double-dealing and deceit in exotic locations, usually very inaccessible, right across the globe. It had the flavour of high society, for bishops, princesses, even presidents of countries, were involved. And it had touches of the bizarre and eccentric, mandatory to the detective story ever since Wilkie Collins set the ball rolling. But what writer could imagine such a villain, who in real life kept strings of salami hidden behind cupboards at Hitler's HQ so that he could eat a slice on the sly and who had a fetish for brown boots which he bought by the dozen?

It was such an impossible story. What writer would dare create a wanted man searched for for fifty years, from the

---

* Brown on account of the uniform the Party bosses wore.

Norwegian fiords to the jungles of Paraguay; and who finally (according to the most recent book on him) ended his days peacefully in Surrey, England, in 1989? No editor would accept such a fantastic story for publication. However, the story of the hunt for Martin Bormann is not fiction. It is *fact*!

Here then is the story of that fat man who began running on that night of 1/2 May, 1945 to start the greatest manhunt the world has ever known – THE HUNT FOR MARTIN BORMANN: THE TRUTH.

Charles Whiting,
York.
August 1996.

I

The Birth of a Legend

I hope the bastard fries in hell!

– HERMANN GOERING, 1945

1

Smoke lay heavy over the shattered city. The Russian rockets crashed down with frightening regularity on the last of the German defences, throwing huge chunks of mortar and brick into the air. Here and there a German 88-mm. cannon cracked in reply, its shell tearing the sky apart with a sound like a huge piece of canvas being ripped open. But in the main the handful of SS men defending the half-square mile of brick rubble which was all that was left of Nazi Berlin – the capital of an empire which was planned to last a thousand years and had survived twelve – had solely their rifles and machine guns with which to fight back against the tremendous Soviet arms superiority.

The middle-aged colonel ran through the smoke, the dirty bedsheet clutched in one hand, the field-cable drum in the other. His face and field-grey uniform were dirty and there was a rip in his breeches, which bore the thick red stripe of the General Staff. The Russian officer next to him panted something and the German colonel dropped instinctively. Not a moment too soon. A Spandau machine-gun – somewhere to their front – cut the air with a high-pitched, vicious burr. A second later it was answered by the slower chant of a Russian machine gun. Colonel von Dufving crouched behind a shattered wall, panting heavily. In spite of the coldness of that May morning, he felt the sweat trickle warmly down his face and his thick uniform clung to him unpleasantly. He felt tired, too; tremendously tired. He dearly would have liked to lie down in the smoking rubble and sleep; sleep forever. But there was no time for sleep. He had to carry out his mission; he had to get back to the *Führerbunker* alive with his news about the Russian terms for the surrender of the survivors of this worst debacle in Germany's history.

The evil-smelling Russian officer in his mud-coloured uniform ordered *"Davai!"*[1] and seized the German colonel's arm. The machine guns had stopped firing again. They could go on. Dufving got to his feet. Body bent, tensed for the blow of steel that must come at any moment, he ran on at the Russian's side. The landscape reminded him of the French battlefields of World War I: death and destruction everywhere.

Now they were approaching the outer line of the German defences. Behind him the cable snaked out across the shell-littered terrain. It was beginning to pull hard. He cursed and hoped that it would be long enough. Otherwise, how were they going to establish direct contact with the Russians? At least in this manner Goebbels could talk to the Russian officers on the telephone without actually giving himself over to their tender mercies in person.

Suddenly the Russian next to him groaned and fell heavily to the ground. A hundred yards off, the SS snipers had opened up. The fanatical last-ditch defenders of the *Führerbunker* picked off anybody who ventured into the "death zone" around the place. The German colonel hesitated and looked down at the man on the ground, his face suddenly deathly pale with the shock and outrage at what had just been done to his defenceless body. Then he told himself he had no time to tend to the Russian. His mission was all-important. He ran on.

When he was within fifty yards of the German line, the cable ran out. He dropped the drum with a curse. Waving his bedsheet frantically, he stumbled on down the shellpocked street, littered with the bodies of the fallen, their arms thrown out in the extravagant postures of the violently done to death. Now he could see a German officer – probably one of SS General Mohnke's men – observing him through a pair of binoculars. He felt the sweat break out all over his body. Although he had crossed over to the Russian lines on highest orders, he knew that if he made one false move, the SS would have no hesitation in shooting him out of hand; they were doomed anyway once they fell into Russian hands. The sniper fire stopped suddenly. Probably the man with binoculars had recognized his uniform. Moments later he stumbled into the German lines, panting hard and exhausted. The officer with

---

[1] Roughly, "Come on."

4

the binoculars strode up to him. He was an SS man, as van Dufving had surmised.

"You're under arrest!" the officer snapped.

"What lunacy is this?" von Dufving raged, telling himself that everyone had gone mad. Quickly he explained his mission and demanded to be connected with the *Führerbunker* at once. But the hard-bitten SS men, with their machine pistols slung around their necks and their dark-ringed eyes filled with the bitter vision of the inevitable death which would be their fate, were taking no more orders from the *Wehrmacht* to which the colonel belonged.

"Only SS orders are valid here," one of them snapped, his mouth like a rat trap under the heavy steel helmet.

"Then get me Mohnke," von Dufving cried, naming their commander, the ex-leader of the *Leibstandarte*.[2]

After some haggling, General Mohnke was brought to the telephone at the other end and ordered his men to let Dufving through. He went on. The last act in the tremendous drama of the Thousand-Year Reich was about to commence.

Von Dufving clattered down the dirty wet concrete staircase into the *Führerbunker* and squeezed his way through the tight, low corridors packed with the frightened civilians and officials who had once been the most mighty in the land. Now they crouched in the narrow ill-lit corridors piled with foodstuffs and supplies right up to the roof, jerking with every fresh detonation or drinking themselves into insensibility.

Finally he fought his way into Minister Goebbels's room. The tiny, sallow-faced Minister of Propaganda, now the most senior official in Berlin,[3] was calm in contrast with everyone around him. He stumped across the tiny concrete cell with his clubfoot, shook the exhausted von Dufving's hand in the Continental fashion and then let him tell his story of General Krebs's (von Dufving's chief) negotiations with the Russian army commanders. Krebs had failed, von Dufving explained in quick excited phrases. The Russian generals were not interested in any terms save one – unconditional surrender.

---

[2] Adolf Hitler's bodyguard division, the premier formation of the SS.
[3] Hitler had committed suicide a few hours before.

Goebbels's calm vanished when von Dufving spoke the words. His sallow face flushed angrily. "*I shall never agree to that!*" he began. "Why—"

Von Dufving did not hear the rest, for just at that moment the total weight of the Russian artillery bombardment descended upon the bunker. The place rocked with the impact and tiny pieces of mortar showered down from the roof. It seemed as if every gun in Berlin had been directed at the last Nazi fortress. A shaken Dufving surmised that General Krebs's disclosure to the Russians of the place's location was the cause of the sudden bombardment.

Gradually it eased off. In the meantime Goebbels had regained his calm. Sitting there in the sparsely furnished concrete cell lit by a single naked bulb in the ceiling, the onetime pupil of the Jesuits and the only intellectual in the party hierarchy spoke clearly and courteously to the middle-aged colonel. "How long can we hold out?" he asked.

"Two days at the most. After that we shall be reduced to isolated pockets," the soldier replied.

Goebbels nodded his dark head as he absorbed the information. Then he asked if General Krebs might have some success in obtaining better terms if he talked with the over-all Russian commander General Chuikov. Von Dufving shook his head. "I don't think so," he said. "The Russians kept insisting on immediate surrender all the time I was there."

Goebbels bit his thin bottom lip and considered what to do next. While he did so, van Dufving stared beyond him through the open door into the corridor. It was clear to the regular soldier who had what he called "a nose for these things" that a panic was about to break out in the bunker. He could read the helplessness of the situation in the wide blank-staring eyes of the civilians who were hurrying back and forth on completely purposeless missions. "Helplessness and panic could be read everywhere," he remembered years later.

Reluctantly Goebbels gave in. "Go and bring Krebs back," he told the other man wearily, "I want to hear what he himself has to say." The little clubfooted Doctor of Philosophy, who reputedly had tossed a coin so many years ago to decide whether he should join the National Socialist or Communist Party knew that his last hope to negotiate with the Russians had vanished; he had lost the toss. Now he knew what his next move would have to be: he would have to pay his last tribute in blood to the master he had served so loyally for twenty years. He would take the life of his wife, six children and himself and allow himself to be burned on the funeral pyre that had done the same service for his master Adolf Hitler which was still smouldering in the scorched, blackened Chancellery garden outside. On this first day of May, 1945, there was no way out for him save death – violent death.

It was midday.

Discipline had begun to collapse in the bunker the day before the Leader and his mistress Eva Braun committed suicide. Now the last surviving remnants of self-control broke down completely. For years the members of Hitler's entourage had carefully hidden their appetites from their master: no alcohol, no meat, no sex. They had been what one cynical observer of the scene had called contemptuously "fried sausage vegetarians"; they pretended to adhere to Hitler's vegetarianism,[4] but secretly stuffed themselves with food. Now they broke into the supplies and gorged themselves on choice tidbits and alcohol.

Frau Junge, one of Hitler's secretaries, who had taken down the Leader's last will and testament, wandered through the damp, labyrinthine passages of the bunker looking for the last food for the Goebbels children, soon to die at their fanatical gnomelike father's bidding. She noted: "It was a world peopled with zombies, whose sole thought was to sing and laugh. They had appropriated some liquor reserves and were stuffing themselves with rolls and caviar. An erotic fever seemed to have taken possession of everyone – everywhere. Even on a dentist's chair I saw bodies locked in lascivious embraces. The women had discarded all modesty and were freely exposing their private parts."

But not all the several hundred men and women were content just to indulge in one last gigantic erotic fling before

---

[4] Hitler was a vegetarian, disdained alcohol, save an occasional glass of champagne and a local Austrian herbal schnapps; and although he kept a mistress, he pretended to the outer world to be uninterested in a sexual relationship with a woman.

their world fell apart. There were several score who determined to escape *now* before death and dissolution caught up with them. But the problem remained *how and to where*.

The exit to the *Führerbunker* lay in the garden at the corner of the famous "Street of the Ministries," the Wilhelmstrasse, and the somewhat narrow Vossstrasse, opposite the front of the so-called New Chancellery. Opposite this lay the burned-out Hotel Kaiserhof, which had been Hitler's staff headquarters until 1933, and Goebbels's Propaganda Ministry.

Now the question was this May midday, which direction should be taken by any escape group? Did a breakthrough to the south via the Wilhelmstrasse offer any possibility of success? The answer was no. The Russians were dug in there in force. What about to the west then, via the burning Tiergarten? Again the answer was negative. To the east, then? Again, no. The only possible escape route open was to the north. In the bunker, those intent on escape believed that if they were able to work their way through the mass of destroyed buildings for some four hundred yards along the famous Unter den Linden eastward, then turn north along a right angle running down the Friedrichstrasse, they might be able to reach the River Spree and break through the Russian lines and head westward to the positions held by Grand Admiral Dönitz,[5] who had just been appointed Hitler's successor. Two parties had already broken out in that direction and, as far as the excitedly planning bunker inhabitants knew, the men who had attempted to escape two days before had been successful.

As that hectic May afternoon passed in drinking and planning, a rough-and-ready escape route was worked out. In all, some four hundred persons decided to make the attempt. The group was made up, in the main, of soldiers and officers of the SS Panzer Grenadier Division *Nordland*, the survivors of *Kampfgruppe Bärenfänger* (a battle group named after its commander, Major General Bärenfänger), several companies of an Air Force field division (or what was left of them), and

---

[5] On the other side of the River Elbe, some eighty miles away as the crow flies.

a few men of the Spanish "Blue Division."[6]

Under the cover of these fighting men, whose main strength was their last three tanks, several half-tracks, and armoured reconnaissance cars, several dozen secretaries, flunkies, and high officials of Hitler's immediate entourage would try to break out along the route already mentioned. They would rally at the Friedrichstrasse railway station, where they would make the attempt to fight their way through the Russian front line and head for the River Spree.

Josef Goebbels, the last of Hitler's major followers, was preparing to commit suicide, telling his adjutant, Gunther Schwaegermann: "Everything is lost. I shall die together with my wife and children. You will burn my body." Meanwhile, those who did not feel any obligation to follow their Führer to perdition prepared for their escape, loading their weapons, packing a few bits and pieces of essential clothing, filling their pockets with what food they could grab.

At the neighbouring Propaganda Ministry, one of Goebbels's loyal servants, long-time radio commentator Hans Fritzsche, protested when he heard of the decision to break out. He went to his boss, the dark-haired, full-faced, exceedingly clever Secretary of State, Dr. Werner Naumann (of whom we are going to hear much more later), and complained bitterly about the breakout. "It's pure madness," he spluttered, his face red with rage at the thought that the party *Prominenz* were leaving the little people like himself to deal with the Russians once they had captured the government administration area, which was inevitable. Why couldn't the *Bonzen* (bigwigs) stay behind and tackle the Russians themselves?

In his anger at what he considered their betrayal he told smooth-talking Naumann, who had been Goebbels's right-hand man those last few years, that he would go to the Russians himself and surrender the whole administrative block to them. Naumann bit his lip and launched into a quick defense of his action in attempting to break out. "Give us time to get away," he pleaded urgently. Fritzsche, the man who had never been at a loss for words all his adult life, hesitated a moment; then he made his conditions. "Only if Martin

---

[6] The one contribution made by Generalissimo Franco to the German war effort during World War II. The division fought mainly in Russia.

Bormann gives the order that the *Werewolf*[7] does not carry out any more offensive actions."

Naumann gave his assent, and the two propaganda men hurried into the garden of the Chancellery. It was full of burning paper fragments as top-secret documents were burned; and occasionally, the hiss of a fist-sized piece of red-hot steel from a Russian mortar bomb was heard. There was not much time left. They would have to make the breakout soon, if they were going to have any hope at all of succeeding.

The man they were looking for was standing in the shelter of a ruined wall, his hard, cunning eyes directed to the west and the safety of the headquarters of the man whom he had appointed Hitler's successor the day before when he had found his beloved master dead by his own hand and had cried out in horrified dismay, "*What shall we do without him!*"

Martin Bormann, the longtime Secretary of the Leader, was a thickset, undersized man with a protruding chin and heavy, powerful shoulders; he had the appearance, accentuated by his gross stomach, of a boxer gone to seed. Now, in preparation for the breakout, he was dressed in the field grey of a general of the *Waffen SS*,[8] devoid of any decorations save the "Blood Order," coveted in Party circles, which he had won twenty years before for his part in a political murder. Over this he had slung a long leather coat which came down to his jack-booted ankles. In his hand he carried a steel helmet.

With unusual courtesy for a man who for so long had been able to make and break other men at the drop of a hat, he listened to the radio commentator's demand, which was punctuated by the soft hush and obscene plop of Russian mortar bombs landing close by. Completely without counter-argument he gave in to Fritzsche's demand. There would be no further Werewolf murders or sabotage actions. Suddenly Fritzsche

---

[7] A Nazi underground movement started in November of 1944. Its aim was to carry out sabotage and other paramilitary operations behind the Allied lines. Its only major achievement was the assassination of the Allied-appointed Burgomaster of Aachen in March, 1945. See C. Whiting, *Hitler's Werewolves*, (New York, Stein and Day, 1972).

[8] The "Armed SS," the fighting arm of the Black Guards, who had nothing to do with the other SS formation which guarded concentration camps.

realized that "MB," as he had always been known by his intimates at Hitler's court during his heyday, was frightened – damnably frightened. He would do anything to save his skin. *Reichsleiter Martin Bormann was going to get out of this mess alive – come what may.*

2

In the bunker the leaders of the various escape groups were giving out their final instructions. There were six groups in all, which would attempt to break out under cover of darkness between 8:45 and 10:00 P.M. At 9:00 exactly, the first group would make a desperate run for the nearest subway station and walk along the tracks in comparative safety until they reached the Friedrichstrasse station. Here they would surface and take their chance of running the Russian barrage, breaking through the Russian lines and crossing the River Spree, the main barrier on their way to Dönitz and safety.

In his private quarters Goebbels had already had his six children poisoned. Dr. Naumann went in to pay his last respects. Goebbels thanked him for his loyal service, but his beautiful wife Magda (who had more than once threatened to leave her undersized husband on account of his womanising yet who had now decided to die with him), could not speak, overcome at the thought of her dead children. She reached out her hand to the pale-faced official in the SS uniform. Naumann bent low and kissed it. Unemotionally, Goebbels remarked he was going to walk up the steps to the Chancellery garden where Hitler lay so that his friends wouldn't have to carry him. He shook hands with Naumann for a last time. The latter watched the gnomelike, deformed Reichsminister as if mesmerized as he dragged himself up the steep concrete stairs for the last time. Then abruptly there was a shot. Naumann started as if he had been hit himself. Then he shook himself out of his daze. Two orderlies clattered up the stairs after Goebbels. Naumann knew what their task was; they were to pour gasoline over the dead "Minister of Hate" and burn his body so that the Russians could not lay their hands on him.

As the oily yellow-and-red flames started to lick viciously up about the body, the first group, led by General Walter Mohnke of the SS and Colonel Gunsche, Hitler's six-foot-five SS adjutant, stole out of the bunker. Most of the group, which included secretaries and Hitler's favourite cook, had not been outside the bunker for over seventytwo hours. The sight which met their eyes hit them in the stomach almost literally. The once-proud government area was now a waste of brick rubble, covered with the smoke of war, illuminated now and again by the violent red of a shellburst or the cold icy light of a Very flare. But they had no time to consider the drastic, terrible change. Under the oaths and urgent pleas of their leaders they hurried through the night toward the sharp crackle of small-arms fire. One by one they crawled through a narrow hole in the Chancellery ruins near the corner of the Wilhelmstrasse and Vossstrasse (Mohnke had spotted it earlier in the day). Then in single file, cook, secretary, politician, admiral, and ordinary soldier dashed across two hundred yards of burning rubble until they reached the subway station entrance opposite the Hotel Kaiserhof.

Mohnke counted them as they came in breathing hard and, in the case of the women, scared out of their wits by the deadly gauntlet of fire they had just run. Then he ushered them down the dark slippery steps of the subway.

The first group of escapers was underway.

Soon thereafter, at 2200 hours, the Naumann group assembled, ready to break out. Bormann approached the propaganda man and asked him if he could accompany his group. Naumann nodded his agreement and told the smaller man. "But keep close behind me all the time." Bormann said he would and the men and women lined up nervously, ready for the order to go.

While they waited, Secretary Traudl Junge stared in at Hitler's room for the last time. His uniform coat and gold-braided cap were still hanging in the open closet. Almost instinctively she went into the room and through it to Eva Braun's bedroom. The favourite silver fox coat of Hitler's longtime mistress still hung there. She fingered the E.B. initials which were in the shape of a four-leaf clover and thought they had not brought the Munich girl much luck. Then she turned and joined the rest again.

Bormann strode across to his own secretary, the jackboots he had favoured ever since his days as a farm manager so long ago making a lot of noise on the naked concrete. He took her hand and for a moment could not speak. Else Krüger – everyone called her Krügerchen (little Krüger) – wondered if at last emotion had penetrated even his hard heart. He shook her hand. It was the last time she was to see him, but she did not know that. She felt she would see him again if and when they got through to Dönitz, and she knew his ankle-length coat concealed a copy of Hitler's last will and testament, which he would show to Admiral Dönitz as proof of his claim to take a major part in any government formed by the former U-boat chief.

"Well, then, good-bye," he said slowly. "I don't think there's much sense in it. I'll try though, but I don't think I'll get through." And with that, he turned and joined the rest.

It was a strangely fatalistic statement from "MB," Else thought. He had never known when to give up all his life; it had been the secret of his success all these years working close to "AH."[1] Then she dismissed the thought from her mind and hurried to her own group.

Lieutenant Colonel Erich Kempka, Hitler's youngish, tough SS private chauffeur, had managed to get his group out of the Friedrichstrasse Station. But just as he had been ready to make a dash for the River Spree they had been hit by a severe Russian artillery barrage. He had cursed violently and ordered them to run for shelter to the ruins of the Admiral Palace Theatre. Now it was nearly two o'clock on the morning of May 2, and the barrage had died away. His pugnacious jaw thrust out hard under his camouflaged helmet, the SS man crept out of his shelter alone to attempt to assess the situation.

A terrible picture met his eyes. In front of him lay the Weidendamm Bridge running over the River Spree. Beyond that was a tank barrier. As he recalled later: "I could hear several shots echoing hollowly. Otherwise the place was as still as death." But all the same, the SS officer knew that sudden

---

[1]Hitler's staff always called him "AH" among themselves.

death lurked darkly on the other side of that barrier. The bodies of the dead and dying men who had tried to advance beyond it lay thick on the cobbles. He made his way cautiously to the handful of SS men defending the barrier. They told him the houses beyond it were full of Russian snipers and infantry armed with their round-barrelled grease guns. Some troops, they reported, had managed to break through successfully, but the great majority hadn't gone more than a dozen metres before they had been mowed down by concentrated enemy fire.

Kempka advanced closer to the barrier which marked the farthest German outpost, and, looking beyond the still shapes of the dead huddled in the gutters, he could make out the gigantic bonfire the Russians kept burning at the far end of the Friedrichstrasse. Its purpose was obvious; the Russians would have a perfect target if anyone tried to break through. The flames would magnify silhouettes to gigantic proportions on the shattered walls which bordered the street on both sides. Sickened by the sight and shocked for a while into inactivity, he doubled back to the Admiralspalast to confer with his group about what to do next.

Time passed. It was now 0200 hours. Erich Kempka was back at his lookout post in the doorway of the Admiralspalast, straining his eyes against the darkness. waiting for an opportune moment to make the dash for the tank barrier and the gauntlet of fire which lay beyond. Suddenly his heart skipped a beat. A small group of uniformed figures were making their way cautiously in his direction, hugging the houses in a short file, as if they were expecting trouble at any moment.

The SS officer's finger crooked around the trigger of his machine pistol. A cold trail of fear traced its way icily down the small of his back. Were they a Russian patrol? Abruptly he relaxed. He recognized the uniform of the first man. It was German! He shouted softly to them. They started, stopped, and then hurried in his direction.

Now, against the dull red of the Russian bonfire at the far end of the street, he recognized them all. They were his former comrades from the bunker: in front there was Bormann in his brown leather coat; behind him came Naumann, also in uniform; and then Dr. Stumpfegger, Hitler's doctor; one-armed Hitler Youth Leader Axmann; Goebbels's adjutant

Schwaegermann; Baur, Hitler's pilot (with Hitler's favourite portrait of Frederick the Great securely tied around his waist under his uniform jacket); and a couple of others.

Hurriedly they crowded together in the doorway while Kempka told them what he knew of the situation beyond the tank barrier. Bormann and Naumann listened attentively, then the former said that the only way they could break out was under the cover of tanks. It was their last and only chance. Kempka shook his head. "It's no good," he told them firmly. "There isn't a German tank left in the whole of Berlin."

He was wrong. A short while later the little group of escapees heard the rusty rattle of tracks and squeaking of brakes that heralded the tanks. They pressed themselves into the shadows. But their caution was unnecessary. The twin blue flames that came from the shadowy iron monsters' exhausts indicated to the trained soldiers among them that the tanks weren't Russian T-34s as they feared, but German Panzers.

There were three of them – Tigers – armed with great over-hanging cannon. Behind them came three half-tracked armoured personnel carriers. Kempka ran out into the street, joyous with relief. Their appearance, he recalled, "was like a miracle."

"Who are you and who is in charge?" he asked.

Out of the darkness a voice answered, "Obersturmführer Hansen!"

They were a section of the SS Division Nordland, which, with its wounded piled high and bloody in the halftracks, was trying to break through the Russian cordon. As young officer Hansen explained, these six vehicles and their crew were all that was left of his decimated company.

Kempka absorbed the information, then rapped out orders of his own. After all, he was a colonel in the SS. His group would break out on foot. The tanks would give them cover. They would form a *Traube*[2] behind the first vehicle once the tank barrier had been cleared. The tanks would then cover them as far as the Ziegelstrasse. After that it was every man for himself.

---

[2] Literally, "grape": a military expression for the infantry tail formed behind a tank during a tank-infantry attack.

In spite of his obvious exhaustion, the young SS officer snapped out a smart "*Jawohl*," and the "grapes" behind the three tanks and the half-tracks began to form up. Behind the lead tank, to its left, Naumann led the way. Close behind him came Bormann, then Dr. Stumpfegger, with Colonel Kempka bringing up the rear.

Cautiously they passed the barrier. Slowly they crawled forward, with the four men bent expectantly near the roaring metallic giant which stank of diesel, its long hooded cannon swinging slowly from side to side like a primeval monster seeking out its prey. Their nerves, as Kempka recalls today, "were taut and ready to break. Every one of us knew that this was a matter of life or death."

They were coming ever closer to the two blocks of houses on each side, which Kempka knew from the defenders of the tank barrier contained the Russian snipers. It was now or never. He felt the hair stand out at the back of his head. Now they were parallel with the first block. Still no Russian fire; no angry shout of surprise and hail of bullets. Perhaps they were going to get away with it after all. Perhaps . . .

The darkness was abruptly torn apart. Tracer zigzagged angrily through the night. A machine gun started to chatter. Rifle fire joined in. Suddenly the night was hideous again with the deathly music of war. Then there was a harsh, frightening explosion. The tank came to an abrupt halt. It shuddered momentarily. A violent bright yellow flame shot up from its side. Kempka screamed out loud as Dr. Stumpfegger slammed into him. Before everything went black before his eyes, he had one last terrible sight of Bormann and Naumann being raised high into the air by some huge invisible hand. Then he fell to the ground and lost consciousness.

His nostrils still full of the acrid smoke of the explosion, Kempka slowly opened his eyes. Somewhere he could hear something burning; he could smell the unpleasant odour of diesel and hear the crackle of flames (it was the tank). But he couldn't see anything. He blinked his eyes several times. Then he rubbed them hard. Still nothing was visible, save bright yellow-and-red stars which shot past his eyeballs in a crazy, frustrating pattern. "*My God*," he told himself with a sob, "*I'm blind!*" Frantically he touched his body all over. He could not find a wound or the hot, frightening dampness of his own blood. He seemed to be all right. But his eyes . . .

Yet in spite of his panic he knew now that he must get away from the spot where he lay. He probably was in full view of the Russian snipers, illuminated as far as he knew by the burning Tiger (if it was really burning; he could not see it). Slowly he began to crawl back the way he had come.

"It was difficult," he recalls today, "crawling on hands and knees for about forty metres. Then I struck some object which I couldn't surmount. I touched my way along the wall. It was probably the tank barrier." Slowly he was able to make out objects again – or at least their outlines. "After some time I could recognize my surroundings again and saw before me a swaying figure. I went toward it and recognized the second flight captain of our Chief [Hitler], Georg Beetz, who had also taken part in the breakout attempt. To my horror I discovered that he had had his head torn open – apparently by a shell fragment – from the forehead to the base of the skull."

The heavily bleeding Beetz told Kempka that his wound had been caused by the tank explosion in which he, too, had seen Bormann and Naumann fly high into the air. Supporting one another weakly, the two men made their way back to the Admiralspalast, fully convinced that there was no hope now of their ever breaking through the Russian ring of steel around the dying capital, and that Martin Bormann was dead.

But the man who had survived so long and who, his enemies maintained, always knew how to rescue his own hide, was not yet dead. In the middle hours of that terrifying May night which dragged down the remainder of the "Thousand Year Reich" in a holocaust of flame and fear (similar to that of a Wagnerian opera which Hitler had so dearly loved), Reichsleiter Bormann was still scurrying through the rubble-littered, death-stalked streets of the capital looking for a way of escape.

Naumann, who, like Kempka, had been knocked out by the force of the tank explosion, came to to find Bormann back on his feet, standing near a crater on the Weidendamm Bridge. With his head ringing hollowly, Naumann staggered to where a group of the survivors had dropped into the crater and were crouched on their haunches excitedly discussing what they should do next now that they had failed to break out via the Friedrichstrasse. Naumann dropped down beside them and peered at them stupidly, his eyes not yet focusing properly.

"There were perhaps eleven of them," he recalled later. "Martin Bormann; Axmann, Hitler Youth Leader; and I also remember a doctor, Dr. Stumpfegger."

Thus we know that Martin Bormann was still alive after Kempka had presumed him killed in the tank explosion.

The band of survivors considered what to do next, while the machine guns chattered and shells tore the night apart with a frightening crash and spurts of fiery red-and-yellow flame. Finally they decided to make one more attempt to break out while they still had the cover of darkness. In spring, dawn comes early in Berlin, and they knew they had only a couple of hours left before the first false light revealed their position to the Russians. Even now the situation was bad enough, with a full moon high in the sky and throwing its cold silvery light on the centre of the battle-littered road. Ripping off all their badges of rank, the golden tresses and gleaming decorations which had once gained them and their kind the disdainful nick-name of the "Golden Pheasants" among the rank-and-file frontline soldiers, they clambered out of the crater. Carefully they started to work their way up the embankment to the railway track that led into the Friedrichstrasse Station.

Once up there, some three metres above the road, feeling like sitting ducks for any Russian sniper, they crouched and waited until the moon slid behind a cloud; then they started to steal along the line through the smoky, acrid gloom like a file of grey ghosts. And they were in luck. They crossed the River Spree without incident. Now they were approaching the shattered, nineteenth-century Lehrter Station, which was behind the Russian line and was in all probability already occupied by the Russians. They decided to leave the embankment before it ran into the station proper. With luck they would be able to work their way around the place, dodging behind the wrecked locomotives and shattered cars which dated from the bombing of the winter, and thus avoid contact with the Russians. One by one they tumbled down the steep embankment, cursing eloquently each time they tripped over a smoke-grimed bush or trailing wire cut by the artillery bombardment. But they made it. Collecting themselves, dusting off their clothes hastily, they set out again; not for long. They had hardly gone a dozen meters when they saw the soldiers camped out in the middle of the road, sitting around what looked like a fire. Naumann bit his lip hard to prevent himself from crying out loud. The soldiers were Russians. *They had walked right into a Russian guard unit!*

There was no turning back. The Russians had spotted them, but they didn't grab for their weapons. They were in a good mood. They gestured for the Germans to come forward, crying in a mixture of German and Russian: "Voina kaputt – voina kaputt!"[3]

Hesitantly the Germans came forward into the light. It was clear that the Russians had been celebrating; Axmann, the one-armed Hitler Youth Leader who was among the first of the group to approach them, realized why. Just as in Germany, May 1, the traditional Labour Day, was a major day of celebration in Soviet Russia. As he recalled much later, "The Russians obviously took us for Volkssturm[4] and offered us cigarettes."

The Germans accepted the coarse, clumsy Russian cigarettes made of black tobacco wrapped in ordinary newspaper, and puffed away in apparent contentment and ease. While they tried to understand each other with a handful of Russian words aided by much German and a lot of dumb play, Axmann showed them how the mechanism of his artificial arm worked. The simple Russian soldiers were delighted. They followed the workings of the specially built limb with wide round eyes.

But danger was looming large on the horizon. Out of the corner of his eye, Axmann spotted "Bormann, followed by Dr. Stumpfegger, leave the group and begin to steal away hurriedly into the shadows, taking off in the direction of the Invalidenstrasse."

It took a few moments for the Russians to tear their gaze from Axmann's arm to the figures disappearing into the gloom. They stared after them suspiciously and, to use Axmann's words again, "They became distrustful of us and we

---

[3] "The war's finished."
[4] A home guard formed by Bormann in late 1944 made up of old men and young boys. It had little fighting value.

felt the danger of what could happen to us." Slowly, one by one, they started to edge themselves tensely out of the circle of light. Now there were four of them making a break for it: Naumann, Schwaegermann, Axmann, and his adjutant, Weltzin. Crouching low and hugging the protection of the nearest wall, they followed the path taken by Bormann and his companion, heading up the Invalidenstrasse in the direction of Alt Moabit, expectantly waiting for the hoarse cry of rage and burst of fire that must come in an instant. But none came. The Russians simply let them go. Perhaps they were too drunk or too tired to care.

Shortly thereafter, Naumann and Goebbels's adjutant Schwaegermann broke away from the others and disappeared into the bushes of the old *Ausstellungsgebiet* (exhibition area) south of the Invalidenstrasse. Axmann and his adjutant marched on alone. But not for long. Suddenly the pudgy-faced Hitler Youth Leader stopped and turned his head to the wind. Somewhere ahead there was the rattle of rusty iron tank treads. He knew what that meant. They were well behind the Russian lines; the tanks could only be enemy!

Digging his adjutant in the ribs, he ordered him to turn around. Hurriedly they ran back the way they had come. Dawn would be upon them soon and they were still trapped.

The fire of the enemy guns intensified. Perhaps a last-ditch-battle was being fought by the SS left behind to defend the Chancellery area. The Stalin Organs, the Russian multiple rocket mortars, opened up with a frightening, stomach-churning howl. The night was torn apart by their roar. The fiery red rockets came down with a rush like a myriad angry hornets. Great spouts of earth and rubble flew into the air wherever they struck. Berlin was in its death throes. It would be all over by dawn. The two men rushed on as if the devil himself were after them. If they didn't break through the Soviet ring soon, they might as well consider themselves dead men.

The Russian fire had reached its peak now. The sky was a terrifyingly burning red. Hot metal shrapnel splinters as big as a man's fist flew through the air in all directions. White-and-red tracer stitched a pattern of death across every road. Over where the last German positions lay, white, red, and green flares hissed into the sky. They were last desperate pleas for help. But no help was forthcoming.

Axmann and Weltzin blundered on, breath coming in huge leather-lunged gulps. Suddenly Axmann stopped. In front of them on the bridge which ran over the tracks leading from the Lehrter Station he saw two still figures sprawled out as if dead. He and his adjutant sensed that they might have belonged to their group. Perhaps Naumann and Schwaegermann? He ran forward, followed a second later by his adjutant.

"We knelt at their side," he recalled later. "Perhaps we could help them. They were Martin Bormann and Dr. Stumpfegger. Any mistake is ruled out. I could see their faces clearly. They lay on their backs, arms and legs stretched out. I touched Bormann. No reaction. I bent over him and could not trace any sign of breathing. I couldn't see any wounds or traces of blood. Had they taken poison?"

But he had no time to consider further. Suddenly Russian sharpshooters started to zero in on the two Party functionaries. He and his companion scrambled hastily to their feet. They began to pelt down the street, the only sound the crackle of small arms fire and the pounding of their heavy boots on the pavement.

Behind them the two men lay sprawled out on the bridge, the hoarse slow chatter of an ancient Russian machine gun firing over their bodies like the chatter of some evil black jackdaw. It seemed to be heralding the death and destruction of all that the little man with the boxer's face had taken so long to build up.

3

The city was in ruins.

Once its medieval streets had echoed to the regimented hard stamp of 100,000 jackboots and the harsh, spine-chilling brass of the military bands. Then a half-million throats, crazed with mass hysteria, had bellowed the enraptured *"Heil Hitler"* as the hoarse Austrian voice had blared forth from the thousand loudspeakers. The red-, white-, and black-crossed flags had flapped defiantly in the breeze and the city had been proud to call itself "the place of the Party Day."

But that had been long ago. Now, since the thirty-minute raid on January, 7, 1945, the day Hitler lost his last gamble in the West (the Battle of the Bulge), the centre of Nuremberg lay in a waste of rust-coloured rubble, dotted here and there by obscenely twisted lamp standards and girders. Crude roads were forced through the waste of what had once been medieval gabled houses by U.S. army bulldozers. Now the only flags which flapped in the breeze were those of the occupiers and the only music which sounded were their strange, hectic, unmilitary tunes; and the regimented hard stamp of the jack-boots had been replaced by the soft, relaxed stride of the rubber-soled combat boots of the victors and the slow, sullen shuffle of the vanquished.

In that summer of victory, 1945, the only building in the centre of the southern German city of Nuremberg which had been rebuilt (after that terrible whirlwind air raid of the previous January) was the Palace of Justice. Here the Germans were to be tried, to be called to account for their five-year domination of Europe from the Channel to the Urals, to atone for what the occupiers liked to call their "war crimes."

Throughout that summer the American Army swiftly rebuilt

the shattered edifice, refurbishing the old paneled courtroom, hanging great velvet drapes across the windows so that not one single ray of light could penetrate. They had constructed a dock at one end of the rectangular room, and soundproof little glass cubicles around the walls for the interpreters, who would be translating back and forth in four languages. In the well of the court, space was made available for the two hundred or so newspapermen and photographers who would cover the "greatest trial in history" for the world. There, attached to every seat, as everywhere else in the court, there was a pair of earphones so that the listener – be he German, Russian, English, American, or French – could follow the monster trial in his own language.

And then at last the old Palace of Justice was ready to face an ordeal it had never known in all its long career, a career replete with legal ordeals. It was a dramatic moment as the accused filed in to face their judges and the flashing lights of the cameramen. For the first time in history an attempt was being made to outlaw war on a global scale; under the leadership of the United States the "new world" had really come at last "to redress the wrongs of the old." Its legality was vague and its morality even more so. The victors who now sat so solemnly in judgment on the vanquished that day had themselves killed 7,000 Poles in cold blood in Soviet Russia,[1] slaughtered at least 100,000 defenceless civilians in Dresden[2] and twice that number with their atomic bombs in Japan. But if the motives of the victorious powers were mixed and their own consciences besmirched, at least they were trying something which was a civilized innovation: to place guilt where it really lay, with the men who had issued the orders, rather than with the little men who had carried these orders out.

The charges levelled at the twenty-one accused were:

1. Conspiring or participating, as leaders or accomplices, to commit crimes against peace, committing specific crimes

---

[1] The infamous massacre of Polish officers in Russian-occupied territory which was discovered in 1942 by the Germans and is usually ascribed to the Russians.

[2] The Anglo-American raids on Dresden in February 1945; a target which had no military value at all.

against peace by planning, preparing, initiating, or waging wars of aggression.

2. War crimes, including murder, deportation for slave labour, killing of hostages, and ill-treatment of prisoners of war.

3. Crimes against humanity, including murder, extermination, enslavement, deportation, and political, racial, and religious persecution.

Thus, as those twenty-one men took their places in the dock, looking for the most part so harmless, haggard, and impotent now that they were stripped of their glamorous bemedalled uniforms, five other accused men sat down with them and picked up the earphones in spirit if not in the flesh: Adolf Hitler, Josef Goebbels, Dr. Robert Ley,[3] Heinrich Himmler, and Martin Bormann.

Starting on October 22, 1945, a public notice was broadcast once a week for a whole month over the two major radio stations operating in the British Zone of Occupation. At the same time, the same notice was published in four Berlin newspapers and appeared in two hundred thousand copies of a placard posted all over Germany, or at least in the three western-occupied zones. Under a poor picture of a scowling becapped Martin Bormann,[4] the notice read:

INTERNATIONAL MILITARY TRIBUNAL
ANNOUNCEMENT

Martin Bormann is charged with having committed crimes against peace, war crimes and crimes against humanity, all as

---

[3] Poor stuttering Ley, who had at first been Bormann's enemy and then became solely a figure of contempt. "He can't help being a swine. After all his father was a cattle-dealer," Irma said of him. Ley hanged himself in his cell before the trial with a towel he had attached to the toilet pipe.
[4] At this stage of the hunt for Bormann, Allied undercover agents were handicapped by the lack of good photos of the "man in the shadows," as Bormann was often called.

particularly set forth in an indictment which has been lodged with this Tribunal.

The indictment can be seen at the Palace of Justice, Nuremberg, Germany. If Martin Bormann appears, he is entitled to defend himself or have himself defended by counsel.

If he fails to appear, he may be tried in his absence, commencing November 20th, 1945, at the Palace of Justice, Nuremberg, Germany, and if found guilty, the sentence pronounced upon him, will, without further hearing, and subject to the orders of the Control Council for Germany, be executed after he is found.

By order of the International Military Tribunal. Harold B. Willey, General Secretary.

But the month passed and no Martin Bormann made his appearance or could be "found."

The prosecution was in a quandary. Could they try a man who was presumed dead or at least was very definitely missing? The President of the Court, aged, bald British Lord Justice Sir Geoffrey Lawrence, who affected gold-rimmed spectacles and an old-fashioned, stiff high-wing collar (and which the Germans who viewed him in the newsreels laughingly called a "father-murderer"), asked the four prosecutors on November 17 if they had any statement to make on the Bormann situation.

Sir David Maxwell-Fyfe, Deputy Chief Prosecutor for the United Kingdom, speaking also for the two Western Allies – France and the United States – replied: "If it please the Tribunal, as the Tribunal are aware, the Defendant Bormann was included in the Indictment, which was filed before the Tribunal. There has been no change in the position with regard to the Defendant Bormann; nor has any further information come to the notice of the Chief Prosecutors. . . . Three members of the party who were with Bormann *in* this tank[5] have been interrogated. Two think that Bormann was killed and the third that he was wounded. The position is, therefore, that the Prosecution cannot say that the matter is beyond probability that Bormann is dead." The elegant British lawyer, star of the

---

[5] Note the error. Even at this early stage the confusion about the tank episode on the Weidendamm Bridge was beginning, although the incident had occurred only a few months before.

Old Bailey, cleared his throat and then added significantly, *"There is still the clear possibility that he is alive!"*

After he had given the court time to absorb the first public pronouncement that Hitler's right-hand man was officially thought possibly still alive, he concluded: "In these circumstances I should submit that he comes within the exact words of Article 12 of the Charter[6] – 'The Tribunal shall have the right to take proceedings against a person charged with crimes set out in Article 6 of this Charter in his absence, if he has not been found.'"

Thus the "trial of the Germans" commenced at 10:03 A.M. on November 20, 1945, with an empty place left in the defendants' dock for Martin Bormann. Two months later, on January 16, 1946, when Lieutenant Thomas Lambert, U.S. Army, the assistant to Thomas Dodd, Executive Trial Counsel for the United States, opened the case against Bormann, it was still empty.

Because of Martin Bormann's unique method of operating as Hitler's "man in the shadows" (of which we shall hear more later), the young officer had difficulty in documenting his case that Bormann himself actually initiated "crimes against humanity." In his official position as Hitler's Secretary, with most of their conversations taking place under what the Germans call "four eyes," who was to know which orders originated from Hitler and which were products of Bormann's own drive for power, prestige, and position?

But the junior counsel struggled bravely on, ending his case with a naïvely worded yet effective statement. "May it please the Tribunal, every schoolboy knows that Hitler was an evil man. The point we respectfully emphasize is that, without chieftains like Bormann, Hitler would never have been able to seize and consolidate total power in Germany, but he would have been left to walk the wilderness alone." He then concluded the strange Biblical allusion to the "wilderness" with a further excursion into religious imagery: "He was, in truth, an evil archangel to the Lucifer of Hitler, and, although he may remain a fugitive from the justice of this Tribunal, with an empty chair in the dock, Bormann cannot escape responsibility for his illegal conduct."

---

[6] Convening the Tribunal.

As the young lieutenant sat down, a little red in the face and drained with the effort of speaking so long, he naturally could not hear the mocking laughter into which Martin Bormann must have burst (if he were still alive and listening) at the religious references. The boy who was baptized "Martin" in honor of Martin Luther by his exceedingly pious mother had hated and persecuted the Church as long as he had been in a position of power.

The young American soldier was followed by his opponent, bespectacled, middle-aged, somewhat pompous Dr. Friedrich Bergold, a local German lawyer who had been given the unenviable task of trying to defend a man whom he did not know and who was not present in court. Yet he tried his best in his typically long-winded German lawyer's way. In essence his defence was simple. He did not attempt to defend his unknown client; instead, he tried to show that Martin Bormann was dead (something he himself passionately believed), and that the court could not try a dead man. Bergold's star witness was naturally Erich Kempka. The months in the interrogation camp had taken their toll. The face of the thirty-five-year-old SS colonel, who had been born one of nine children and had joined the National Socialists in 1932 out of poverty,[7] had lost its well-fed, fleshy look. Now he looked yellow, tired, and underfed, and there were new lines around his eyes that had not been there when he had fled from the bunker a year or so before. Now, on July 3, 1946, he took the stand, still full of hatred for Bormann, of whom he said, "Those of us who had to work for long years in close proximity to this diabolical personality hated him."

Dr. Bergold got down to business at once and took him through the usual legal hoops.

"Witness, in what capacity were you employed near Hitler during the war?" he asked.

Kempka told him and added that during this period of time he had met Martin Bormann.

---

[7] His father had been a miner in the Ruhr; at age fourteen Erich Kempka had left school to become an apprentice mechanic. In 1932 he had become Hitler's chauffeur and, like all the immediate entourage, achieved high rank once the Leader came to power (even Hitler's valet held the rank of colonel in the SS).

Dr. Bergold then asked, "Witness, on what day did you see the defendant Martin Bormann for the last time?"

Kempka replied, "I saw the Reichsleiter – er – the former Reichsleiter Martin Bormann on the night of May 1/2, 1945, near the Friedrichstrasse railroad station, at the Weidendamm Bridge. Reichsleiter Bormann" – again he excused himself for his slip of the tongue – "*former* Reichsleiter Bormann asked me what the general situation was at the Friedrichstrasse Station and I told him that there at the station it was hardly possible . . ."

"You are going too fast," Sir Geoffrey Lawrence interrupted him severely, cupping his hand behind his ear. "*He asked you what?*" Here and there a counsel hid a smile behind his brief and told himself the Britisher was getting a bit too long in the tooth for this sort of thing.

Dr. Bergold pulled his black robe a little more tightly around his ample frame and looked fiercely at his witness, as if Kempka were letting him down by talking too quickly.

Kempka licked his thick bottom lip and started again. "He asked me what the situation was and whether one could get through there at the Friedrichstrasse Station. I told him that was practically impossible, since the defensive fighting there was too heavy. Then he went on to ask whether it might be possible to do so with armoured cars. I told him that there was nothing like trying it. Then a few tanks and APCs came along and small groups boarded them and hung on. Then the armoured cars pushed their way through the anti-tank barrier and afterward the leading tank – along about at the middle of the left-hand side, where Martin Bormann was walking – suddenly received a direct hit, I imagine from a bazooka fired from a window, and this tank was blown up. A flash of fire suddenly shot up on the very side where Bormann was walking and I saw . . ."

It was at this crucial moment, with the body of the court hanging on to the hectic, hard-breathing female interpreter's words as she sweated in her hot little glass cage, that Sir Geoffrey chose to interrupt again.

"You are going too fast," he lectured the witness crustily. "You are still going much too fast. The last thing I heard you say was that Bormann was walking in the middle of the column. Is that right?"

Kempka was grateful for the pause, but as he looked up at that grey old face he could not quite repress a little shudder; there was death in the dark eyes of the old Englishman who often enough in the past had placed the little square of black silk on his stiff white wig and said those fateful, solemn words: *"You shall be taken from this place and in due process of time be hanged by the neck until you are dead."* He would undoubtedly say them again before his own life came to an end.

He hurried on with the testimony, eager now to get it over with and be away from that old man with the eyes of death. "Yes, at the middle of the tank, on the left-hand side. Then, after it had got forty or fifty metres past the anti-tank barrier, this tank received a direct hit, I imagine from a bazooka fired from a window. The tank was blown to pieces right there where Martin – Reichsleiter Bormann – was walking. I myself was flung aside by the explosion and by the person thrown against me who had been walking in front of me. I think it was *Standartenführer*[8] Dr. Stumpfegger. And I became unconscious. When I came to myself I could not see anything either; I was blinded by the flash. Then I crawled back again to the tank trap, and since then I have seen nothing more of Martin Bormann."

Now Dr. Bergold came into his own. In a couple of quick questions, he made Kempka emphasize the impact of the explosion. "Witness," he asked, "did you see Martin Bormann collapse in the flash of fire when it occurred?"

"Yes indeed, I still saw a movement which was a sort of collapsing. You might call it a flying away."[9]

Bergold followed up rapidly. "Was this explosion so strong that according to your observation Martin Bormann must have lost his life by it?" In his eagerness, Bergold leaned forward to catch his witness's words.

Kempka nodded solemnly and answered slowly but deliberately. *"Yes, I assume for certain that the force of the explosion was such that he lost his life."*

---

[8] Roughly, "Colonel" in the SS.
[9] Wegfliegen.

4

But the self-satisfied smile with which Dr. Bergold received that final sentence of Kempka's testimony would have vanished if he had known at that moment what was going on in the heads of the prosecutors. Hitler Youth Leader Axmann had been captured by a joint Anglo–American team in December, 1945, after living "underground" with a group of his *Hitlerjungend* for six months. His testimony made Kempka's look silly. According to the one-armed Youth Leader, Martin Bormann had still been alive one hour after the incident at the tank barrier.

Dr. Bergold's self-satisfaction would have taken another blow if he had known something which the Russians were still keeping concealed from their Western Allies. They had managed to capture another of the escapees from the Berlin bunker, Hitler's pilot Hans Baur. While imprisoned in Russia he had been questioned and cross-questioned for weeks on the last days in the bunker. As he recalled in his book *I Flew the Mighty of the Earth*: "I was offered money, a job in Chile; they [the Russians] would even let me live in Russia if I did not feel safe in Germany, so long as I told them where Hitler was now. It was a crazy business."

But the Russians were not interested only in Hitler's whereabouts; they were also interested in Bormann, and they heard from Baur a different tale than Kempka's.

As Baur recalled the incident:[1]

"We got as far as the Weidendamm Bridge. That's where the Russian front line was. I had asked Bormann to wait at the

---

[1] In an interview with the German magazine *Bunte Illustrierte* (No. 2, 1965).

corner of the Friedrichstrasse and Schiffbauerdamm till I'd found out whether we could break through. About there I told Bormann that we didn't have much chance of breaking through. . . .

"On account of the heavy bombardment I left Bormann on the steps of a wrecked corner house in the Friedrichstrasse. From this position he could survey the whole street. Bormann remained seated here for a long time. I went off and recce'd where we might get through without opposition. I got as far as the Ziegelstrasse. But the Russians were everywhere. When I got back – it was about one o'clock at night – Bormann asked me to stay, because I was the only person on whom he could still rely. We then pushed on to the corner of the Ziegel- and Friedrichstrasse.

"I led Bormann into a wrecked house. A little later I heard the noise of shooting in the yard. I ran up to the first storey . . . and saw that there were at least twenty Russian soldiers in the yard. I ran down to the house entrance and told Bormann that the Russians were already in the house. All they needed to do was to look through the door and they would have us!

"At that time I was with Secretary of State Dr. Naumann, SS Dr. Stumpfegger and Bormann. As we had no other choice, we decided to try to break through in spite of what might happen.

"Dr. Naumann ran ahead first. Bormann followed at about twenty metres' distance. Then Dr. Stumpfegger. Behind him – me. We ran through the pitch-black Ziegelstrasse eastward in order to get to the brewery in the Schoenhauser Allee. The Russians were firing with machine pistols and machine guns . . . so that the dead and dying lay thickly everywhere. I got as far as just before the University clinics where I threw myself down. I called the names Bormann and Stumpfegger several times. The only reply I got was from other comrades. There was no trace of Reichsleiter Bormann. He must have been killed. The only one who got through all right was Dr. Naumann. Dr. Stumpfegger was killed and I was badly wounded."

Thus Baur had yet another version of the events of that fateful night, and the manner of Martin Bormann's "death."

Like the Russians, the Americans, too, were not revealing all they knew about Martin Bormann. Unlike them, however, the Americans were not concerning themselves solely with the events of that evening of May 1/2, 1945; they were occupied with the present; with, in particular, the day-to-day life of Frau Gerda Bormann, the missing man's wife.

The American Counterintelligence Corps had discovered her whereabouts in unusual circumstances. One day in May, 1945, just after the war had ended, a distraught German appeared at the Munich CIC headquarters to complain that his child had been kidnapped by Gerda Bormann, the wife of the Secretary of the Führer, and had been taken from her home at Obersalzberg to somewhere in the Italian Tyrol. Eagerly the CIC seized at the opportunity offered by this lead, assigning to a German-speaking Belgian Jew who had escaped from a German forced labour unit the task of finding her.

In company with a German civilian also working for the CIC, the Belgian, named Alexander Raskin, drove to the rugged mountain area. If we are to believe his report, he spent four days searching the remote valleys around the city of Bolzano on muleback.[2] In the end he found his quarry, living under the name of "Frau Bergmann," with her youthful sister-in-law, their children, and a couple of others who had been residing at the Bormann house at Obersalzberg just before they had been forced to flee before the advancing Americans.

The once-robust thirty-seven-year-old Frau Gerda Bormann, who had borne her husband ten children in fifteen years, was a shadow of her earlier self. Her face, once brown and fit from the Alpine sun of her mountain home, was pale and emaciated, and her blond hair was lackluster and brittle. Her eyes had the shadow of death in them. Gerda was dying.

Raskin checked with the local Italian partisan doctor who had examined her. He told the CIC agent that Gerda Bormann was in the final stages of cancer of the womb. Unknown to herself, she had been suffering from the disease since at least 1943. At that time her own doctor, examining her to check her fitness to have yet another child, had discovered it. Gerda's

---

[2]Although the cities in this area were predominantly Italian, the rural areas were 100 percent German-speaking and pro-Hitler. In other words, the local farmers would not be inclined to betray anyone such as Frau Bormann if she were hiding out from Allied justice.

family does not know whether the doctor told Bormann about it. But the doctor did warn Bormann that his wife should not have any more children. However, Bormann, proud of his virility and his family, had insisted.

Raskin reported his news to his HQ in Munich and settled down to watch her every movement in case she tried to contact her husband or, more likely, in case he tried to contact her. [3]

Gerda Bormann is long dead and we do not have her testimony for this period of time. But her youthful companion of that miserable winter is still alive, the wife of Gerda's younger brother, Hermann Buch. A much decorated and much wounded (seven times) SS officer, he, like Martin Bormann, was missing in 1945.

As Frau Buch recalls today:[4]

"We fled from the 'Berg' [a familiar name for Obersalzberg in the Bormann circle] at the end of April, 1945. It was bitterly cold and the bus we fled in was badly shot up. The windows were all broken. But we packed the kids in – there were fifteen of them altogether – while Gerda checked what she would allow us to take with us.

"The day before we left, some sealed packing cases had arrived from Berlin, containing the most precious possessions of the Bormann family. She sorted these out, taking four watercolours done by Hitler, his wedding present to Bormann – a set of Meissner porcelain with a dragon design – and some private papers (these were Bormann's letters, notes on Hitler's table-talk etc.). And then we were off.

"Gauleiter Hofer[5] [the gauleiter in charge of the Tyrol] had arranged everything. We left the cases with him – we never saw them again and then we went to Wolkenstein in the Grodner Valley.

"It was terrible. Everything was confused – chaotic. The Italian partisans had taken over and nobody was safe on the

---

[3] Raskin was sure that his news got through right up to General Patton, then Governor of Bavaria where Munich is located. Later an intelligence officer on Patton's staff told him: "The general feels that the woman should be left to die in peace."

[4] In a conversation with the author in 1971.

[5] Nazi Germany was divided in 42 regions or *Gaue*. The highest ranking Party official in the regions was called the *Gauleiter*.

streets. They shot up everything. But Gerda was getting worse. She was normally a very quiet person, cultured, perfectly happy when she could play her guitar or do her drawings. Now she couldn't hide her pain. So I sent one of the maids who could speak some Italian down into Bolzano to get a doctor.

"He came up. He was with the partisans, but he spoke broken German and told us Gerda had cancer; she needed an operation immediately. But where were we going to get the fees? We had no money. So we sewed clothes and swapped them with the farmers for butter which we hoped that we could sell on the black market for money.

"But my visit to Bolzano to find out about the operation was a fiasco. The Italian partisan doctor told us that the only place where it could be carried out was in Munich. So I tried to find out how we could get there. By chance I heard there was a train going north to Munich once a week. Immediately I hurried off to the Town Commandant – I think he was called Kaufmann. He was American. 'Yes,' he said to me, 'there is a train going to Munich weekly.'

"I then told him about Gerda and who she was.

"Kaufmann shook his head. 'Yes, there is a train all right. But it's not for your sort – Nazis. It's reserved for those who have suffered – concentration camp victims.'"

Sitting in the quiet book-lined study in the southern German town in which she now lives, Gerda Bormann's sister-in-law twists her face at the memory, more with pain than with bitterness. "Of course, that was Gerda's sentence of death. She didn't live much longer after all. She knew she hadn't a chance without the operation."

Outside, the little cobbled street is silent save for the far-off rattle of the ancient blue trams which still transport commuters in this area of the world. In the corner of the softly lit room the clock ticks away the minutes with metallic inexorability. I thought of Gerda Bormann, simple, naïve, gentle – Speer called her "modest somewhat browbeaten . . . although blindly devoted to her husband," – sentenced to death, not for what she had done but because of her mistake in marrying the "man in the shadows."

Then I asked the question I had travelled so far to put:

35

"During this time did you hear anything of Martin? *Did he try to contact you?*"

The woman shook her head. "No. All we heard was a radio broadcast saying he was dead. No, both of us thought he had been killed trying to escape from Berlin. *Martin Bormann is dead.*"

Meanwhile, Dr. Bergold was fighting on on behalf of his unknown client. In his summing up he said: "The case of the accused Martin Bormann whom I have been empowered by the High Court to defend is an unusual one. The accused lived in the shadows as the National Socialist Empire flourished. In this case he remains in the shadows and now in all probability he is again living in the shadows – as the ancients described the fate of the dead."

Sir Geoffrey breathed out hard. Did the German presume to teach him his classics!

But Dr. Bergold did not notice His Lordship's impatience and continued: "He is the only one among the accused who is not present against whom Article 12 of the Charter is being applied. It is almost as if the history of the continuity of the *genii loci* is being maintained and specifically here in Nuremberg . . . where we have the saying, dating back from the Middle Ages, stating 'don't hang a man you don't hold' . . ."

And thus Dr. Bergold rambled on until the British judge snapped down at him, "*Dr. Bergold!* This is not a suitable place to discuss this question [that of trial *in absentia*] after we have already opened the case against Bormann! We've given you a long time to make an application to have this decision [i.e., to try Bormann] re-examined. Can't you follow my explanation?"

Bergold stuttered, "I haven't quite understood the last sentence."

After Sir Geoffrey had ordered him testily to adjust the dial of his translation apparatus, the plump German finally got down to the essence of his plea, basing his statement on Kempka's evidence. "Bormann therefore was in the centre of the explosion which was so powerful that the witness [i.e., Kempka] was convinced he must have been killed. . . . Even if Bormann hadn't been killed on that occasion, he was certainly so badly wounded that he would have been unable to flee. In that case he would have fallen into the hands of the Soviet troops who according to the affidavit of the witness Krüger[6] were close to the Chancellery at that time and occupied it on May 2nd; the U.S.S.R – who in view of the loyalty they accord this court – would certainly have handed him over to the Tribunal."

In the light of what was to happen in years to come, Dr. Bergold's comment about Russia was of the highest significance, but in that year of 1946, Soviet Russia and the United States were still allies and the latter still trusted implicitly in the good faith of their Eastern ally. Thus the comment was overlooked in the court's eagerness to hear Dr. Bergold's final words. "There are," he concluded, "only two possibilities, according to my way of thinking at least, namely, that Bormann fell into Russian hands wounded – which has been proved did not take place. So that remaining possibility is the only likely one – Bormann died." Bergold paused and took a deep breath. *"Therefore I am of the opinion that there is sufficient proof that Bormann is dead."*

On July 22, 1945, Dr. Bergold petitioned the court accordingly "to suspend the proceedings against the defendant Bormann until he is personally heard and can personally state his case." The Tribunal turned his application down and thus the one empty seat in the dock remained there as the "trial of the Germans," the greatest legal proceeding the world has ever seen, reached its climax.[7]

The same day that the news of the Tribunal's decision to try Bormann appeared in the world's press, a certain Jakob Glas, who had been fired from his job as Bormann's chauffeur in 1944 because he had – according to Bormann – stolen vegetables from the Obersalzberg garden,[8] hurried to the offices of the Munich CIC. For a while the CIC agents could make no

---

[6] Bormann's secretary.
[7] Although the Court concluded in its summing-up that Dr. Bergold had "labored under difficulties" and that "if Bormann is not dead and is later apprehended, the Control Commission for Germany may, under Article 29 of the Charter, consider any facts in mitigation and alter or reduce his sentence if deemed proper," he was sentenced to death with eleven other defendants on the afternoon of October 1, 1946.
[8] Bormann was a passionate gardener.

sense of Glas's statements; he was too excited and talked in a thick Munich dialect accompanied by a lot of arm-waving. But finally he calmed down and told them that he had seen his former boss.

He was "absolutely certain" that he had seen him riding a car in the neighbourhood of Munich's central Karlsplatz. He was riding as a passenger and was dressed in shabby clothes. At first the Americans did not believe Glas, but the ex-chauffeur persisted. "I know Bormann," he insisted, "and the man I saw was Bormann." His behaviour and vehemence convinced them.

The local bureau chief ordered an immediate search. The agents accompanied by armed MPs swarmed out to search the busy area around the Karlsplatz, entering houses here and there, poking through the odd patches of ruins. But in the end they had to give up. As the summer light began to fade, they returned tired, hot, and angry to their headquarters. Their search had been fruitless.

But the Glas search was the herald of things to come. Soon reports of other Martin Bormann "sightings" would come pouring in from all corners of the world, from Brazil to Bulgaria and from Denmark to Italy. Week after week, month after month, year after year. The legend of the missing Secretary of the Führer had been born. The hunt was on.

II

The Man in the Shadows

To win this war, I need Bormann!

– ADOLF HITLER, 1943

5

Martin Bormann's entry into big-time politics was dramatic enough, perhaps too dramatic for the undersized yet tough-looking farm manager running the estate of the aristocratic von Treuenfels family in the central German province of Mecklenburg.

In 1923, when it all started, Martin was exactly the same age as the century. Four years before, he had left his native town of Halberstadt to join the German Army. But the young gunner had never seen any action. Instead, he did a year's army service and had then been released into a beaten Germany where jobs were hard to find, especially for people like himself who had no profession and no training save how to lay a cannon. As a result, he had drifted into farming, taking a job as a trainee manager with von Treuenfels, an ex-officer and extremely right-wing nobleman, who had one of his many farms near the little Mecklenburg town of Parchim.

It was here on the farm, Gut Herzberg, helping to run Hermann von Treuenfels's 810-acre farm, that Bormann first came into contact with politics. There were half a dozen "labourers" on the farm, ex-soldiers whose main job was to keep an eye on left-wing agitators or anyone else suspected of trying to "turn the workers red." These tough mercenaries, who had all served in the mud, mire, and blood of the Western Front during World War I, were members of the Rossbach Organization, an illegal paramilitary organisation commanded by ex-Lieutenant Rossbach, a swaggering, cynical, hard-boiled soldier of fortune. A few months before, the organisation had been banned, but it had gone underground and managed to survive by quartering its members all over the Province of Mecklenburg on farms such as that owned by Hermann von Treuenfels. He, like his fellow right-wing landowners, was eager to pay and support the mercenaries in return for the protection they offered against the "red threat."

In 1923, Bormann was still politically naïve. He had joined the "Society Against the Presumptuousness of the Jewry" soon after he had been discharged from the army, but his main concerns were managing to keep alive in a Germany stricken by inflation and running the von Treuenfels estate efficiently.

Trouble began for Martin Bormann with the advent of one Walter Kadow, a twenty-three-year-old member of the Rossbach Organization. The ex-schoolteacher, soon making himself popular with his comrades at the farm who bunked together in the long barn on the estate (which is still there), had gotten into debt with them and had borrowed thirty thousand Reichmarks from Bormann, who was acting as the Rossbachers' treasurer. This was a fatal mistake, since a short while later Bormann was forced to fire Kadow from his job in the farm's brickyard with the sum still outstanding.[1] In addition, some of his comrades began to suspect that Kadow was working with the Reds. He boasted of the trip he had made to Moscow and had been to the Ruhr area several times under suspicious circumstances, especially as the Ruhr had recently been occupied by the French who were busy interning all members of right-wing outfits such as the Rossbach Organization. The questions they whispered to one another behind his back were whether Kadow was a spy for the Communists – and perhaps also for the hated French.

Thus it was that when the twenty-six-year-old salesman Massolle turned up at the farm on the afternoon of May 13, 1923, to report breathlessly that Kadow had made an appearance in a local inn – the Luisenhof – in nearby Parchim, Bormann knew something had to be done about the "traitor." Smiling coldly in that way of his, he told the other man that "the best thing they could do" was to "give him a good beating."

Massolle needed no urging, but there was a hitch; his ancient motorbike had acquired a puncture on the rough track leading up to the farm. Bormann didn't hesitate. In his capacity as manager he was also in charge of the place's small vehicle park.

---

[1] At the rate of exchange current at that time, all of five dollars!

He lent the salesman a small horse and cart to get back to Parchim. Then waving good-bye and warning Massolle to "take it easy with the beating," Bormann went off on one of his never-ending rounds of the farm, leaving Massolle to collect nearly a dozen more Rossbachers for the task of dealing with the renegade.

By midnight that same day, Kadow, still unsuspecting, was drunk out of his mind, flattered by the attentions and generosity of his comrades who kept insisting on buying yet another *korn* (a kind of grain schnapps) in the sleazy little inn. Without hesitation he allowed himself to be loaded drunkenly onto the waiting cart "so we can go to another place and really get a skinful." But when the horse left the main highway and rattled off down a narrow cobbled country road, it dawned on even his fuddled brain that his "comrades" were up to no good. Rudolf Hoess, a tall, blue-eyed ex-machine-gunner who would one day achieve notoriety as one of the most sadistic men of our time,[2] was the first to confirm Kadow's growing suspicion. He smashed his clenched fist into Kadow's face. A second later pale-faced Jurich, who was dying of TB and had been in and out of mental homes for the last four years, brought his club down on Kadow's head with a sickening thud. "Have you got any last message for your mother?" he cried crazily. Then they all joined in.

Desperately the bleeding Kadow pleaded with them; held his hands across his face, trying unsuccessfully to protect himself against the blows raining down on him from all sides, while the cart swayed back and forth. "Let me go!" he screamed. "Let me go! *I'm no Communist! Honest!*"

But there was no saving him now. Kadow was dragged from the cart and thrown to the ground. Hoess picked up a branch lying on the ground and threw it down again because it was too thin. With all his strength he pulled a two-inch-thick pine sapling from the earth and brought it crashing down on Kadow's skull. Something cracked. Kadow let out a scream. Dark red blood shot from Kadow's nostrils. Another Rossbacher, who at the trial confessed he was sexually excited by the sight of blood, drew his knife and slashed it across the dying man's throat. And so it went until some time later an

---

[2] He was to become the commandant of Auschwitz Concentration Camp.

end was put to the merciless butchery by one of them firing two shots into the body at close range. Kadow jerked frighteningly for one last time and then he lay still, with the others staring down at him blindly, their chests heaving as if they had run a great race, all energy drained from them.

It had to come out, of course. The half-crazed Jurich blabbed to the editor of a Socialist paper what had happened. The editor went to the police, and one after another the murderers were arrested until finally Martin Bormann, who pleaded that he had only lent them the cart and had warned them to "take it easy," was also taken into custody and lodged at Leipzig Jail to await trial.

For the unmarried farm manager in his early twenties it must have come as a great shock to realize that he was considered a dangerous criminal by the prosecutor, who personally went over the heads of the judges to ensure that Bormann was tried.[3] It must have come as even a greater shock to Bormann to find himself sentenced to just under a year's imprisonment. But in later years when he came to describe the events of the trial in Hitler's own paper, the *Völkische Beobachter*, he made light of that shock. For him it had been a patriotic exercise, with him and his fellow prisoners singing defiantly as they were led to the Black Maria through a cordon of guards:

> If you're run through by the sword, keep fighting nonetheless.
> Give yourself up for lost, but not your flag
> Others will wave it when they bury you
> And win the glory that hovered over you.[4]

Thus, Martin Bormann's real political education began in Cell 273 of the Elisabeth Street Prison in Leipzig. Abruptly this son of solid, God-fearing middle-class parents, who felt he was a victim of a miscarriage of justice, was plunged into the new, frightening, and violent world of the political criminal, the hired killer, the mercenary, the fanatical ex-soldier nationalist – people who were prepared to kill at the drop of a hat for the

---

[3] The judges maintained that they did not possess the right to try Bormann after they had concluded the case against the main accused.
[4] "*In den Kerkern der Republik*" ("In the Dungeons of the Republic"), Martin Bormann

price of a loaf of bread or for the sake of the "cause." His cell-mate, ex-infantry officer Bruno Fricke, had been born in his home town but, unlike Bormann, he had volunteered to fight for his Kaiser at the front at the age of sixteen. He filled Bormann's head with the new theories of hate and aggression current in nationalist circles: "the stab in the back,"[5] the "November criminals," the "international Jewish conspiracy."

Standing emptying his nightly slops into the filthy, reeking earthern latrines, sitting sticking envelopes closed, plodding endlessly around the cobbled prison exercise yard, Martin Bormann learned his fanaticism. He lost the belief in God that his pious, fat Lutheran mother had drummed into him throughout his youth; he started to hate the soft, easygoing "mealymouthed" bourgeois world into which he had been born. He learned that the only solution for his problems and Germany's problems was a simple one – violence and yet more violence until the "criminals" who had committed this dastardly crime against him and his "Volk" were eradicated for good.

As he himself wrote: "The punishment did not break us. Indeed it hardened us. . . . It deepened our love for our people and at the same time strengthened our hatred of all those who have abused this people. . . . One day before my release the judge called me to his office. He told me to keep away from the Nationalists. I should think of my future and my career. The success of his attempt? One day after I was released I was back in the ranks of my old comrades."

When Martin Bormann was released from prison in March, 1925, he was indeed filled with a burning hatred of the "system." By that year, things were changing for the better in Germany. The inflation was conquered and the French had withdrawn from the Ruhr; a minor boom was underway and it seemed that the ill-fated Weimar Republic had overcome its birth pains. Soon Germany would sign a treaty of non-aggression and friendship with its traditional enemy, France, and, as a result, she would be accepted into the League of

---

[5] The theory that Germany was not defeated at the front but "stabbed in the back" by traitors such as the "November criminals" who in November, 1918, made peace with the victorious Allies.

Nations: a sign that she had become once more a respected member of the European family of nations.

As a result, the extreme right-wing groups lost ground rapidly. Their members returned to normal "respectable" civilian jobs, admittedly disappointed, but believing that there would be no armed revolution against the "government of traitors." The battle-hardened young officers comprising such Free Corps as that commanded by Rossbach, who had felt they had nothing to lose when they had joined, now discovered they did have after all. They began to look for jobs, get married, produce children, buy houses, get fat, and forget the hectic, bloody life of the front.

But Martin Bormann could not return to the comfortably boring bourgeois existence from which he had been wrenched so rudely two years before. He tried for a little while, at his old job on the estate. But there he found he was little better off than the labourers he supervised . . . he began to hate the von Treuenfels; they were just as stuffy and conventional and money-grabbing as the bourgeois class which he now hated so passionately. Yet what would he do if he left the farm? After all, he was *vorbestraft* – an ex-convict – a stigma that would follow him with his records to the end of his days.[6] Who would want to employ him, especially as he had nothing to offer save a poor school record and his training as a farm manager?

The more he thought about it in those months after he was released from prison, the more he realized that the only solution was to enter politics. But in what capacity and in what party? The old Rossbach Organization was finally wound up. Besides, even if Rossbach had been prepared to employ him full time, the ex-soldier had hardly enough money to keep himself, not to speak of paying Bormann.

In the end, Martin Bormann made his decision. He knew he had no talent as a speaker. His metier was the backroom office, where his undoubted organisational talents and his ability to work hard could come to fruition far from the public eye. He offered his services to a relatively small, basically southern German political party, whose rightist aggressive policy had

---

[6]In Germany, everyone has to register with the police every time he changes his address. Accordingly, every police station would know of his crime."

46

attracted some attention in the year he had been sent to prison. It had suffered a decline ever since its leader had been sent to serve a five-year term in the fortress at Landsberg. In fact, the shockhaired foreign-born leader – Bormann believed he was an Austrian – had been released prematurely, but had been forced to swear that he would not address a public meeting again until the ban on his speaking was lifted.

Yet although the party, which had its centre in the Bavarian capital of Munich, had little power in his own far-off province and was admittedly on the decline, Bormann saw membership in it as the only escape from his present untenable position. Thus it was on February 17, 1927, that young Martin Bormann joined the National Socialist German Workers' Party; an obscure, balding young man, inclined to corpulence, whose high party number (#60,508) indicated that he was a Johnny-come-lately. Within the next ten years he was destined to become the most powerful man in Germany after Adolf Hitler himself.

6

The late twenties were lean years for the National Socialist Party. The old Prussian spirit of self-sacrifice and devotion to the state seemed dead. Germany in the last years of that decade was a free, ultra-modern country whose art, architecture, music, and literature were envied by the rest of Europe because of their boldness, their frank, open quality, and delight in experimentation. Indeed, the country, and in particular Berlin, was becoming the Mecca of daring young men and women from all over the Continent. These new Germans, who had not gone through the hell of World War I, were an easygoing, sun-worshipping, hedonistic lot who regarded life as their personal oyster to be cracked open eagerly and enjoyed to the full. And most of all they were apolitical; if they ever mentioned "the funny Austrian with the moustache," it was to make fun of him and his strange hoarse rantings against all and sundry.

The 1928 elections revealed to just what extent the Nazis had lost their grip on the nation. In that year, Hitler's party polled exactly 810,000 votes out of a total of 31 million and won a miserable six seats out of the 491 available in the national parliament, the Reichstag. The actual paid-up members of the Party itself numbered exactly 108,000 in that same year.

It was therefore not surprising that Hitler set about recreating his organisation with a fury almost akin to despair. In the main he had two objectives in the late twenties: to concentrate all the power in his own hands and cut out any possible rivals for leadership; and to re-establish the National Socialists as a political party which would seek power not through revolution, as he had attempted in his ill-fated *Putsch* of 1923, but by constitutional means. As he told one of his cronies while still in prison at the fortress at Landsberg: "When I resume active work, it will be necessary to pursue a new policy. Instead of working to achieve power by an armed coup, we shall have to hold our noses and enter the Reichstag against the Catholic and Marxist deputies. If outvoting them takes longer than outshooting them, at least the result will be guaranteed by their own constitution. Any lawful process is slow. . . . Sooner or later we shall have a majority— *and after that, Germany!*"

To carry out his bid for power by legal, constitutional means, the hoarse-voiced, hypnotic-eyed leader needed a new kind of follower. The old street-corner bully boy who had first rallied to him in 1920 was no longer the type he wanted to pursue his new policy. He needed hardworking, sober-minded bureaucratic types – not the revolutionaries – but the technocrats of power. And unknown to him, in faraway Saxony the man who was one day to be the classic example of this type was already working hard for his new employer.

But if Hitler was not yet aware of Martin Bormann's undoubted organizational and bureaucratic talents, other members of the Party were. In 1928, after only a year in the NSDAP, he was promoted to assistant to Captain von Pfeiffer, a crusty ex-regular soldier and head of the Storm Troopers in the Munich area. It was a chance to get close to the centre of Party power and Martin Bormann seized it eagerly with his fat, heavy hands, even though Captain von Pfeiffer was a typical *Kommisskopf*[1] who wanted nothing better than to turn the Storm Troopers into a second regular army.

Martin Bormann's big breakthrough came after he had been in Munich for nearly a year. In the year before the Great Depression, more and more unemployed workers started to flock to the swastika flag, lured by Hitler's promise of *Brot und Arbeit*, – "Bread and Work"; a simple slogan but an attractive one in 1928 with already over one million Germans unemployed. Faced with ever-increasing audiences, Hitler decided he needed a permanent home for his undoubted rhetorical talents and found it in the winter quarters of the *Zirkus Krone*, a well-known German circus. Here he and other

---

[1] "An old sweat," as the British would say. An old soldier, in other words.

leading members of the Nazi Party used to speak regularly to the enthusiastic audiences of unemployed workers, Party members, and representatives of the solid middle classes whom he was now trying to attract into the Party.

And it was here that the twenty-nine-year-old Martin Bormann met twenty-two-year-old Gerda Buch, daughter of Major Walter Buch, a former regular soldier, longtime Hitler friend, and Chief Party Judge.

Gerda was tall (taller than Bormann) – a slim young girl with her hair drawn back in a bun in the fashion popular in Party circles but ridiculed by the short-skirted marcel-waved emancipated young women elsewhere. She was a dreamy person. As her brother Hermann remembers today:[2] "She had been trained as a *Kindergärtnerin* (nursery school teacher) and she was never happier than when she was with children, drawing with them or making lino cuts. . . . In contrast to Martin, who was realistic, down-to-earth, she was a completely impractical person." But if she was inclined to be a little withdrawn, scared of society and large gatherings, Gerda Buch had learned her political creed right from the cradle from her straightlaced, deeply honest father, who was regarded as "somewhat of a political fool – a typical soldier[3] within the Party. Gerda – like her father – rejected the Versailles Treaty, the Jews, the Catholics (the Buchs were strict Protestants), and believed Germany's problems could only be solved by an ultra-right-wing nationalist party such as the National Socialist.

But as Gerda Buch strolled home with her father after the tremendous enthusiasm of the meeting, the cheering, the promises, the heady promises for the future, her mind was not on politics; it was on Martin Bormann. "He's got such lovely eyes," she breathed absently to her somewhat amused father. "I *do* hope he'll be there next time."

But young Bormann was not. Nor the time after that. Perhaps he was a little scared of Major Buch, who had the reputation of being exceedingly moral (and Martin Bormann's bachelor life at that time was not so moral). Perhaps he was

---

[2] In a conversation with the author, 1971.
[3] Comment made to the author in 1971 by "Putzi" Hanfstaengl, Hitler's first press chief.

put off by the entranced looks Major Buch's daughter had given him at the meeting. Or perhaps he simply did not like the fact that Gerda Buch was half a head taller than he was.

In the end, after Gerda had mooned around the house unhappily for a couple of weeks, sighing at nothing and playing her guitar half-heartedly and without her usual happy enthusiasm, Major Buch decided to take matters into his own hands. He sought Bormann out and almost ordered him to come to eat at the simple wooden Buch house on the outskirts of Munich. Bormann obeyed, and thus the relationship between the two unlikely partners began: on the one hand, the tough, undersized Saxon who had both feet planted firmly on the ground; and on the other, the artistically inclined young Munich girl whose only joke was to say in company, "Let's play at reading," then open a book and immerse herself in it, forgetting everyone else around her.

The affair began to progress. Bormann met Hitler in the Buch house. He started to realize that a more permanent relationship with Gerda might be useful. The family, too, obviously liked him. Hermann, the nine-year-old, and his teenage brother Walter both got on well with him, and Frau Buch often proclaimed, "We want a Martin in the family."[4]

In the end Bormann succumbed. On April 13, 1929, he went walking in a nearby park with the whole of the Buch family. While the rest strode purposefully ahead beside ex-infantryman Walter Buch, the young couple lagged behind, but when finally Gerda returned home that evening, starry-eyed and flushed, the family knew what had happened even before she opened her mouth to tell them. *Her* Martin had asked her to marry him.

They were married five months later on September 2, 1929, in a little wooden church, after a civil ceremony where for the first time in German history the officiating burgomaster wore the Nazi brownshirt. The marriage was honoured by the presence of two men as witnesses who were going to dominate the rest of Martin Bormann's Party career – Adolf Hitler and sunken-eyed, dark-skinned Rudolf Hess.

---

[4] She, like Bormann's own mother, was a strict Lutheran and wanted a son-in-law named after the founder of her church.

51

Promotion came quickly for the young, full-time Party official after that. In the same year that his first child was born – and naturally was named "Adolf" after the Leader as well as "Martin" – the tireless and devoted Bormann was appointed head of the NSDAP *Hilfskasse* (the Party Aid Fund) which was slated to provide financial assistance for those members of the "movement", who were injured in the ever-increasing street brawls with the Communists and Socialists.

It was a real jump forward. Undoubtedly the fact he was married to Gerda helped to get him the job, but once he had taken it over, the success of the undertaking was due solely to his own efforts. And not only did it place hundreds of future Nazi officials who had been injured in his debt, but it also supplied Adolf Hitler with a valuable source of funds at a time when money was very scarce.

At the time this book was written ex-Nazi Putzi Hanfstaengl, half-American, a former Harvard scholar and friend of Franklin Delano Roosevelt, said of the Bormann he knew in those early years: "I always thought of him as disciplined, dutiful and informed. Now, his father-in-law Buch was a good officer but in politics, he was – " desperately the huge, former joker of the Party, who had entertained Hitler[5] in the very room in which he and I were presently sitting, sought for the appropriate term, finding it finally in the slang of fifty years ago " – A real – real *pinhead*. An absolute pinhead in politics.

"Now, Martin was different. He didn't concern himself with politics. When he moved into the *Hilfskasse*, he really organized it. At that time I thought, thank God, we have a man who knows how to look after the finances of the 'Brown House' [the HQ of the Nazi Party]. Up to that time everyone had been filling their pockets without any kind of checks. A thousand for Goering – I've had that fat bastard in here many

---

[5] Dr. Hanfstaengl, scion of a wealthy family, had joined the Party in 1923 when he had lent it $1,000, a tremendous sum in those days. In the years that followed he came close to Hitler and it was said that his clowning and piano playing "soothed" Hitler. Just before the outbreak of WWII he fled Germany when he thought Hitler was trying to have him killed. During WWII he was "interned" in Washington, but in fact, by virtue of his friendship with FDR, he acted as an unofficial adviser on German affairs to the US Government; it must have been a role that amused everyone who knew, both in the U.S.A. and Germany – not least the big man himself.

a time," he added, with a huge grin on his broad face dominated by a large bulging nose. "Fifteen hundred for Goebbels. *No receipts! No nothing!*

"But when Bormann came along, all that changed. Within three months he had knocked the *Hilfskasse* into shape." Putzi paused and considered how to formulate his concept while the clock ticked metalically in the stillness of the book-laden, untidy study filled with the mementos of the great who are long dead. Then he found the phrase he wanted. Expressing himself in those Bostonian accents he had acquired over half a century before, he boomed, *"In the final analysis, Martin Bormann was the star of the bureaucrats."*

It was a sentiment that was echoed by all those who knew him in those early years; one shared by Adolf Hitler. Six months after he came to power, therefore, he approved Rudolf Hess's choice of the thirty-three-year-old official as his chief of staff and made him *Reichsleiter*, one of the highest office-holders in the state, belonging to that group which had direct responsibility to the Leader himself.

But Martin Bormann did not let himself be seduced by the heady atmosphere of that first year of power. He remained his modest, hard-working self, content to function behind the scenes, to become the "man in the shadows" who despised the outward trappings of power, intent instead on *real* power. As he wrote to his wife many years later: "I have deliberately avoided this type of notoriety [the outward signs of having 'arrived'].If ever there is a memorial ceremony after my death, there must – under no circumstances – be a cheap exhibition of cushions with rows of medals and so on. These things give a false impression. Any nitwit who has been chasing after that sort of rubbish can have several cushions covered with it!"

For Bormann, power lay in talking over the administration of the Party, placing his men in the key jobs, seeing he had the Führer's ear, ensuring that those who couldn't be bought were at least scared of him. Within months, he had begun to ensure that Party promotions, demotions, and appointments lay within his hands and his hands alone. As his first and closest colleague, white-haired, art-loving, surprisingly gentle (for a former SS colonel) Heinrich Heim remembers today:[6]

---

[6] In a conversation with the author, 1971.

"He was correct, realistic, vital, and purposeful. But of course our job at first – there were only the two of us on Hess's staff – wasn't very promising. It was to help Party members who needed aid in any form from the leadership. In other words, a completely unpolitical activity."

But Bormann wanted more. His boss Hess, the Cairo-born World War I pilot, given to mysticism and astrology, the man who had copied down Mein Kampf while imprisoned with Hitler in Landsberg, was no organizer; indeed, he had as much interest in such things as did his supreme chief Adolf Hitler, who considered himself an artistic bohemian and acted accordingly. Although he now held a high position in the new regime, Bormann felt that Hess was letting the power slip through his fingers. Bormann knew that Hitler only wanted decisions; he did not want discussion or argument. Yet Hess was never present when the other high officials at Hitler's court made those decisions. As a result, Hess's role – and naturally Bormann's, too – was diminishing rapidly.

One year after Hitler had come to power, Bormann called Heim, who had previously practised law in Munich, into his office. He was in one of his frequent rages, which Heim suspected was the way he let off the steam accumulated behind the frozen bureaucratic mask he assumed before Hitler and Hess. "We can't go on like this!" he thundered. "Hess gets called to meetings only when the decisions have been made. Our office has no purpose if we don't have the power to make decisions ourselves or at least have some part in their making!" Heim nodded calmly. In the period of time he had worked with Bormann he had quickly acquired a thick skin. The coarse rages that stocky little Saxon was given to in private no longer worried him. Indeed when, a few years later, Bormann had bawled him out violently in the presence of "AH" himself, he had jerked a contemptuous thumb over his shoulder at the red-faced, trembling Bormann and said casually, "What do you expect from that farmer there!"[7]

When Bormann's anger of that particular moment had

---

[7] Throughout all his subsequent career he remained true to his old profession, rearing pigs and chickens just after his marriage to Gerda and running a model farm on the Obersalzberg later when he became much richer.

calmed, Heim suggested they should both draw up a paper and forward it to Hitler personally. In it they would propose that they should be represented at all important committee meetings, even if Hess had no time for the job. Surprisingly enough, Hitler, who had little time for such memos, agreed and as Heim remembers thirty years later, "In one scoop we were part and parcel of the decision-making process."

However, Martin Bormann was careful never to abuse his new-found power. "Martin Bormann's strength," as Heim puts it, "lay in the fact that he never overstepped the mark. He always kept within the boundaries of his own sphere. He was like a lawyer almost. He knew everybody's job and anyone who overstepped the mark was punished at once. Indeed, as the thirties passed, the representatives of the other departments were only too glad *not* to have to make the decisions any more. They left that to 'MB.'" But as the third decade of the twentieth century progressed and Hitler moved from one strength to another (and with him Bormann too) there remained one black spot on the little bureaucrat's horizon: the person of dark-eyed Rudolf Hess, the Führer's Deputy.[8]

---

[8] Hess had been wounded in the lung in World War I and as the thirties drew to an end he became increasingly concerned with his health and less with his job.

7

The Messerschmitt came in low over the little Scottish village of Eaglesham. Then it soared up steeply into the spring sky. Below the twin-engined German fighter, which was still on the secret list, the small, white-painted crofters' cottages were reduced to tiny boxes. At 650 feet the pilot levelled out; he had reached the minimum height at which he could safely parachute out.

Now the heavy-set forty-eight-year-old with the deep eyes and bushy black eyebrows started to work with remarkable speed for a man of his age and weight. He cut the ignition. Hastily he set the prop feathering. It was almost on zero. Now the wind would not be able to spin the twin screws. He had no desire to be dashed against the killing blades when he jumped.

Reaching up his hands, he felt for the canopy release. To his horror, the tremendous air pressure thrust him back against his seat – hard. "It pressed me up against the back partition as if I was glued to it," he recounted much later. "In spite of the great care I had taken to find out about *everything* from my good friends at Messerschmitt's there was just *one* thing I had overlooked. I had never asked about how to jump; I thought it was too simple!"

It wasn't, and as Dungavel Hill raced up to meet him at a terrifying rate, the middle-aged pilot sought desperately for some way out of the trap in which he found himself. Then, as he struggled to raise himself yet once again, he remembered the advice another old flier had once given him: the easiest way to get out of a crashing plane is to swing it upside down and fall out. The middle-aged German grabbed frantically at the stick. The ground fell away from him. Centrifugal force thrust him into his seat again. The blood drained from his brain. Stars flashed before his eyes in red-and-silver explosive bursts. Just before he lost consciousness, he told himself, I am only just above the ground and flying straight down. Soon the crash must come. *Is this the end?*

It wasn't – yet, though there were many of his fellow citizens in faraway Nazi Germany who would be soon wishing that it had been. Almost unconsciously the stunned pilot began to carry out the moves he should have made right at the start as he planned to jump. He brought the plane out of its curve and turned it almost on its tail. The blood rushed back to his brain. He felt sick and nauseous. But he was conscious again.

Somehow he pulled up his long legs and kicked himself up and out. Instinctively he pulled at the ripcord. There was a great jerk under his armpits. The crazy rush through the May sky halted. He drew in a huge gulp of fresh air in relief. Below in the moonlight he could see the fields and the village beyond. There were no lights and no visible signs of movement (the country had been blacked out after nightfall for three years now). He might have been falling into a dead world.

And then he hit the ground hard. Unconsciousness threatened to swamp him again. He fought it off and found the parachute harness. Somewhere far off he could hear faint shouts – whether they were of welcome or rage he could not tell. All he knew was that he, Rudolf Hess, deputy leader of a nation which ruled in this year of 1941 from Spitzbergen in the north to the Brenner in the south and from Brest-Litovsk in the east to Brest in the west had landed in enemy territory. "Only gradually," he wrote much later, "as the shouts of the Scottish farm labourers grew ever closer did it become clear to me that I had reached my goal – or rather a new beginning.... Alas, it was more of a beginning than I dreamed."

The man he had left behind who had represented him for over eight years at Hitler's court was Martin Bormann. For him, too, it was the beginning of a new life. Albert Speer, who was present at Hitler's residence on the Obersalzberg when the news of Hess's flight to England to make peace was revealed to the Leader, remembers: "At the time it appeared to me that Bormann's ambition had driven Hess to this desperate act. Hess, also highly ambitious, could plainly see himself being excluded from access to and influence over Hitler. Thus, for example, Hitler said to me sometime in 1940, after a conversation with Hess lasting many hours: 'When I talk with Goering it's like a bath in steel for me; I feel fresh afterwards With Hess every conversation becomes an unbearably tormenting strain. He always comes to me with unpleasant matters and won't leave off.' By his flight to England, Hess was probably trying, after so many years of being kept in the background, to win prestige and some success. For he did not have the qualities necessary for survival in the midst of a swamp of intrigues and struggles for power."

Martin Bormann did, however. As soon as Hitler bellowed *"Bormann at once! Where is Bormann?"* upon hearing the news of Hess's defection, Bormann went into operation. After warning Hess's pale-faced military adjutant, who brought the news of the flight to Hitler, not to involve him, he let the adjutant eat and make his report, then presented himself at the dinner table with two armed SS officers, who towered above him. "Karlheinz Pintsch," he said in a rasping voice to the young Air Force adjutant, "you are under arrest. You will be held under house arrest at Obersalzberg until a court of inquiry can be held into your part in the events of today. Heil Hitler!" In the hastily summoned conference held a few hours later, he convinced the Nazi *Prominenz*, including Hitler, that they should declare Hess insane; it was the only way to convince their erstwhile ally Russia, whom they would soon attack, that they were not trying to sign a separate peace pact with England.

One day later, Bormann stepped into his own for the very first time. It was at the special conference of the gauleiters. During this conference Hitler informed them that the news of Hess's flight had made him so physically sick that he had "almost fainted for the first time in his life" on opening the letter brought by Captain Pintsch.

Gauleiter Karl Wahl, World War I sergeant who was in charge of Swabian *gau* and knew Hess well (Hess's plane had come from Augsburg, Wahl's home) remembers that meeting on May 14, 1941. "I smelt a rat straight away," he recalls;[1] "there was something in the very air of the place. After Hitler told us about his not feeling well when he had opened the Hess

---

[1] In a conversation with the author, 1971.

letter, he then ordered Bormann to read it out to us. Bormann stood up and read it. But in a derogatory manner – I couldn't understand half of it. He swallowed down the bits where Hess explained why he'd flown to England.

"But the radicals and the arse-crawlers who supported Bormann were happy. You could see the happy look on their faces around the table. They knew by then that he'd got Hess's job. But I wasn't. Without Hitler, Bormann was nothing: with him he was everything."

That evening as he arrived back in Augsburg, Wahl came across the first announcement of the Hess flight. It explained: "Party Member Hess, because of an illness of many years' standing, which was becoming worse, and who had been forbidden by the Führer to do any flying, went against this order and obtained a plane on Saturday May 10. At 6:00 he left Augsburg in the plane and has not been heard from since.

"A letter which he left behind shows from its confused writing the unfortunate traces of a mental derangement and it is feared that Party Member Hess sacrificed himself to a fixed idea. It is felt that he crashed somewhere on this trip and probably died. The Führer has ordered the immediate arrest of Hess's adjutants who alone knew of the flight and the fact that such flights had been forbidden by the Führer."

Small, completely bald Wahl, who had been severely wounded in World War I and had built up the Nazi Party from almost nothing in his own area, read on: "The Leader has announced the following order. The Office of the Deputy to the Führer will now be called Party Chancellery. It will come under my direct control. *Its leader will be, as up to now, Party Member Martin Bormann.*"

Gauleiter Wahl, who like so many of the older gauleiters hated Bormann with a passion, considering him an upstart and interfering busybody, experienced a sinking feeling. As he recalled later: "This order was the death sentence for the Nazi Party! It was the commencement of Bormann's extension of his own personal power, which – with Hitler's aid – became ever larger during the course of the war until finally Bormann had complete control in his hand."

Thus at the age of forty-one, the ex-farm manager had reached the top at last. He had become increasingly gross and pugnacious in appearance. Schellenberg, the smart young lawyer who was the head of the SS Secret Service, described him at that time: "He was a short, stocky man with rounded shoulders and a bull neck. His head was always pushed forward a little and cocked slightly to one side and he had the face and shifty eyes of a boxer advancing on his opponent. . . . The contrast between him and Himmler was really grotesque. If I thought of Himmler as a stork in a lily pond, Bormann seemed to me like a pig in a potato field."

Hitler had long lost control of the civilian apparatus in wartorn Germany. He himself admitted in a moment of confidence: "[I have] totally lost sight of the organisations of the Party." His main concern was the conduct of the war. Now it was left to Bormann, who had waited so long and so patiently for his chance, to assume charge of the entire Nazi Party machine which extended far beyond the boundaries of Germany itself and controlled the destinies of nearly two hundred million people.

In his new office he appointed every new Party official and only allowed those already appointed to retain their jobs if they pleased and served him well. But his power did not limit itself to the Party; it extended for obvious reasons to the Army and the government, too. Now he had a hand in virtually every decision, and although he was not directly concerned with military operations, he did interfere in the relationships of the soldiers and generals with the populations of the occupied territories. (For reasons of his own, he was the main opponent of any attempt made by the Army to arm the millions of Russian prisoners of war under its control who wished to fight against Communism. It was a key decision which was not reversed until it was too late, and it contributed greatly to Germany's loss of the war in the East.)

Even before he was finally appointed "Secretary to the Führer" in 1943, everyone who was anyone within Nazi circles knew that the way to Hitler's ear was through Bormann. He, and he alone, controlled the people who spoke and wrote to Hitler; and even when his opponents managed to break through the defensive cordon he had built up around the person of the Leader, it was Bormann who carried out any decisions Hitler made. As a result, anything which was not to

Bormann's liking was simply "overlooked"; it got placed in a desk drawer and was conveniently forgotten.

Heinrich Hoffmann, one of Hitler's oldest and most loyal followers, Hitler's official photographer and the man who had introduced him to his mistress, Eva Braun, once appeared to criticize Bormann. Hitler lost his temper with the plump Bavarian who had made a fortune for himself (and the Führer) by the sale of his monopoly on Adolf Hitler photographs. "Get this quite clear in your head," he told the stunned little man, "and tell it to your son-in-law too.[2] To win this war I have need of Bormann! It is perfectly true that he is both ruthless and brutal . . . but the fact remains, one after another, everybody has failed in their implicit obedience to my commands – but Bormann never!" Hitler stared in that half-crazed hypnotic way of his and then his voice rose to a scream. "Everyone, I don't care who he may be, must understand this one fact clearly: whoever is against Bormann is also against the State! I'll shoot the lot of them, even if they number tens of thousands, just as I will shoot those who babble of peace! Far better that a few thousand miserable and witless fools should be liquidated than that a people of seventy millions should be dragged down to destruction!"[3]

---

[2] Baldur von Schirach, former Hitler Youth leader and Gauleiter of Vienna, to whom Hoffmann had once wanted to marry Eva Braun but who had eventually married Hoffmann's daughter.

[3] Later Bormann became aware of Hoffmann's dislike of him. He spread the rumour that both Hoffmann and his son were suffering from a contagious disease. He knew this was something which would repel Hitlcr, who was always almost pathologically afraid of disease. (Told to the author by Hoffmann's son in an interview, 1971.)

8

To outsiders the Nazi regime looked like a tightly knit and tremendously threatening structure in 1943. But the typical observer of the Nazi scene from England or the U.S.A. or from one of the occupied countries was blinded by his own fears of the jackbooted monster; it admittedly had been badly wounded at El Alamein, Stalingrad, and numerous smaller battles, yet it was still capable of battling against the combined might of the Western Allies and Russia.

But in reality the Nazi form of government was remarkably sloppy, loose – almost Bohemian, like the man who had originated it. No one really knew who was responsible for what, save that the real centre of power was located in the person of Adolf Hitler. Yet the overwhelming question still remained for the German enquirer: *How did the Führer exercise that power? Where did he get the information to allow him to form his decisions and how exactly were they put into operation?* One skilled observer of the German scene at that time, Hannah Arendt, deduced that "real power began where secrecy began." She maintained that this is "the only rule of which everybody in a totalitarian state may be sure."

By 1943, Martin Bormann was the most powerful man in Germany after Adolf Hitler. His shadow had fallen over and blocked out those stars of the Old Guard such as Goering, Ley, Ribbentrop, Himmler – and even Goebbels only kept his position by joining the Bormann camp. New stars such as Albert Speer, Hitler's "fellow artist" who could do no wrong in the Führer's eyes, also failed in their attempts to break Bormann's power; and Speer had to admit ruefully of the Leader's Secretary (he called him "the man with the hedge clippers"): "Our grand assault on Bormann had come to grief."

Yet in spite of the immense power he had at his disposal, the calculating, clinical Saxon (of whom Speer said despondently, "A few critical words from Hitler and all Bormann's enemies would have been at his throat") still disdained the outward show; he saw power alone, not its trappings. He was "the man in the shadows," the "Brown Eminence" – in short, a man of "darkness and concealment," as seventeenth-century Cardinal Richelieu called his own Bormann, Père Joseph.[1]

Bormann was always at Hitler's side in his badly fitting uniform, briefcase under his arm, making notes on slips of paper which he tucked in his cuff, listening, considering, plotting, with an expression of eagerness on his broad "Slavic" face (many of his enemies thought he must be of Slavic origin; to them he simply couldn't be German), as if he were ready to pounce on some unwary victim at any moment.

According to German writer Joachim Fest, Bormann divided people into two categories: "those he could win over and subordinate to himself and those he had to fear, and he distrusted everyone." Working silently and secretively in the background, he assiduously collected information on his personal card index about everyone and anyone and showed himself to be a master of court intrigue, dropping a hint here, a whispered aside there, breaking a reputation over the *Eintopf* (a kind of stew) served at Hitler's table, making one over the cream cakes and tea which the Leader loved so greedily. It is not without reason that Bormann has been often compared with Stalin in the days when the latter was second man after Lenin and was already planning for the time when he would take over absolute power from the dying Communist dictator. By this time Bormann, who knew everything, must also have known that Adolf Hitler did not have much longer to live.

The intense secrecy with which Bormann functioned makes it exceedingly difficult to know what was going on in his mind at a time when he, more than anyone else, knew how badly the

---

[1] In the spring of 1943 Speer had tried to mobilize Goering, Goebbels, and Ley against Bormann. Then Goering had exclaimed excitedly: "He's always putting in a word edgewise, torpedoing me below the water line. But that's ending right now! I'm going to see to it, gentlemen." But when it came to a showdown, both Goering and Goebbels backed off.

war was going for Germany. It was an almost pathological need which extended beyond politics to his private life.

His brother-in-law Hermann Buch remembers:[2] "In those years we could never go and visit my sister when he was there at the Obersalzberg. On the odd occasions when we went, we were always invited when he wasn't there. . . . But he liked his food all right. Indeed, one of my old comrades Richard Schulze told Hitler in 1942: 'My Leader, you've got a lot of hypocrites around you here. [They] pretend to be vegetarian and then fill themselves with meat.' Hitler looked at Richard who was a bit of a comic and said, 'What do you mean? Who are you talking about?' But Richard refused to give the name. 'If I told you, my Leader,' he replied, 'I'd be kicked out of the Party.' Thereupon Hitler smiled and said, 'Oh I know who you mean.' And Gerda always used to say, 'They must have terribly bad food at Hitler's HQ; when Martin comes home, the first thing he starts looking for is sausage.'"

These secretive eating habits were confirmed by Henrich Hoffmann's son[3] who remembers that "at the Führer's HQ in East Prussia, he always kept a loop of sausage hidden behind the closet in his room, hanging on a nail. When no one was present who might blab on him, he'd move it and cut himself off a piece."

Similarly, he was secretive about his sex life. It was known that Martin Bormann had powerful sex drives. To his intimates he boasted that no woman "could resist" him; undoubtedly he had several mistresses and occasional love affairs with the secretaries attached to the Leader's HQ. Yet in his diary found after the war,[4] the references to his mistresses are kept in the same secretive manner as everything else in his life, as, for instance: "M" Dresden *Weisser Hirsch* (the name of an inn probably); "Theatre" which referred, in fact, to the Dresden movie actress, Manja Behrens, who became his mistress after he had dropped his former one in 1943; "IR" (again written in the same secret shorthand), his former mistress.

---

[2] In a conversation with the author, 1971
[3] In a conversation with the author, 1971
[4] We'll come back to the diary later.

The only person in whom he seemed to confide to some extent was his wife. In 1944, after he had been sleeping with the minor movie actress Manja Behrens for some six months he wrote his wife (whom he called *Mutti*; i.e., Mummy) a blow-by-blow description of the relationship. Dated January 21, 1944, the letter reads in part: "[I kissed] her without any further waste of time and quite scorched her with my burning joy. I fell madly in love with her. I arranged it so that I met her again many times and then I took her in spite of her refusals. You know the strength of my will, against which M was naturally unable to hold out for long. Now she's mine and now – lucky fellow – I am, or rather I feel, doubly and unbelievably happily married. . . . What do you think, beloved, of your crazy fellow?"

Gerda, a long-suffering mother weakened by too much child-bearing in spite of her (previously) robust constitution, replied at once. "I am so fond of M myself," she wrote, "that I cannot simply be angry with you, and the children love her, too, very much – all of them." She then went on maintaining it was "a thousand pities" that Manja Behrens should be denied children because her fiancé had been killed in Russia. Her husband, she advocated, should change this state of affairs. "But then," she wrote, "you will have to see to it that one year M has a child and the next year I, so that you will always have a wife who is mobile. . . . We'll put all the children together in the house on the lake and live together, and the wife who is not having a child will always be able to come and stay with you in Obersalzberg or Berlin."

However, the suggestion of this potentially piquant sexual situation which held the promise of a *ménage à trois* apparently offended Bormann's desire for secrecy, for he wrote on the margin of Gerda's letter that it was a "wild idea" but that it "would never do! Even if the two women were the most intimate friends. Each stays by herself. Visits, all right, but even that without exaggeration."

And in the end one doubts whether Bormann even confided in Gerda to whom he wrote (after she had allowed him to make love to Manja in their house on the Obersalzberg): "I believe she [Manja] loves me very much. Of course, it doesn't go as deep as our love does; fifteen years of one's youth, rich in

65

shared experience, and ten children weigh heavily in the scales."[5]

Bormann repeatedly told his wife that all he desired was to get away from it all and become a farmer again. In October, 1944, for instance, he wrote her: "My beloved Girl – You cannot imagine how much I am looking forward to life after I'm pensioned off. . . . As soon as our Führer no longer needs me, or as soon as there is a new Führer, I shall retire to private life and live – at last – a few years in peace, according to my inclination" He wrote this at a time when he was eagerly consolidating his own power by doing what all the important members of the Old Guard, whom he'd cut out in the last two years, had done before him: establish a private army, the half-a-million-strong *Volkssturm*, a home guard made up of teenage youths and men over military age. In addition, he was getting ready for the final showdown with the last men in Germany able to stand up to him: the gauleiters, who had a great deal of independence in the running of their *Gaue*. Were these the actions of a man who really meant that his major concern was retirement and a return to quiet private life on a farm?

What then was going on in Bormann's mind in the last year of the war? There is no doubt that he completely realized that Germany was heading for a defeat and the rats were about to desert the sinking ship. In a letter from his wife in February, 1945, she wrote, obviously in answer to one he had written her: "My darling Daddy – We have now reached the parting of the ways; all those who have not absolute faith in the Führer are faltering and losing their courage." Gerda ended with a compliment for him: "Do you remember the Führer saying to us during the struggle period that, if in 1918 there had been a body of ten thousand men under strong and determined leadership, everything would have been very different? Well – today we have, thank goodness, very many more fine men than that – *and not all of them at the front either.*"

In his last letter to his wife, dated April 2, one month before the end, he wrote: ". . . but we must not be downhearted; whatever comes, we are pledged to do our duty. And if we are

---

[5] One child died before the war due to Bormann's insistence that the child should drink uncooked or "raw" milk; it contracted bovine tuberculosis.

destined, like the old Niebelungs, to perish in King Attila's hall, then we'll go to our death proudly and with our heads held high!"

Was Bormann planning to go down with the ship? His intimates thought so. Heinrich Heim, the reserved ex-Secretary of State who had known him since 1929 and was his closest colleague, maintains today: "MB made no plans to escape from Berlin. He was completely loyal. He wouldn't try to run away." Former Chief Editor Schwaebe of the National Socialist daily *Westdeutscher Beobachter*, who had known Bormann since 1931, gives a more practical reason for Bormann's decision to stay in Berlin. "What was he without Hitler? He was the Leader's mouthpiece. As soon as Adolf Hitler was dead, Bormann would be a nobody. He was no politician after all – simply a bureaucrat. For that reason he wouldn't make plans to run away."[6] It is an opinion shared by his brother-in-law Hermann Buch, who said, "Martin didn't look that far ahead. He was part and parcel of Hitler's daily life. Without Hitler he didn't exist. What would the future hold for him even if he had have gotten out of Berlin? Without Hitler he was a nothing."

Yet when finally Bormann found himself with Hitler in the bunker, the only one of the paladins left (apart from Goebbels), there is no indication that he felt he was going to die there, violently or otherwise. After all, even when the Russians had surrounded Berlin, there were still ways and means of getting out by both land and air; and most of the parties and individual aircraft which fled the beleaguered city got through to the west – albeit with casualties.

Nor did his actions in those last few days seem to indicate a man who had resigned himself to death. While the "lack of fresh air became unbearable," according to Cavalry Captain Gerhard Boldt, who was adjutant to General Krebs, "and the people . . . sank into a dull brooding mood," Bormann was busy sending out a steady stream of telegrams to the remaining operational commanders in the West.

His behaviour in those days did not indicate that he had given up his overriding will to live. Admittedly he got drunk more often than he had done earlier, but that meant very little in the

---

[6] In a conversation with the author in 1971.

hectic, chaotic atmosphere of the fetid, evil-smelling bunker; everyone was getting drunk. Once during the course of one of these drinking sessions, a drunken General Burgdorf told Bormann[7], his already red face growing purple with rage: "Nine months ago I approached my present task with all my strength and idealism. I tried again and again to coordinate the Party and the Forces, I have gone so far in this that I have been looked at askance, even despised by my comrades in the Forces. I have done the impossible to try to eradicate from Hitler and the Party leaders their mistrust of the Armed Forces and I have finally been called a traitor to the officer caste in the Armed Forces. Today I must confess that these accusations were justified, that my labours were for nothing, my idealism was wrong and not that alone, it was naive and stupid."

General Krebs, who was also present at the drunken scene, tried to calm his comrade. But Burgdorf was not to be stopped. He railed at Bormann and said the sacrifice of the German Army had been in vain. It had not been ". . . for a decent clean Germany. No. They have died for you, for your life of luxury, for your thirst for power. In their faith in a good cause the youth of a nation of eighty million has bled to death on the battlefields of Europe. Millions of people – innocent people – have been sacrificed while you, the leaders of the Party, have enriched yourselves with the property of the nation. You have feasted, have accumulated enormous wealth, have robbed estates, wallowed in abundance, have swindled and oppressed the people. Our ideals, our morals, our faith, our souls, have been trodden in the dirt by you! Man for you was nothing but the tool of your insatiable craving for power. You have anni-hilated the German people. That is your terrible guilt!"

No one had dared to talk like that to Martin Bormann for years – not even Hitler.[8]

Yet it is indicative of Bormann's mood at that time that he did not lose his temper or launch into a spirited defence of his action (as so many of the bunker's inhabitants were now

[7] Overheard by Captain Boldt and reported in his book, *Die Letzten Tage*.
[8] His brother-in-law, on guard at the Reichs Chancellery before the war, remembers his comrades pulling his leg because Hitler had *angeschissen* (literally, "shit on,') Martin because the latter had failed to have an automobile waiting for the Leader on one occasion.

doing, now that they knew their end was near). Instead, Bormann replied in a voice which Boldt, listening with his ear pressed to the wall of the other room, recalls as "cool, premeditated and oily": "My dear fellow, you ought not to be so personal about it. Even if all the others have enriched themselves, I at least am blameless. That much I swear to you on everything that I hold sacred. Your health, my friend! *Prosit!*"

Indeed Bormann's last political action indicates that he felt he would survive and that he hoped to enjoy a political role in the post-Hitler Reich. How else can we explain the careful and cunning way that he dealt with the Grand Admiral Karl Dönitz, designated as Hitler's successor, between April 30 and May 1/2, 1945?

At 3:30 P.M. on the afternoon of April 30, two shots rang out in the bunker.[9] In the near-by conference room, Bormann, Gunsche, Hitler's SS adjutant, and Heinz Linge, the Leader's valet, started. Then they rushed to Hitler's rooms. They found him sprawled face down across a little coffee table. He was dead.

Unnerved, Gunsche staggered back and almost bumped into Kempka.

"For God's sake Otto," Kempka snapped. "What's going on? You must be crazy to have me send men to almost certain death just for two hundred litres of petrol!"

Gunsche slammed the door closed and faced the chauffeur Kempka, his eyes wide and staring as if drugged. "The chief's dead," he breathed.

For a moment Kempka did not speak. Then he stuttered, "Where's Evi?" (He meant Eva Braun, the Führer's new wife.)

Wordlessly Gunsche pointed into the next room.

Kempka staggered in the direction of his gaze. His eyes fell on Bormann trying to lift Eva Braun. Suddenly rage overcame him. He knew what Eva had thought of Bormann, although she had managed to conceal her dislike of the squat "skirt-chaser" (as she called him) who was even too dangerous for

---

[9] Nothing is clear about Hitler's death – even twenty-six years later. Were there two shots or only one? Did the Russians find his body or not? Was he even shot? Did he perhaps take poison? *Or did he even die at all?*

her, the Leader's long-term mistress. "Not one more step," Kempka snapped. "I'll carry Evi!"

Bormann stopped, then shrugged and handed his burden over to the broad-shouldered, tough-looking miner's son. Both his master and his mistress were dead, Bormann's eyes seemed to say; now he had to look after himself.

Thus while the chauffeur, the valet and the adjutant – each of whom held the rank of SS colonel – paid their last homage to their *Brotherr* (the man who gave them bread), Bormann, the incurable optimist, set about assuring his own personal future.

Almost immediately, even before the macabre funeral ceremony got underway in the shell-pitted garden outside, he sent a brusque, highly uninformative telegram to Grand Admiral Dönitz, the onetime head of the German U-boat service. It read:

Grand Admiral Dönitz – In place of the former Reichsmarschal Goering, the Führer appoints you, Herr Grand Admiral, as his successor. Written authority is on its way. You will immediately take all such measures as the situation requires.

—Bormann

Not one word of the Führer's death and what the situation was in Berlin.

Dönitz, the thin-faced, cold-eyed sailor who had brought the British Empire almost to its knees with his submarines in 1942, was puzzled but relieved. "I'd been considering stopping the war at sea and committing suicide for days," he recalled much later.[10] "But now everything had changed. I had a relatively clear-cut task again. I could do something."

One day later Dönitz, at his headquarters in faraway Plön, received yet another enigmatic telegram from the squat little man in the beleaguered bunker, who, now that Goebbels would soon be dead, would be the last of Hitler's paladins with any real power in his hands. It read:

The testament is in force. Coming to you as soon as possible.

---

[10] In a conversation with the author, 1971.

Until then you should, in my opinion, refrain from public statement.

Again the vitally important foci that Hitler was dead was not mentioned!

A few hours later the Admiral, who had lost two sons himself in the war, but who was still resolved to continue fighting as long as he could save German soldiers and civilians fleeing from the East and the Russians, by holding open the "Elbe Gap" against the advancing British, received the final communication from Martin Bormann. [11]

This time he revealed that the Führer was already dead, for the radio message stated:

> Führer deceased yesterday at 3:30 P M. Testament of April 29th appoints you Reichspresident. Minister Goebbels Chancellor, Reichsleiter Bormann Party Minister . . . Reichsminister Bormann will try to get to you today to orient you on the situation. The form and time of announcement to the troops and public are left to you.
> Confirm receipt.
>
> Goebbels-Bormann

"This is utterly impossible," Dönitz exclaimed, his thin, worn face flushing angrily when he got the radiogram. Turning to his adjutant Lüdde-Neurath, he snapped, "Has anyone else seen the radio message yet?"

The tall, skinny adjutant with the Iron Cross on his breast assured him that the news was known only to himself and the radiotelegraphist.

Dönitz then swore them both to secrecy, and turning to Speer, Bormann's deadly enemy, who was present, he asked, "What will we do if Bormann and Goebbels actually arrive?"

---

[11] This was the only escape route from the East across the River Elbe to the comparative safety of the West which Dönitz knew would be soon occupied by the Anglo–Americans It was an escape route used not only by ordinary soldiers and civilians, but also, by those who knew they would have to answer to Allies on account of "war crimes." Among the latter the most prominent was Himmler, who managed to hide from the British for nearly three weeks before he disclosed his identify. The presence of this escape route westward is an important point to bear in mind in the Bormann case.

Then before Speer could answer, he snapped, "I absolutely will not cooperate with them in any case!"

"That evening," as Speer remembered many years later, "we both agreed that Bormann and Goebbels must somehow be placed under arrest."

Speer and Dönitz need not have feared; Bormann, as we know, did not turn up. And in this particular case we can take both men's word for it. Unlike such witnesses as Axmann, Kempka, and Naumann, who had no reason to tell the Allied investigators after the war the truth – why should they? *After all, Bormann was one of them* – Speer hated the squat little Party Secretary with almost pathological intensity; and as for Dönitz, he had little contact with Bormann and did not assess him very highly. As he told this author, "Bormann did not appear on my scale of values – either up or down. For me he was of no importance."

Yet all the same, Bormann obviously intended on that first day of May, 1945, to try to get to Plön. He was not prepared to die. As Albert Speer was to tell the press many years later: "Bormann was a born survivor. If anyone got out it would be him."

Today we can reconstruct his own conception of his future role after Hitler's death along the following lines. With Hitler's death, Bormann's power automatically ceased and was transferred elsewhere – from the bunker to Dönitz's HQ. He knew this and also that the only means of continuing that power, which he loved so dearly, would be somehow to be the bearer of the news that Hitler was dead. But would that be sufficient? Bormann evidently thought not. So instead of leaving immediately with the group that left the bunker carrying copies of the Leader's last will and testament (and it should be noted that each of these men got through successfully to the West), he decided to stick it out with Goebbels, who had every intention of committing suicide like Hitler, and try to arrange a peace with the Russians. The inhabitants of the bunker had already managed to raise radio contact with the surrounding Russians and receive an affirmative answer to their request for a meeting with them.

If – accepting the fact that this was Bormann's reasoning – he could secure an armistice, or a peaceful surrender of Berlin on the basis of whatever terms the Russians demanded, he could then demand a plane or other means of transportation to leave the city. Naturally he would not tell the Russians what his real intentions were. Perhaps he would offer himself as an emissary to Dönitz so that they would gain the grand kudos of having *all* the German forces surrender to them, instead of to Montgomery as was soon to be the case. In fact, he thought he would arrive at Dönitz's headquarters in the role of *deus ex machina*, who had saved what was still to be saved in Berlin and was now prepared to accept an important role in the Grand Admiral's government which undoubtedly would be supported by the Western Allies once the latter became aware that the real threat to their safety lay in the East and turned against the "red hordes".[12]

By the small hours of the night of May 1/2, Martin Bormann had become aware that his carefully laid plans had come to naught. Yet, as we have already seen, he was still prepared not to succumb to the heady attraction of suicide as a final solution to all his problems, as a means of escaping the destruction which he had helped to bring upon Germany. Unlike Hitler, Goebbels, Himmler, Ley, and Goering, who all took this way out, Martin Bormann was ready to fight for his life like a cornered rat.

And like a rat, Bormann exhibited bitter, desperate courage, and more cunning. The man who had worked for so many years in the shadows and had raised himself up from a minor, completely obscure position to become what Professor Trevor-Roper has described as "the most powerful individual in the internal affairs of Germany between 1943 and 1945"[13] was not a man who would do anything without a plan. As we have seen, even in the midst of the complete breakdown of authority and discipline within the bunker, Bormann was still planning and calculating. Would such a man "the star of the bureaucrats," simply run? Would he blunder blindly after the others – the admittedly tough but minor figures such as Kempka, the

---

[12] Then, as even today, many older Germans simply could not believe that the Anglo–Americans did not see the danger from the Communists. They cannot understand why the British and Americans did not continue the war, this time against their allies of the last four years.
[13] In a letter to author.

chauffeur; Linge, the valet; Secretary of State Naumann; the radiotelegraphist; Axmann, the one-armed SS man? Would he not have a plan, however crude and last-minute, for the continuation of his journey once he had broken through the exceedingly loose cordon the Russians had thrown around the centre of the city?

Forgetting Axmann's, Baur's, and Kempka's testimony (and that of the round dozen other "witnesses" of "Bormann's death" who would join them in the years to come) for the moment, let us have a look at the escape possibilities open to the Reichsleiter on that terrible, shell-rocked day of May, 1945.

They can be reduced to three.

The first is the escape route to Dönitz; the obvious one. As we have seen, if Bormann did take the westward route and managed to get through, he did not make an appearance at Dönitz's HQ; the Admiral would have arrested him.[14]

The second is the most unlikely one, but one we shall examine in due course. It is eastward to the Russians, a people Bormann had always hated with a passion – at least outwardly – and of whom he said: "They only need to learn to be able to count up to ten in German and read our signposts." For him the Russians were "red scum" and "raping monsters." It would seem, therefore, hardly likely that he would take that particular route.

All that remains is the third one: southward through Bavaria and on to the snow-locked mountains and deep, lonely valleys of southern Austria and northern Italy. In other words, the Tyrol, inhabited on both sides of the border by granite-hard, fanatically loyal German-speaking peasantry, an area which in May, 1945, was still causing headaches for Allied intelligence officers from Major General Kenneth Strong, Eisenhower's Chief of Intelligence, down to the most unimportant battalion S-3 of the U.S. Seventh and Third Armies, which were still fighting their bitter way into the harsh, snow-filled valleys.

---

[14] In order to lend his "administration" credibility in the eyes of the Allies, the Grand Admiral had kept it clean of Nazis. In this way he hoped to gain Allied support for the continuance of the rump German government at Flensburg. (For further details see the author's *Finale at Flensburg*.)

The "Alpine Redoubt," as the area was referred to on the Allied situation maps, was regarded by Eisenhower as the place where the fanatical remnants of the SS would fight to the last. Was it not here that the toughest and most desperate of them were concentrating – Skorzeny, the scarfaced giant who had rescued Mussolini and who was now featured on the Allied wanted lists as "the most dangerous man in Europe"; Müller, head of the Gestapo; Kaltenbrunner, the chain-smoking, scarfaced Austrian-born head of the German SS Main Office; and all the rest of the men who had held Europe in fear and trembling these last six years?

As the war which had cost the lives of some twenty million soldiers and civilians came to an end that May, agents from a dozen different countries started to slip into the mountain fastness. Some came to help those who wished to escape from Allied justice; others to prevent that escape. And the hunt for Martin Bormann was on.

III

The Hunt Begins

The greatest manhunt in history is under way from Norway to the Bavarian Alps.

– ANTHONY EDEN, British Foreign Secretary, 1945

III

The Hunt Begins

9

In the silent, snow-capped mountains they waited that month for fate to overtake them or offer them the unbelievable chance of a new start. Down below in the green, sun-drenched valleys the *Amis*, as they still called the GIs contemptuously, buzzed busily to and fro in their jeeps, whistling gleefully at the buxom, barelegged Bavarian and Austrian girls, avoiding the plodding, bullock-drawn carts with superb ease and casualness, as if they had been driving in the mountains all their life, resting on their laurels after the miserable mud of Metz, the blood and snow of the Ardennes, and the costly fight through central Germany. It was all over for the bright-faced twenty-year-old veterans of Patton's and Patch's armies. *Their* war was over.

But in the lonely ski huts and isolated farmhouses of the mountains with their enormous green-tiled stoves which reached up to the roof and their carnation-bright wooden balconies, decorated with blue-and-white paintings of happy farmers in short leather trousers and buxom farm maids in billowing dirndls, some waited for the knock on the door, the impatient scrape of heavy boots and the inquiry which might mean death– or a way across the mountains to a new start in Spain or South America. For, as British Foreign Minister Anthony Eden told the House of Commons in that month of victory, the greatest manhunt in history was under way from Norway to the Bavarian Alps.

At the foot of the aptly named Austrian Totengebirge, the "Dead Mountains," in the tourist village of Alt-Aussee, Ernst Kaltenbrunner knew the war had ended. The six-foot-three, scarfaced, rotten-toothed Ernst, formerly SS chief in Austria and more recently (after 1942) Chief of the Reich Security Police and Security Service, knew that time was running out. But the chain-smoking giant did not wait for the Allied patrols to come and capture him. Almost immediately he set off with a fake Army paybook which bore a forged Red Cross seal identifying him as a doctor.

Before he left he had met for the last time one of his most notorious subordinates: a small, balding, hook-nosed SS officer with an everyday sort of face distinguished only by dark colouring unlike the SS-preferred pink-and-white Aryan complexion. His name was Karl Adolf Eichmann; he was the Gestapo man in charge of "Jewish Problems."

A short time before that, "Gestapo Müller," the ex-cop (of whom we shall hear more soon) who had become head of the Gestapo, had offered Eichmann faked papers testifying that he had worked for a civilian firm during the war. Angrily Eichmann had stalked into Müller's office at that time and confronted the latter with that look in his cold dark eyes which had sent off so many millions of Jews on their last journey on this earth.

"Well, Eichmann." Müller had inquired, "what's the matter with you?" "*Herr Gruppenführer*" he announced, "I don't need the papers." He tapped the pistol at his belt. "This is my certificate. When I see no other way out, it will be my last remedy. I have no need for anything else."[1]

However, Eichmann's previous attitude had changed. Within a matter of weeks, his face had sunk and his eyes were dull; in spite of the brilliant sunshine outside, his usually dark face looked wan and sickly. At this, their final meeting, Kaltenbrunner, who was sipping cognac (he usually finished a bottle before lunch) and playing solitaire, asked almost casually, "What are you going to do now'?"

Eichmann licked his thick underlip uneasily. He avoided the other man's eye, as he explained he was going to go into the mountains and fight a last-ditch battle along with other Nazi stalwarts.

Kaltenbrunner looked at him cynically. "That's good! Now

[1] A little later Eichmann told his own men: "I will gladly jump into my grave in the knowledge that five million enemies of the Reich [he meant the Jews] have already died like animals."

1 & 2. Always in the shadow of his master: Bormann with Hitler, seen below shaking hands with Himmler.

3. A rare photograph of Martin Bormann's wedding to Gerda Buch in 1929. The witnesses include Hess (left), Hitler (second from right) and Bormann's brother Albert (right).

4. A bust of Gerda by Arno Breker

5. Bormann in the 1930s. With him is Field Marshal Keitel.

6 & 7. Reinhard Heidrich, the only man who might have stood in Bormann's way, seen below with his wife and child.

8. Rudolf Hess, Bormann's boss (see p.59).

9. Reichsführer Heinrich Himmler, one of the 'Old Guard'.

10. Wachenfeld, Hitler's residence on the Obersalzberg, established by Bormann.

Himmler can talk to Eisenhower differently [Himmler had explained a little while earlier that he was going to negotiate with the Supreme Commander]; he'll know that an Eichmann in the mountains will never surrender – *because he can't!*"

Eichmann stared at the big Austrian open-mouthed. He knew Kaltenbrunner's drunken moods but he had never seen him like this.

Suddenly Kaltenbrunner snapped down a card. Eichmann jumped at the noise. "*Es ist alles Scheisse* [It's all crap]," he said quietly, as if he had abruptly made up his own mind about the future. "The game is up."

By the end of that glorious May of 1945, there were many others hiding in the mountains who thought so, too.[2] Otto Skorzeny came down from his hiding place and surrendered himself to the astonished Americans, still in possession of his pistol and decorated with his chestful of medals for bravery. General Reinhard Gehlen, head of Eastern Intelligence, of whom we shall hear more, did so as well and to his indignation was imprisoned in a common POW camp until the Americans became aware of whom they had caught. They then flew him secretly to Washington where he would spill all he knew about the secrets of the United States enemy of the future – Soviet Russia.

Some Nazis surrendered as part of their escape plan, for example, Eichmann, now known as Corporal Barth of the Lwftwaffe. Naturally he was put into a POW camp. But that wasn't good enough cover for Eichmann, who knew the intelligence services of a dozen countries were already looking for him. He promoted himself to SS Lieutenant and assumed the name of Otto Eckmann. Who would believe that any German that year would deliberately put himself in danger by claiming to belong to the SS? Lieutenant Otto Eckmann was obviously a small, harmless fish. One year later he escaped from the camp without difficulty and fled down the Odessa escape route to South America, where, fourteen years later, he was captured by Israeli agents in Buenos Aires and smuggled to Israel for trial. He was sentenced to death.

But some wouldn't or couldn't surrender – they did not dare take the risk that Eichmann had.

---

[2] Kaltenbrunner was arrested on May 15 and was hanged at Nuremberg.

There was the cold, secretive head of the Gestapo, Heinrich Müller, who, as SS General Schellenberg remembers, played Bormann's game: "Privately Müller established good relations with Bormann, while pretending to oppose him strongly." He was a man described by one of his subordinates as possessing an "imposing head and sharp features, curiously disfigured by a thin gash of a mouth that had no lips." At the end of the war he was thought dead, killed in the fighting in Berlin. When his grave was dug up later, it was found to contain the bones of three different men, none of them Heinrich Müller. Where was Müller?

Simon Wiesenthal, born in Polish Galicia, who made his business the hunting of the ex-Nazis, reported the presence of a "strange lieutenant with the everyday name of Schmidt" in the mountains that summer. The "locals found it strange that a man of about fifty and a humble lieutenant in rank" could give orders to high-ranking officers of the SS and Army. On May 5, 1945, the locals reported their suspicions to the American garrison. The latter sent a task force under a Colonel Pearson to apprehend the group led by the strange lieutenant. But before they could make contact, they had to fight their way through Austrian Communist partisans. The latter did not put up any great resistance, but by the time the task force had reached the spot where "Schmidt" was reported to be, he had fled with his followers – *eastward!*

Wiesenthal, an ex-concentration camp inmate who had relinquished his profession as architect to become one of the most feared amateur detectives in history, drew one conclusion only: the man who had run the Gestapo for so long, who had tortured and murdered Communists by the hundred, had gone over to his most deadly enemy – Soviet Russia.[3]

A tall, lanky, bespectacled Englishman came into the mountains as the scores of agents, sensation-seekers, and journalists, eager for such a good story, began to depart disappointedly. He was not interested in Kaltenbrunner, Skorzeny, Eichmann, Müller, and the rest. His deceptively mild-mannered gaze was fixed on the image of one man only – Martin Bormann. Let us

---

[3] Some authorities think-as we shall see-that Müller had been a Soviet agent from 1943 onward.

see if we can capture something of the personality of this man who was to take such a crucial role in the hunt for MB.

Professor Hugh Trevor-Roper is the epitome of the upper-class English scholar. He was educated at the exclusive six-hundred-year-old public school of Charterhouse from whence he passed to Christ Church, Oxford, where he was later to become a distinguished professor. He is a tall, finely limbed man. In spite of the relatively poor salary earned by an Oxford professor of history, he was given to wearing expensive clothes and riding to hounds (he once broke his back doing so), with a little salmon fishing in Scotland in winter thrown in. Like the other members of his class, he pretended to disdain seriousness and was much given to practical jokes.

During the war, for instance, he had been attached to the famous Dambuster Squadron as an intelligence officer.[4] As a result of his participation in one of the squadron's missions, he and a dozen more officers and NCOs were to be suitably decorated by King George VI at Buckingham Palace. They were packed in two special train compartments; in one were the "respectable" officers, accompanied by their wives; in the other, the "bloods" (to use the upper-class term which Trevor-Roper favoured), pockets filled with bottles of rationed gin and whisky.

The party got under way as soon as the train left the provincial station bound for London. In the "respectable" compartment the officers were chatting politely to their wives dressed in their best "floral bonnets" and the WAAF officers in their best blues,[5] when a bewildered radio operator appeared, immaculately dressed, his buttons shining and blue collar crisp and stiff with starch – dressed, that is, in everything *save his pants!*

"Losht my pantsh," he mumbled. "Very awkward. Can't see the King without pantsh."

One of the senior officers of 617 Squadron jumped up and bundled the drunk man away from the giggling WAAFs and

---

[4] This squadron had the highly dangerous and decidedly tricky task of creating breaches in the dams that fed the German Ruhr with water and power by a new "skip and hit" type of bomb. They were highly successful.

[5] Female RAF officers.

the shocked wives. Shoving him into the toilet, he walked along to the "bloods" compartment where a nonchalant Trevor-Roper was playing cards with a fellow officer. "I say," Humphries, the man in question said, "have any of you chaps by any chance seen Brian's pants?"

There were stifled bursts of laughter.

"Why, Adj," someone asked innocently, "has he lost them?"

"You know he has," Humphries replied angrily. "It's not really so funny. He just walked into a compartment where there were a couple of ladies."

There were louder bursts of laughter.

"Quite well made, isn't he?" someone said.

By this time Trevor-Roper, the originator of the pants-stealing trick, was eyeing Humphries's trousers sinisterly. Humphries looked back sternly. "You wouldn't think it was funny if it had been your girl friends," he said.

"Have a Scotch before you go, Adj," Trevor-Roper said, and before the other could answer had poured him a cupful. The Adjutant knew that it was either the drink or his pants, so he drank the strong liquor down in one gulp. Thus the drunken party proceeded to London to receive their decorations *en masse*, including one Hugh Trevor-Roper, who received the Distinguished Flying Cross for Gallantry Under Fire.

The former Oxford scholar, who was one day to become Regius Professor of Modern History at the same university,[6] was at the time he arrived in the Tyrol a typical product of his class and training: a man who concealed an exceedingly sharp intellect and a recognized degree of bravery behind the flippancy and casualness which his type of Englishman had cultivated for centuries. And now this apparently mild-mannered man had finally reached the remote valleys as part of the greatest manhunt in history.

---

[6] This is perhaps the highest honor obtainable in the field of history teaching in the United Kingdom. The Regius Professor is – as his title indicates – appointed by the Monarch himself.

10

Three months earlier, in September, 1945, the tall, bespectacled Englishman had been assigned a task. It had now
brought him to these remote, snowbound valleys. He had
been told at the highest level to discover what the true
circumstances of Hitler's death were – if indeed the German
leader had really died in the surrounded Berlin bunker. Even
then, there were rumours enough going around: that Hitler
had been murdered by his own officers; that he had escaped
by submarine to a lonely, fog-shrouded island in the Baltic;
that he was with a group of bearded guerrillas in the mountain fastnesses of the wildest part of Albania. And there were
those in defeated Germany who were prepared to swear on
oath and penalty of a long term of imprisonment that Hitler
was still alive after the bunker was taken by the Russians.

Thus it was that British Intelligence decided to send
Trevor-Roper to collect all the known facts to prevent the
rise of a new Hitler legend – one of a leader hidden away in
some remote refuge, biding his time, waiting for the day
when he would descend once more and rescue his long-
suffering people from the oppressive Allied yoke.

However, Hugh Trevor-Roper, trained historian and
intelligence officer, knew that "anyone who undertakes an
enquiry of such a kind is soon made aware of one important fact: the worthlessness of mere human testimony." As
a result, he decided to limit himself to a search for those men
and women who had remained behind in the nearly
surrounded bunker on April 22, 1945, when Hitler had
ordered a mass exodus of those who wanted to flee and save
their skins before it was too late. As he wrote later: "It was
necessary to look for representatives of all classes – for

guards and typists were likely to prove as good witnesses as politicians and generals."

But how were these witnesses to be found? That was the problem in Germany, whose communications system had been violently ripped apart in the last month of war. Forcibly divided into four zones of occupation with both the French and Russian authorities refusing to cooperate, Germany had some ten to fifteen million people of a score of different nationalities on the road, wandering back and forth purposelessly. But the former jester of the Dambuster Squadron was undismayed. The problem, he thought, was less difficult than may appear. They were all described as "missing"; but in fact people do not disappear or evaporate, even in a period of catastrophe. They either perish or remain alive: there is no third possibility. . . . If they are prisoners they can be found in prison camps – at least if they are prisoners of the Western Powers; if they are free they must be found elsewhere, and most probably in their own home districts, where friends and local knowledge will enable them to survive, but also where enemies (and German enmities are strong) may easily betray them.

Following this theory, Trevor-Roper had paid particular care to the birthplaces of the men and women he sought, and also to any information he could obtain about their places of residence prior to the breakout from the bunker; this method had paid off. Already he had found and interrogated Fräulein Else Krüger, Bormann's secretary, and Erich Kempka, Hitler's chauffeur. With the testimony they had given him, in addition to that of a dozen other witnesses of those last terrible days in the bunker, Trevor-Roper had come to the conclusion that Hitler had committed suicide on April 30. In November, he submitted his report to the headquarters of British Military intelligence in Germany and returned to the grey Gothic halls of his Oxford college. But he was not there long. Scarcely had he arrived and exchanged his uniform (for the last time, he thought) for his shabby, chalk-marked black gown, when he received a signal from British HQ. A document had been found which purported to be Hitler's will.

Trevor-Roper realized the importance of the discovery at once. Genuine or not, this will, with its promise of a Nazi bequest to the German people – the names of those who were supposed to continue the Hitlerite heritage – would contribute enormously to the propagation of the Hitler myth which the Englishman had set out to destroy two months before. He didn't hesitate. On a cold, bitter, rainy day he set off once more, leaving the mellow grey-yellow stones of his beloved Oxford behind to return to the brick wastes of a bombed, sombre Germany. As he traveled, his mind raced with the possibilities opened up by the testament. He already knew that when Bormann had sent Admiral Donitz the message about Hitler's death he had mentioned the will. Furthermore, Dönitz had sent a plane to fetch out a bearer of the will. But although the pilot had made contact, he had been forced off by heavy Russian fire and returned to Dönitz's HQ empty-handed. In addition, British Intelligence also knew by now that four messengers had set out to take copies of the will from Berlin to Admiral Dönitz in Plön; to Field-Marshal Schoerner, commanding an army group in Czechoslovakia; to Bormann's Party Archives in Munich. Trevor-Roper's thoughts were grim as the khaki-coloured staff car drove through the barbed wire entanglement which surrounded Montgomery's HQ at the little German town of Bad Oeynhausen, not far from the place where in the previous May the Field Marshal had accepted the surrender of the German Armed Forces. To prevent the possible start of a new Nazi legend, Trevor-Roper would have to find three men among the grey-faced, grey-uniformed mass of German ex-soldiers who were trudging the streets of their beaten country. *Three men out of six million.* It wasn't going to be easy.

But Trevor-Roper had unexpected good luck. In the first week of November, a Luxembourger named Georges Thiers, who said he was a journalist and was able to give information about what had happened in the bunker during the last days of the war, was still under British arrest because he had been unable to identify himself satisfactorily when, looking for work the summer before, he reported to the British authorities. In that same week in November, during the course of a routine search, a set of papers was discovered sewn into the lining of his shabby brown suit.

The British agents soon deciphered them. They were a copy of Hitler's last will and testament! Georges Thiers soon broke down under intensive grilling. His real name was Heinz

Lorenz, and he had worked under Goebbels during the war assessing the value of foreign news broadcasts. Toward the end of April he had received orders from both Goebbels and Bormann to take a set of the vital documents to Munich, where Heinrich Heim would file them away in the Party archives for posterity.

While the fascinated British Intelligence agents listened intently, the pale-faced, skinny ex-radioman poured out his story, stumbling over his words, eager and glad to get rid of his knowledge of those final, terrible days.

With three companions he had managed to break through the Russian cordon and reach the little island of the Pfaueninsel on Lake Havel, not far from Berlin. There they had waited all day on tenterhooks, alternately hiding and searching the smoke-filled April sky for the plane from Dönitz. But it had never come.

The next day the Russians had swamped the island with a massive artillery bombardment. In panic, Lorenz and the others had seized a canoe from a nearby boathouse and paddled furiously to a yacht anchored in the lake. Here they were but little safer. The yacht had no sails and they did not dare move because of a blazing munitions ship, which coloured the lake a blood-red, lighting up the sky every now and again in violent explosion of brilliant red-and-yellow shells, which went zigzagging crazily in all directions. As the four men crouched miserably in the bowels of the yacht, waiting expectantly for the thud of a shell and the first gigantic spout of water nearby, which would indicate the Russians had spotted them, they told themselves the end was not very far away.

Then their fortune changed. That same night a roaring, three-engine seaplane slid down over the lake, cutting an enormous black shadow on the water against the blood-red flames. "*It's a Ju!*" one of the four fugitives shouted, "*a good old Auntie Ju!*"[1]

It was indeed, but this time the familiar outline of the plane was altered by floats. And they guessed why at once. It was the Dönitz plane, flown from one of the North Sea naval bases! They threw caution to the winds. Their rescue was at hand.

---

[1] The name given to the standard troop transport, Junkers 52, by the German soldier.

Grabbing two canoes, they paddled to the plane, whose scared pilot, his eyes searching the other bank for the Russian positions, was keeping his engines running at full revolutions. Frantically they hammered at the corrugated metal fuselage, while another of their number on the yacht signalled with a blue flashlight.

Lorenz felt fear clutch at his heart. They were so close to rescue yet the pilot, a black silhouette in the cockpit, didn't know they were even there. And then, to the radioman's relief, he spotted them. Hoarsely they shouted against the roar of the three engines that one of their number was still on the yacht; they would have to fetch him.

The scared pilot roared. "Fetch him then – *quick!*"

In a flurry of sweated activity they turned their flimsy craft. But tragedy struck the next moment. One of them upset his canoe. He plunged into the crimson waters of the lake. Hurriedly the other two fished him out. They righted his canoe. But the Russians had spotted them now. Huge spouts of water began to flush upward. Hot metal flew through the air. Machine-gun bullets cut the surface like heavy summer rain. Feverishly, knowing that they had only seconds to spare, they paddled back to their companion stranded on the yacht. *Too late!* The frightened Junker pilot was not prepared to risk his life any longer for the unknown men in the water. He revved his engines up to an ear-splitting roar. The three of them in the water stopped simultaneously in midstroke. Their hearts sank. The big seaplane was skimming across the water, a white bone in its teeth. Moments later it was airborne, followed by the frustrated zigzag of bright red Russian tracer. One minute later it had vanished behind the dark clouds. Their hopes were shattered. They lay across their paddles, oblivious to the continued Russian fire, like dead men.

But in spite of their disappointment, they managed to get out after all. Just before dawn on May 3 they had set out once again and, landing in the Wannsee Swimming Pool just outside Berlin, they had made their way to nearby Potsdam and from there to the demarcation line between the Russians and Americans. This was near Magdeburg on the River Elbe. Disguised as foreign workers, they managed to avoid patrols from both armies and in the end they crossed to the safety of the West.

By that time the Armistice had come into force and they knew Admiral Dönitz and the others would no longer be needing the documents they carried. As a consequence, they split up and went their separate ways. Now they would have to start a new life; the great days were over.

The British intelligence agents had listened attentively and in complete silence to Lorenz's long and adventurous story, but now they interrupted the garrulous journalist "whose vanity and indiscretion led accidentally to the discovery of these important documents" (as Trevor-Roper put it). They asked the one and overwhelming question which filled their quick minds: *Who were the other men?*

Lorenz hesitated. First he named the most unimportant of the other three. He was a soldier called Hummerich and he had nothing to do with the vital missing documents. This the intelligence men (putting together two and two from what they themselves knew and what Lorenz had told them) had already guessed. Who were the others? they persisted.

Lorenz licked his lips. Garrulous and vain as he was, he still possessed a kind of loyalty to those who had braved that terrible flight from Berlin with him. But in the end he gave up; he told the British agents the names of two remaining men.

Trevor-Roper soon found the first of them. Major Willi Johannmeier, who had been ordered by Hitler himself to carry the will to Field Marshal Schoerner, was living with his parents in his old home at Iserlohn, not more than a couple of hours' drive on the autobahn from British HQ. But ex-Major Johannmeier, a tough combat soldier, was of different mettle than Heinz Lorenz. He wasn't talking. As Trevor-Roper recalls: "[he] was too proud, too courageous to yield the truth."

The "straightforward soldier, of unconditional loyalties and unpolitical courage" denied that he had ever been in the bunker. But when Trevor-Roper pointed out that he had sufficient evidence to prove that the German had been, he changed his story. All right; admittedly, he had been present in the bunker and had broken out with the other three. But his task had been a purely military one. The tough soldier, who had been Hitler's Army adjutant and whose chubbiness belied his iron will, maintained that it had been his job simply to guide the others out of the Berlin trap; no more and no less. Their mission was unknown to him and it had been none of his business to ask.

In the end, it was Trevor-Roper, who couldn't help having a sneaking admiration for the German's honesty and loyalty, who gave in. As he wrote of Johannmeier much later: "Nothing could shake him from this position and in spite of the discrepancy between his evidence and that of Lorenz, he almost convinced his interrogators." Yet the Englishman knew he was lying. There were three copies of the will. Two were known to be in the possession of Lorenz and the other member of the remaining trio. Why then should Johannmeier be the exception? Surely he must be the bearer of the third copy? Besides there was the evidence of the secretaries whom Trevor-Roper had interrogated earlier. Yes, the chubby ex-major with the stony, guarded face was his man all right. But how was he going to get him to talk?

Eventually the lanky Englishman decided that he was wasting his time for the present with Johannmeier. In order to get him to tell where he had hidden the papers, he would have to find the third man. If he could be found and made to talk, then the stubborn ex-major would sing; he was certain of that. In the end, he knew, they all talked.

Thus it was that in December, 1945, one of the coldest winters in memory, Trevor-Roper set off for the Bavarian capital to look for the third man – SS Standartenführer Wilhelm Zander, the man who had been supposed to break through to Admiral Dönitz with a copy of the will; and the man who had once been the personal adjutant at the Leader's military HQ to no less than – *Reichsleiter Martin Bormann.*

11

When Martin Bormann had summoned him for the last time and told him he was to make an attempt to break out with the precious will, Wilhelm Zander had felt that his last hope of a *Strich unter die Rechnung*[1] was over. He had served the Party loyally for these last twelve years, returning from his profitable business in Italy for the sake of his country. Now all he wished for was death; there was no hope, no bright future for him. He preferred to die here in beleaguered Berlin.

One week before, when a flight of planes had arrived in Berlin to evacuate those who wanted to live, he had refused. He did not want to survive the destruction of the "Thousand Year Reich" which had lasted exactly twelve years. He wanted to remain in the doomed capital and share the dire fate of his Führer and his Fatherland.

All this he told Bormann, protesting that the Reichsleiter must find someone else to take the document to Admiral Dönitz. With unusual tact, for him, the undersized, bull-like Reichsleiter had accepted Zander's protest without complaint and had borne it back to Hitler himself.

A little while later Bormann had reappeared and told a disconsolate Zander that he had to go. "The Leader had ordered it." Then he handed the unhappy SS colonel copies of Hitler's wills and his certificate of marriage to Eva Braun. And that was that. They had shaken hands for the last time and Zander had departed to collect a machine pistol and change into a camouflaged SS smock for the hazardous escape, although, as Trevor-Roper records it – "[He didn't want to be]

---

[1] Literally, "to draw a line under the sum," i.e., to put an end to it all

ordered out to begin again, without guidance or purpose, his half-wasted life."

That had been in April, 1945. Since that time, Zander had wandered southward in the general direction of the Alpine Redoubt, which was not, in truth, much of a fortification. Arriving at the village of Tegernsee, the picturesque prewar tourist centre on the Bavarian lake of the same name, he had hidden the precious documents in a trunk and left it with a friend. Then he had attempted to break completely with the disastrous past. Leaving his wife in Hanover, he had changed his name, his identity – everything. He had told a handful of friends they must regard him as dead from now on; they spread the word that he had been killed in the last few days of the fighting. Thereupon Wilhelm Zander had slipped out of the world of power and pomp he had known the previous twelve years, with its shining jackboots, smart uniforms and rakishly angled caps. He reappeared as the simply dressed, humble market gardener Wilhelm Paustin, prepared to begin a new life in the remote Alpine village of Aidenbach. The past was dead.

It wasn't.

Frau Zander was cooperative. She told Trevor-Roper she had not seen her husband since the end of the war, and readily supplied him with photographs of the missing man and names and addresses of his brothers and mother. But Trevor-Roper did not trust her; he sensed she was trying to protect someone – she was a little too cooperative. Was her husband alive after all?

A visit to Munich told him that he was right. Zander was still alive and living somewhere close at hand; it was becoming clear to the Englishman, as it was to many more Allied investigators of that winter, that there was some kind of *organized* escape route out of occupied Germany; its various north-south routes all led to the rugged Bavarian frontier, which could not be effectively checked, and from thence to Italy and a new life in Spain or South America.

By Christmas of that year, Trevor-Roper felt he had discovered Zander's whereabouts: he located him at the same address as one of Bormann's former secretaries at Aidenbach near the ancient cathedral town of Passau, close to the Austrian frontier; an ideal location if one had to"disappear" quickly.

Trevor-Roper contacted the local branch of the U.S. CIC. The Counter-Intelligence Corps readily agreed to cooperate. Perhaps Zander would lead them to his master – if he were still alive. Swiftly the Allied intelligence group planned a raid on the house to take place at the classic time for such operations, three o'clock in the morning; the hour at which a man may most safely be trusted to be asleep in his bed.

The raid was carried out on the morning of December 28. The snow was piled high on the approach roads to the little village. It muffled the sound of their jeeps. Everywhere the inhabitants were still abed, kept there - in spite of the soft lowing of the animals as the Counter-Intelligence Corps passed silently – by the intense cold and the curfew. The December world was one great, silent white desert.

It was a success. Wilhelm Zander was caught in bed and forced to dress in the rough blue drill suit of a Bavarian farmer even before he had become really aware of what was going on. For Trevor-Roper he was "a disillusioned Nazi idealist who saw that his former world was shattered and spoke freely." He soon had all the information he had come so far to find. Now he knew he could go back to Johannmeier and convince him that he, too, must surrender his copy of the will.[2]

The Englishman now had time for questions about someone else – Martin Bormann. As he wrote to me: "I have some grounds to *suspect* that he [Bormann] reached Bolzano, but I cannot prove it: I would merely say that the present balance of evidence points in that direction." So, although it was not his main purpose, he interrogated the downcast prisoner concerning his former chief.

Zander could not throw much new light on the subject. He did not believe that Bormann had planned an actual escape

---

[2] Johannmeier kept up his pretence of knowing nothing for two hours under questioning in spite of the evidence to the contrary. But finally he broke down and revealed that the vital copy was hidden in a bottle in his garden. Observing, "*ich haber die Papiere,*" he broke the frozen ground with an axe, dug them up and handed them to Trevor-Roper. In my opinion, based on conversations with those who were close to Hitler, there could be yet another copy of this priceless collector's item still hidden outside of Germany: one that Bormann is reported to have had on him when he left the bunker.

94

route in advance; if he had attempted an escape, it would have been on an improvised basis, and obviously – as he, Zander, saw it – in a westerly direction toward Dönitz's HQ. That was the route that everyone else had taken and there was no earthly likelihood that Martin Bormann, that *Kommunistenfresser* (literally, "eater of Communists"), would venture eastward to the Soviet Russian lines.

With that, the Englishman gave up. Zander was led off to an internment camp and Trevor-Roper returned to the north to deal with the obstinate Major Johannmeier. Yet as he drove away from the snowy mountain fastnesses that December, he was not satisfied. Two points still troubled him greatly: "The ultimate disposal of Hitler's body, and the fate of Martin Bormann" [as he wrote one year later]. The key source of information on both subjects was the one-armed Hitler Youth Leader who had been one of Bormann's companions in the original escape. Artur Axmann, who had been captured three weeks earlier after six months in hiding in Bavaria, had been questioned by the Americans on the basis of a brief supplied by Trevor-Roper. According to information at the Englishman's disposal, Axmann had been given a box with Hitler's ashes. But he denied any knowledge of the disposal of the corpse of his Leader; in addition, he was the last witness to swear he had seen Bormann and that Bormann was dead at Dr. Stumpfegger's side on the bridge. As Trevor-Roper saw it, why should this devoted and convinced Nazi give any other answer than one which would puzzle the Allied interrogators and throw them off the scent? Why, indeed! The proof of the death of Bormann rested on the evidence of Axmann only, and although other points in Axmann's testimony rang true, the trained, logical mind of the English professor asked itself: Was Axmann deliberately lying to protect Bormann?

Hugh Trevor-Roper drove away to another world far from the sudden, heart-stopping knocks in the middle of the night and thin, greasy sweat on the faces of scared witnesses; far from the abrupt deflation of the fat-bellied, much-decorated men who had once been great; far from the hard-faced cynicism of those who had seen everything and didn't like what they had seen.

He returned to the sherry parties, the high table, the brilliant little "chats" and other semi-social gatherings that played so active a part in the life of the great grey university which trained his country's elite. But in the years to come he could never quite forget the riddle of the pot-bellied son of an army trumpeter whom he had never seen. Was he alive or was he dead?

Fifteen years after that December 1945 arrest of Wilhelm Zander, the disillusioned Bormann adjutant, Trevor-Roper wrote to Lev Bezymenski, who was also looking for the missing Reichsleiter (but for completely different reasons):

In my opinion, there is no definite proof of his [Bormann's] death. One can conclude from a number of things that he escaped from Berlin on the night 1/2nd May 1945, at least out of the area of fighting. I am firmly convinced that the reports of his death given by Erich Kempka and others do not correspond to the facts. I also don't believe in the testimony given by Axmann during his interrogation by the Americans, viz., that he saw Bormann's body on the railway lines.

All in all I think the lack of proof that he died must force us not to accept this fact. I know a few things which lead me to conclude that he reached Bolzano where his wife was living. I can't swear to it naturally, but I wouldn't be surprised if one day it came out that he had managed to escape.

12

Many people reached the same conclusion as Professor Hugh Trevor-Roper. In the years that were to follow, the late forties and early fifties, a veritable Martin Bormann fever seemed to grip Europe.

Fourteen days after the Nuremberg war criminals went to their death on the gallows under the supervision of heavyset, hard-hitter Master Sergeant Wood, who acted as U.S. Seventh Army Chief Executioner, a German named Joachim Borsburg was found marching somewhat dazedly down the main street of one bombed southern German city, dressed in the full uniform of a colonel in the *Waffen SS!*

He was arrested immediately. But the Americans who interrogated him found he was no die-hard Nazi or some latter day Rip Van Winkle who had reawakened a year or more after the war had ended. The explanation was simpler than that. The unshaven, medium-sized German told them seriously that he had just been promoted to the rank of colonel at a midnight ceremony held in – of all places – *the local cemetery!*

The CIC agents, now aware of what kind of person they were dealing with, nodded understandingly and asked sympathetically who had conducted the initiation.

Borsburg, who in reality was a simple private in the infantry who had gone mad during captivity and since then had been committed to a mental home, from which he had escaped a couple of weeks before, leaned forward confidentially and whispered out of the corner of his mouth "*Reichsleiter Martin Bormann natürlich!*"

But all the people who spotted Martin Bormann in Europe that year and in the years to follow were not mad; nor were they sensation seekers. The Flensburg writer Heinrich Lienau, who had been imprisoned in Sachsenhausen Concentration Camp for a long time, certainly wasn't. He maintained that he had seen Bormann in the town of Lüneburg, where Field Marshal Montgomery had signed the surrender agreement of all German forces in 1945.

Lienau remembered Bormann because the latter had once visited Sachsenhausen with a group of higher-ranking Party officials. Bormann had stepped out of a Red Cross ambulance in Lüneburg's medieval town square, with its picturesque houses and cobbled marketplace, and had gotten into the same goods train as Lienau had taken northward.

In this encounter, they had crouched in the evil-smelling wagon facing each other in uneasy silence for nearly three hours, until they had reached the border town of Flensburg (the crossing point to Denmark). There Lienau had rushed out to warn two passing British Tommies; but too late! Bormann spotted them. Before he could be stopped, he had jumped another train just leaving the shattered station and escaped.

The Danish doctor's report that Bormann had landed on a Danish island in the Baltic in the first month of the peace could also not be dismissed just like that. Nor could one dismiss the Egyptian report that Bormann was hiding out in that anti-British, anti-Zionist country of pro-Nazi~ leanings, where, indeed, a goodly number of Germans wanted by the Allies did "surface," once the British had gone. Then there was the report of the serious, well-liked Josef Kleemann, former head of the German Seaman's Union, who maintained he had seen Bormann in Sydney, Australia.

In 1949, Albert Bormann, formerly Hitler's adjutant and a man who had always felt himself looked down upon by his older brother as *a Manteltraeger* (a coat-holder; in other words, a flunky) surfaced after living as an agricultural labourer for nearly five years.[1] He, too, maintained to the press that he was not satisfied with the stories that he had heard to the effect

---

[1] Martin had refused to allow his brother, who was a head taller than he yet nicknamed by the family "Little Albert," to marry a secretary at Hess's HQ. Subsequently there was bad blood between the two brothers. This author, after searching for Albert for over a week, finally found him, only to be told over the phone: "I'm not talking about him. He had nothing to say for me when he was alive; I'm not saying anything about him now that he's dead,' and with that Albert Bormann hung up.

that his brother had died in Berlin. He told the court that tried him as a former member of the Party and SS that Martin was in the hands of the Russians; after all, they were interested in finding the Nazi big shots, with one exception – *Martin Bormann!*

One year later, Bjorn Hallstrom of the Danish paper *Kristeligt Dagblad* who had travelled through South West Africa, which had been German up to 1919 and still had a sizable German colony, reported that Bormann was hiding out in a lonely African farm, enjoying the bright hot sunshine of the bush. In his opinion, there were so many Bormanns in the local telephone directories that one of them must be Martin's relative and hiding him.

Two years later, the great hunt hit the headlines yet again.

From Rome came the report that one month after the Italian ex-partisan leader Luigi Silvestri told newspapermen in February, 1952, that he had seen Bormann in Bolzano on May 10, 1945,[2] a certain Herr Eberjard Stern, a former official of Albert Speer's Ministry of Armaments, had by chance spotted a monk in the San Antonio Franciscan Monastery in Rome. Stern had recognized the man immediately although it was seven years since he had last seen him in Berlin. It was Martin Bormann!

Reporters from all over the world sped to the Italian capital to get in on the scoop. But Stern chose to sell his red-hot story to the Associated Press. In an interview with its representative, he showed the reporter a photograph he had taken of the monk in question, who now bore the name Frater Martini, and who had not denied his true identity. He had, indeed, told Stern: "You see, I am alive and I don't want to be disturbed."

Stern went on to say that he had received an invitation a little earlier from a former gauleiter, Hartmann Lauterbach, who had fled from a British internment camp at Bremen and had joined up with the Italian Fascist movement (which was legal

---

[2] He had stepped out of a Mercedes and entered a Dominican monastery which served as Italian Red Cross HQ. There he posed as head of a German organisation concerned with the release and exchange of Italian and German POWs.

again) to meet Bormann in person. Unfortunately Stern had not been able to meet Lauterbach because the latter was again serving a prison sentence. But he had met another ex-SS man named Giesauf, who had fled Germany after the war and knew for certain that Bormann was hiding out in a monastery, where he kept up his contacts with the Italian Fascists and an escape route from Germany (of which we shall hear more soon). On the basis of this information, Eberhard Stern had made his way to the San Antonio monastery and confronted Bormann.

Obviously, the AP man thought, as did the other reporters who managed to get in on the sensational scoop, the next step was to go and visit Frater Martini.

"But the whole story has been made up – drawn out of the air completely," thirty-five-year-old Brother Martini laughingly assured the assembled reporters a few days later as they fumbled, fussed and shoved in their eagerness to get pictures of the monk.

"But what about the photo?" someone at the back of the excited multinational crowd cried.

"*Yes, the photo!*" There was a chorus of approval, followed by simultaneous cries in half a dozen European languages.

The photograph in question, which Stern had supplied, did show a somewhat toothless, fat-faced man who bore a striking resemblance to Bormann in his middle years.

Brother Martini could not answer that one, but the Vatican did a few days later. A spokesman maintained that Stern, for some reason known only to himself, wanted to damage the reputation of the monastery, and went on to state: "Bormann was never here and isn't here today." As for the photograph, it was the likeness of seventy-six-year-old Antonio Romualdi, also a Franciscan monk, who remembered having been stopped on the street a few weeks previously by a man and two girls who had wished to take his photograph. Being a good-hearted and friendly man and thinking it was a typical foreign tourist whim, he had agreed.

Stern, who had now gone home to Berlin, still contended he had seen Martin Bormann in the monastery. Indeed, he had sent him a letter, addressed to "Frater Martini Bormagione" (which the monk had admitted receiving) in which Stern had written: "Dear Herr Martin Bormann. I am very grateful to have had the opportunity to see you during my visit to Rome and would like to thank you once again for your friendly reception." For his part, Frater Martini insisted energetically that he had never even seen Herr Stern. But by now neither Stern's accusations nor the monk's denials interested the authorities or the press; they had a new sensation. Bormann had been spotted yet once again – some five thousand miles away in the thick, barely penetrable jungles of the border area between Chile and Argentina!

The man who had spotted him was Paul Hesslein, a sixty-two-year-old German who had been a member of the Reichstag with Bormann prior to 1933. After the Nazi takeover he had fled Germany and taken out Chilean citizenship, supporting himself by journalism. He was one of the many exiles living in that hospitable backwater, struggling to keep his head above water as best he could. That is, until belated fame – or perhaps notoriety – came to him in the early fifties.

"In February, 1948," he told the reporters in 1952, "I was a guest at the farm of my friend Count Hans Ulrich von Reichenbach, which is located in Chilean jungle. Towards the end of my visit I decided to hike to the little landing place at Llifen which is at the southern end of Lake Ranco Sur. Even before I started out, people warned me that Martin Bormann might be hiding out in the southern part of Chile or Argentina – the area called Patagonia.

"I was also told that a whole group of Nazis had landed in the southern part of Argentina from a couple of U-boats in 1945. One of them was Martin Bormann who had taken the cover name of Juan Gomez. And my informant told me I had better be careful. Then it would be hard to trap Bormann. . . . Whole regiments of soldiers wouldn't suffice to find him in the thick jungle. Besides, there were a lot of large landowners in that area who were pro-Nazi [and would help him]."

In spite of the warning, the sixty-two-year-old German set off on foot, armed with a revolver and accompanied by two large and fierce native dogs; apart from any Nazis who might be hiding in the lush tropical forests, he had to be wary of pumas, not to mention lurking Indians, who were known to be hostile to the whites who had done their best to wipe them out over the last three hundred years.

But let Hesslein tell his story himself.

"Halfway between my friend's farm and the little township of Llifen, I saw three horsemen approaching me. They were dressed in the Araucan[3] manner, with big hats and ponchos.

"The dogs grew uneasy and I clicked my revolver off safety. I stood in the middle of the track as the riders got slowly nearer. I seemed to recognize the face of the one in the centre. Then I knew him. *It was Martin Bormann!*

"In the nick of time I jumped to one side. The riders began to pass. Suddenly the one in the center reined in his horse. His face twitched. Then he gave the order to speed up. In German! And as they sped away I heard him say quite clearly: *'That was Hesslein!'*"

The former deputy's adventure in the jungle did not end there. He walked on, pondering this strange meeting with a man whom he had known well enough prior to 1933 when Bormann had been one of the noisy, unruly, brown-shirted Nazi faction in the Reichstag. He reached the little tumble-down, tin-roofed bar at Llifen. Still shaken by the fact he had seen a man sought by the whole world and yet thought dead by most people, he asked for an *onze*, as the natives called breakfast, and slumped down on a rickety cane chair under the slowly twirling fan. Sunk in his thoughts, his hands still trembling with shock, it took him some time to become aware of the man behind the counter who had served him his coffee.

"The man wore a jacket like that worn by motorcyclists and brown 'Nazi' breeches. He told me he had emigrated to Chile in the twenties. Then he asked me where I came from. I told him I came from Germany, but I now possessed Chilean nationality."

During the course of their conversation, the man told Hesslein that the Nazis wouldn't have lost the war if Hitler had not been betrayed by his generals. Hesslein nodded and didn't say anything. He did not feel at ease in the bar. His strange meeting of a while before and now this encounter with an obviously Nazi German in the midst of nowhere unsettled him. Then he took his courage in both hands and leaning forward across the fly-specked, stained bar, he whispered, "How's our friend Juan Gomez getting on?"

"You know about him?" the other man asked, a little

---

[2] The Araucanians are the Indian people native to that area.

surprised. Then he relaxed. "You're pretty well informed . . . Gomez has been living locally for a little while now and this afternoon he went out riding."

Hesslein nodded as if he was fully aware of everything.

"You could have easily bumped into him today in the jungle," the other said.

Hesslein recounted that then "he became very talkative as the bar was completely empty. He informed me that he [Bormann] would return to Chile after his ride across the border to the Argentine. This time he would live in the neighbourhood of Lake Todos los Santos. Thereafter Martin Bormann, alias Juan Gomez, would return to Europe. He'd certainly find an opportunity to hide in Spain until his hour came."

As the other man chatted, Hesslein became aware of the danger of his position. The barkeeper took him for one of his own. But if Bormann returned unexpectedly, he would recognize Hesslein for what he was: a longtime opponent of the National Socialist Party. Hesslein had to move fast. As he recalled three years later: "I'd seen Martin Bormann. Now after hearing this confirmation, I knew it was time to get out. I caught a truck going back the way I had come and arrived back at my friend's farm that same night as darkness fell."

The handful of agents and journalists who were able to follow up the lead given by Hesslein soon dropped out of the picture. Hesslein had been warned by the Chilean police authorities to keep his mouth shut.

According to these investigators however, a German U-boat had landed passengers on the coast of Argentina some time in 1945. They had been put up at the second-rate Hotel Colón in the small town of Encarnación for a while before setting out for the remote plantation at Alter, owned by a former Nazi named Alban Krug. There the group had settled down to farm and laze; its leader, Bormann. (Incidentally, if this is true, a remarkable coincidence must have taken place; only a dozen miles away in *another* small German colony, Martin Bormann's ex-cellmate from his Leipzig Jail days was eking out a poor living as a teacher. Ex-Lieutenant Bruno Fricke had fled Germany in 1930 after breaking with Hitler and had gone to Paraguay.)

Zvi Aldouby, an ex-spy for Mosad, the Israeli Intelligence Service, told the *International Herald Tribune* much later that a bored Bormann, sick of loafing and reading, had decided soon afterward to return to his old love – farming. He had moved to Chile and bought a farm. But he had not felt himself safe enough and had moved yet again, to Paraguay, "where there are fourteen colonies of emigres and some 50,000 Nazis, ex-Nazis and Nazi sympathizers close to the Argentinian border."

There, according to the ex-agent, Bormann: "employs a quasi-Mafia network known as the *cuchilleros*, the 'knife fighters,' to protect his life against agents with an urge to kill or capture him. Two years ago the Poles lost two men booby-trapped by mines. . . . Tito got it into his head that somehow he ought to settle accounts. He sent his people and the Yugoslavs lost four intelligence agents."[4]

Reports continued that Bormann was hiding out in some remote area of Argentina, Chile, or Paraguay, but the European authorities had neither the money nor the interest to send search teams to find him. Neither the United States, West Germany, the United Kingdom, nor any of the other Western Powers wanted to upset the delicate balance of South American politics, in which the rich, hardworking German colonies, dating from the nineteenth century, played an important role both politically and economically. Germany and the United Kingdom were concerned about their export trade to the rich South American markets. The United States, long a sore point with the *gringo*-hating intellectuals of Latin America, had no desire to occasion a fresh outburst of anti-Americanism in the highly volatile political atmosphere of the Southern hemisphere.

In Argentina, the country to which Bormann would undoubtedly flee (if he were actually in South America), the powerful hand of the then Argentinian dictator Juan Peron would, at the least sign of danger, lie protectively over those who fled from the ruins of the beaten Fascist empires of Italy and Germany. Although Hesslein was a man who might indeed have let his imagination run away with him during the course of his somewhat scary expedition through the jungle,

---

[4] The Paris-based *International Herald Tribune*, July 27, 1971.

he was also a man who knew Bormann personally. However, this promising lead was dropped – until that day in May, 1960, when an apparently drunken second officer was shoved on board an El Al plane bound for Israel: an undersized, dark-skinned man with a prominent hooked nose – a man who had lived in South America for the last twelve years or so — a man named Adolf Eichmann.

13

The promising lead given in South America had ended in frustration. But back in Europe, those still intent on solving the Martin Bormann mystery began to re-examine the whole case. Assuming that the Reichsleiter had not been killed during his attempt to escape from the dying German capital, and that he had somehow been able to make his way to the West unrecognized, what, they asked themselves, would he have done next?

For most of those concerned with the hunt, which was already becoming the most protracted one known to modern history, the answer was simple. In 1945, Germany was occupied by nearly six million British, French, Russian, and American troops, all of whom had orders to keep a weather eye open for men who were considered Nazi war criminals like Bormann. In addition, the Western authorities, and later the Germans themselves, had launched a nationwide denazification programme which covered every German adult, who was forced to fill in an extensive questionnaire about his role during the recently ended Nazi regime. Hardly anyone was able to escape this check; that is, if he wished to be able to work and receive rations, neither of which was possible without registering with the police.[1]

If Bormann had been alive then, the solution to his particular problem of the summer of 1945 would have been to get out of Germany as soon as possible to a nearby country where Allied troops were not present in such numbers, where the

---

[1] In those days every German had to register with the police of the place in which he lived. If he left this place he had to check out and re-register in his new place of residence within seven days.

administrative checks were not so thorough, and where the breakdown of the former Fascist regime was not so over-whelming as it had been in Germany; in other words, Italy – especially that part of the country where there were large "Germanic," pro-Nazi populations located in remote valleys which would make ideal places to hide from prying Allied agents. The Tyrol.

But how would he get there? What would he use for money, food, papers in a Germany where there were checkpoints at every bridge, every crossroad, every station? And even if he managed to cross the River Rhine, a major barrier in his progress southward, who would guide him through the Alps into Italy? Alone a man in his physical condition (after all he was forty-five years old, out of condition, and, Speer thought, was seriously ill from a liver complaint resulting from excessive drinking) probably would not make it without collapsing in the snow or revealing himself to the border guards at the Austrian-Italian frontier if he attempted to take the easier way across the Brenner Pass. How, then, would he make it – and who would help him?

There were some in the fifties in Europe who believed that the Nazis had built up an escape organization to deal with just such problems long before Germany had lost the war. These people dated the organization back to *Aktion Bernhard*, the greatest counterfeiting operation the world has ever known.

Aktion Bernhard started in 1942, when the Gestapo had combed the concentration camps for skilled forgers and printers. The latter were grouped at Oranienburg Concentration Camp where they were employed in producing huge quantities of British five-pound notes and U.S. twenty-dollar bills. The Nazis intended to debase the Allied currency by circulating them throughout the world and dropping them by plane over Britain and possibly the United States.[2]

Little came of this plan and in '44 the operation was closed down with many millions of counterfeit dollars and pounds remaining buried in various locations all over Austria and

---

[2] The Allies carried out a similiar operation, to a limited extent, with postage stamps and probably with currency too, though the details have been kept secret to this day.

Bavaria, in particular near the lakes which dot that area. (Eight hundred million dollars were found in a brewery at Redl Zipf, for instance. After the war the British government was forced to change the format of its five-pound note because of the danger presented by these almost perfect forgeries.) Thereafter most of the forgers were sent back to the camps, but a select number were assembled at Alt-Aussee to prepare for a new operation, *Aktion Birkenbaum* (Operation Birch Tree). Under the command of the notorious SS Major Alfred Naujocks,[3] who played a role in most of the SS undercover operations right from the start and who in 1945 actually went over to the British to work for them before changing sides once again in the postwar world, the plan was to produce birth certificates, ID cards, marriage licenses, etc., for those Nazis who felt it would be better to leave a defeated Germany.

Today, even those who do not believe that the Nazis had a carefully worked-out escape organization admit for the most part that there was such an operation as Aktion Birkenbaum; enough of the leading SS personalities, from Himmler through Kaltenbrunner down to Eichmann, were later proved to have possessed faked identification papers at some time or another in the days and weeks immediately following the Allied victory in Germany. But the question still remains whether, as some maintain on the available evidence, the Naujocks operation dovetailed into anything larger – a well-prepared escape organization of the kind that a man like Bormann, who knew everyone and everything, would know of and turn to if he had escaped from Berlin.

Simon Wiesenthal, the most persistent of the Nazihunters, and the man who chased Eichmann for nearly fifteen years, thought there was an escape organization. On his release from the death house at the Mauthausen Concentration Camp in May, 1945, he swore he would make the Nazis pay for the crimes perpetrated against his people. The medium-sized, overweight ex-architect suspected he recognized a secret Nazi escape organization right from the start.

---

[3] In 1939, he had been in charge of the SS raid on the German Gleiwitz Radio Station which was faked to make it look as if the Poles had raided the place; this was the immediate "act of provocation" Hitler used for invading Poland.

It seemed, in the event, that there were two such organizations working together. One, called *Die Spinne* (the spider), operated an evacuation plan for Nazis on the run "right through Germany and Austria to Italy. Occasionally I followed their trails, leading from Bremen via Frankfurt, Munich and Memingen . . . to Lindau and from there to Bregenz and on to Geneva." Or: "Via Innsbruck – Merano to Rome. . . . The main line was called the 'B–B line in Nazi circles, i.e., 'Bremen–Bari.'

"I found out that along the 'B–B Line' there were *'Anlaufstellen'* [roughly, collecting or refuge points] every thirty or forty miles or so. They were staffed by two to five people who knew only the names of the next two *Anlaufstellen* [presumably one on each side of their own]."

These *Anlaufstellen* along the "B–B" route were controlled by the escape organization located at the southern German city of Augburg, "which decided who could leave Germany and Austria with their help and would provide them [the escapees] with papers and transport."

Simon Wiesenthal found the end of the B–B Line in Rome – in *the person of a Catholic bishop!*

In 1951, in the course of his search for Eichmann, Simon Wiesenthal met together with a former member of the SS Secret Service. The latter asked him why he was interested in ODESSA (*Organisation der ehemaligen SS Angehørigen*, Organization of Former SS Members – the Spanish branch of the escape route for SS people, run by Otto Skorzeny, and the second of the two organizations working as a sort of relay team).

Wiesenthal replied that he thought that it might lead him to the man he was looking for.

The German, who a few years before would have arrested the portly Jew in an instant – or done worse than that – then asked, "Does the name 'Hudal' mean anything to you?"

"I've heard the name once – I think in 1949, when there was some talk of an amnesty for the Jews," Wiesenthal replied.

"Not bad," his informant said easily. "Well, Hudal is a bishop. Perhaps he's of Austrian extraction. He was there during the war and had good contacts to the Germans. . . . Our colleagues of Amt VI – you know, Schellenberg's lot?[4] – knew him well. He was one of the few in the Vatican who prayed for a German victory."

Wiesenthal said it was hard to understand that and asked if Hudal was a Nazi bishop.

"I don't think so. . . . After the war he tried to get Austrian POWs released from British and American POW camps. But he kept in touch with right-wing circles in Germany and Austria. They say he had trouble in the Vatican on that account."

Simon Wiesenthal's mysterious informant, whom he does not name save with a commonplace "Albert," then went on to tell him that Hudal played a key role hiding Nazis on the run in various monasteries around the outskirts of the Italian capital until they were ready to continue their escape to Spain, Egypt, or even farther afield to South America.

In fact, Bishop Hudal was a Croatian nationalist who probably felt a great deal of sympathy with the Nazis because the latter had aided the separatist wartime Croatian puppet government in its attempt to settle an old score with the Serbs, who were the major prewar group in Yugoslavia and were Greek Orthodox to boot (the Croatians were Roman Catholic).

When the war ended in a defeat for both the Nazis and the Croatian puppet government, Hudal undoubtedly used his considerable influence in Rome to aid those who had been forced to flee. In addition, it cannot be denied that he kept some form of contact with the surviving right-wing organizations in Central Europe. Indeed, there seems to be evidence enough that he actively hid fugitives from Allied justice in the Via della Pace in the Italian capital.

But whether he was an active and established link in a well-organized escape route as Simon Wiesenthal and others after him have maintained leaves much to be proven; as does, more important for us, the allegation that he aided Martin Bormann. Martin Bormann's son was receiving some of his spiritual training under Hudal's auspices before entering the priest-hood "to atone for the sins of my father," as he once told an

---

[4] General Schellenberg, the clever young head of the SS Secret Service who was in charge of special undercover missions.

Austrian journalist.[5] But as for the rest, it undoubtedly never will be proven on Hudal's own admission – for the Bishop disappeared from Rome in the mid-sixties in mysterious circumstances – whether on orders from the Vatican or because of some more sinister cause we do not know. As a result, it was necessary to seek elsewhere for someone who could give us valid information on whether or not an organization existed – whether Die Spinne or ODESSA – to plan, finance, and execute a large-scale flight of wanted Nazis from Germany, through Austria to Rome and from thence to the safe harbours of Spain and South America; Otto "Scarface" Skorzeny, for instance, the hulking Viennese commando who by the end of the war was regarded in the Allied camp as the "most wanted man in Europe."

The meeting with Otto Skorzeny was a little like the first confusing half hour of one those grade B movies they used to make at the height of the Cold War in the fifties. The scene was a freezing December day in northern Germany with sleet whipping the windows of the train, with the "guide" (who had picked me up so surprisingly at 6 o'clock on that wet, pitch-black morning) leafing idly through his magazine and occasionally glancing suspiciously at the rest of the passengers in the compartment.

But his sudden appearance that morning on the platform was only the first of many surprises. We descended one stop before the station printed on the tickets we had purchased at the start, and pushed our way through the winter-clad crowds of shopping *Hausfrauen* and leather-trousered schoolboys to the exit. A BMW drew up smartly with a squeal of brakes as if its driver had been waiting close by, weighing the situation before he decided whether to pick us up or not. Mumbled introductions and the little gray car was off like a bat out of hell, breaking every German speeding and traffic regulation.

We landed in a suburban, middle-class apartment with a view over the winter park and the rain running down the panes. A meal was already prepared. Scotch was served. More

---

[5] After Gerda's death, all of Bormann's children became Catholic (with the exception of one), which is highly ironic in the light of the Reichsleiter's rabid anti-Catholicism.

scotch and yet more. Telephone calls were made in the other room. Whispered conversations were held just out of earshot. And then when we thought the interview we had come for had fallen through, the grey BMW drew up again outside and we were off in a wild, hectic dash through the great port city in which Skorzeny found himself (fighting for his life, as I was soon to learn), the car pausing only for telephone calls made en route, rather like cops reporting in to HQ.

Fifteen minutes later we were ushered into the top-floor suburban hospital room occupied by "Herr Schmidt," who was still living up to his reputation for deception, subterfuge, and mystery – over a quarter of a century after his fighting days were over. But the bold giant who had once rescued Mussolini and changed the course of the war in Italy, who had kidnapped the son of the Hungarian ruler and forced that country to remain allied to Germany, whose eighty-four man commando team outfitted in American uniforms had caused more confusion behind the Allied lines during the Battle of the Bulge than two divisions could have done, was now scarcely recognizable. Dressed in grey pyjamas that echoed the grey of his face, his hand trembling as he slumped in his chair and drank from a medicinal cup, his gigantic six-foot-four body seemed to have shrunk, while the brutal scars from his student dueling days in Vienna, which had been his most outstanding feature when he had later been in charge of Germany's commando operations, were now merged all but invisible into the shrivelled skin of his sunken face.

Otto Skorzeny had been rushed to Germany to face an operation which gave him only a one-in-ten chance of survival. His doctors in Madrid had discovered a tumor located on his spine, but when the German surgeons had come to operate, they had discovered yet another tumor underneath the first one. They had succeeded in removing both of the growths, but now the onetime "most dangerous man in Europe" was paralyzed from the waist down, his mind seemingly gone, his voice barely able to produce more than a whisper. There was no information to be gained about ODESSA from Otto Skorzeny.

As we shuffled out of his room, embarrassed in the presence of death, with the cold winter rain beating furiously at the window as if it wished to force a way in and wipe out all this

11. Walter Schellenberg, head of the German Secret Service; he thought Bormann was working for the Russians.

12. Herta and Reinhard Gehlen in the 1930s. After the war he became head of the German Secret Service.

13. Martin Bormann junior (right) gives communion to his brothers and sister after the war. In 1971 he left the Roman Catholic church to marry a former nun.

14. 'Tall, exceedingly thin Jochen Von Lang' (p.213) who did much to clear up the mystery of Bormann's death.

15. The author with Dr Putzi Hanfstaengl, head of Hitler's Foreign Press Department. He cordially disliked Bormann.

16. The author with Lina Heydrich, widow of the former gauleiter of Czechoslovakia, Reinhard Heydrich, who was assassinated in Prague in June, 1942.

17. Arthur Axmann, the one-armed Hitler Youth leader who escaped with Bormann, in the 1970s.

18. The former Post Office worker Albert Krumnow points to the spot where he claimed to have burried the bodies of Bormann and Dr Stumpfegger on 2 May, 1945. Excavation in 1965 revealed nothing but in 1972 the two skeletons were found 12 metres away.

misery, I whispered to my guide, "He'll be dead within a month."

But I had underestimated him. Otto Skorzeny regained his strength and his ability to walk. Returning to Madrid, where he had made his home since his escape from an internment camp after the war, he wrote that he had never gotten on with Bormann and toward the end he had anticipated a real showdown with the "Führer's Secretary" because he had placed one of Bormann's Party men before a court-martial on a charge of cowardice.

Skorzeny's role in ODESSA (and Die Spinne) may have been variously interpreted by this and that one – including himself – and no wonder, in the light of a still further tantalizing clue in the puzzle.

Apparently, the Madrid correspondent of a German daily whom Skorzeny knew well had been approached by a certain Herr Graf – but let the ex-commando chief tell the story in his own words:

"This swindler, Herr Graf, wanted to make a lot of dough with a Bormann story. In brief, he stated that at the end of the war he had come to me in Berlin – to my command post, which consisted of five cars in a train. (The whole train was made up of 12 to 15 cars.) Now I am supposed to have given him a personal order to search through the last four cars to check whether or not I had left any documents behind.[6]

"However, I had ordered him not to enter the first car *in any circumstance*. Naturally the clever Herr Graf did exactly this, being a very curious person. And who did he find? No other than Mr. Martin Bormann! . . . As if I couldn't have ordered the car to be locked."[7]

Imagine my frustration. In my attempt to solve one mystery, I had landed yet another: that fabricated by Herr Graf in Madrid. Or was it a fabrication? Although the inference may have been implicit, Skorzeny had not actually denied that Bormann had been in the car.

---

[6] Skorzeny was preparing to evacuate Berlin and drive to the "Alpine Fortress."

[7] In a letter to the author.

My frustration at so many stages in 1972 must have been similar to that of all those concerned in the whereabouts of Martin Bormann nearly twenty years before. For in February, 1953, when everyone – especially those who believed him dead – thought that by now they had sufficient facts about the dramatic events of May 1/2, 1945, to support their contentions, a bombshell exploded and seemed to destroy their carefully built-up theories.

A West Berlin newspaper reported an interview with a certain Joachim Tiburtius, who was now a grain dealer but who had once been a major in the SS Division Nordland. On May 1, 1945, he had commanded a group of four hundred officials, both male and female, plus a handful of troops attempting to escape from the Reich Chancellery. During the course of the breakout, he had seen Bormann trotting next to the tank just as it had been hit by the Russian bazooka. Bormann had been thrown to one side by the blast, but he hadn't been killed as Kempka, Baur, and the rest had maintained. Tiburtius had seen him shortly afterward near the Hotel Atlas on the far side of the Weidendamm Bridge, *and he was dressed in civilian clothes!*[8]

The onetime SS major concluded his statement with the words: "We pushed on together toward the Schiffbauerdamm and the Albrechtstrasse. Then I finally lost sight of him. . . . *But he had as good a chance to escape as I had . . .*"

Tiburtius's statement hit the headlines; even more interest was generated when he followed it up by explaining that a former comrade had seen Bormann a little later in the town of Komotau. Bormann had been wearing a green uniform and hat and looked like a forester. (In Germany forestry officials wear a paramilitary uniform of green jacket with badges of rank, and dark breeches.)

Again interest in the fate of Martin Bormann reached fever pitch. People began reasoning that if Tiburtius could get out of Berlin, as well as a lot of other people who had escaped from the bunker, why couldn't the Reichsleiter have escaped as well? After all, people like the ex-SS major were "nobodies." Bormann was a "somebody." Surely he could have made it, even though he was older and not as fit as the soldiers! After

---

[8] A highly important point which the reader should bear in mind.

all, he had had enough skilled and combat-experienced SS troopers around him who were prepared to help.

Tiburtius's statement had first aroused public interest in Europe; however, those in the know in NATO's intelligence agencies were already busily engaged with the problem and had been for the past month. Exactly one month before Major Tiburtius made his startling announcement, a man long thought dead returned – seemingly from the region of the shades. *Dr. Werner Naumann, the propaganda expert who had fled from the bunker with Bormann that fateful May night, had suddenly turned up.*

IV

The CIA Takes a Hand

Let the suspicion linger that the second most powerful
Nazi leader is still alive as a reminder not to forget the horrors
of the Third Reich.

—Dr. BRODERICK, Head of the Berlin CIA, 1953

14

In January, 1953, the dapper Sir Ivone Kirkpatrick, British High Commissioner in Germany, decided to strike, although doubts were expressed by his political advisers. Counter-intelligence agents working throughout the Ruhr industrial district of West Germany were flooding his office with their reports of the Nazi groups' activities. According to the under-cover men, the "neo-Nazis," as Kirkpatrick was already labelling them in his own mind, were becoming more powerful every new day that dawned. They had already successfully infiltrated the major West German political parties and were making a real bid to put their people into the leadership of the country's smallest party, the Free Democratic Party (the German Liberals).

Sir Ivone's profound knowledge of the German political scene, which dated back to World War I, told him what that meant. The neo-Nazis knew that in the forthcoming election, the FDP, although the smallest party, held the balance of power between the two major political groupings, the Socialists and the Conservatives. Whichever one of the two major groups gained power in the autumn election, it would need the FDP to give it a working majority. If, then, the neo-Nazis were able to take the liberal FDP over, they could – despite their small numbers – decisively influence the future of the new West German democracy.

A few weeks earlier the British diplomat, whose soft brogue indicated his Irish origin, had already warned the leaders of the FDP about the danger to their party. But they had pooh-poohed his warnings; they had had "a nose full of the Nazis," they said, using the German phrase; they were on their guard against any neo-Nazi takeover. And privately they joked among themselves about the Briton's ability to see Nazis where there were none: the High Commissioner saw jackbooted, brown-shirted ex-Nazis in every brokendown has-been who had not managed to find a place in the booming postwar German state.

But Sir Ivone, who had been the man picked by Churchill himself to interrogate Bormann's boss Hess when he had flown to Scotland in 1941, was a man with a suspicious mind. He had concerned himself with German affairs for nearly forty years. He had seen the rise and fall of the Nazi Party and knew well that Hitler had often boasted that his Party (and march to power) was based on the work of "just seven men." Couldn't the handful of conspirators in Dusseldorf pull off the trick once again? They were smart, well disciplined on the whole, had excellent connections in both industry and the government, possessed financial resources and a large potential following of unrepentant Nazis who might rally to their flag if their appeal were strong enough.

All that cold grey January he pondered what to do, as he stared out of the large picture window of his office at the sluggish silver of the River Rhine below, dotted with its industrious brown barges filled to the gunwales with raw materials for Germany's booming factories. He knew the dangers inherent in any action he might take. Germany's politicians and press were jealous of their newly won freedom. (West Germany had gained its independence in 1949.) They wouldn't like it one bit if he went over their heads and arrested the neo-Nazi conspirators. Yet he knew he must act, and act soon, if he were to prevent the FDP from being completely taken over before the September election. For a while he considered giving the evidence in his possession to the German authorities and letting them arrest the group. But then he dismissed that course of action. As he wrote later: ". . . I discarded the idea because . . . they [the neo-Nazis] had agents everywhere and there was a risk they might be warned in time to destroy documents." In the end he decided to go it alone and chance having his whole long diplomatic career ruined by ordering an action, behaviour which was very definitely undiplomatic and unusual for the suave and exceedingly cunning Foreign Office career man. In the second week of January, 1953, he called his Director of Public Safety into his office and began to lay out his plans for the apprehension of the neo-Nazis. This resulted in a simple, but significant order: "ARREST WERNER NAUMANN!"

Werner Naumann the dark, exceedingly intelligent man who had been Secretary of State in Goebbels's Propaganda Ministry, walked with the slight stoop that very tall men often assume. He had managed to escape capture on that terrifying May night eight years before. But not for long. He had been apprehended by the Russians; however, they had taken him for an ordinary Wehrmacht soldier and had released him a short while later in 1946.

The dark-skinned university graduate, who looked a bit like the conventional picture people have of Sherlock Holmes, was quick to make the most of the opportunity of escape given to him. Swiftly he slipped across the "green border" (the unguarded part of the frontier which separated East and West) into the French and later the American Zones of Occupation. There, his astute mind told him, he was in a little less danger than he had been in the Russian Zone; but he was in danger nonetheless.

Naumann had joined the Nazi Party at the age of nineteen and had given up his dreams of an academic career to join Goebbels. The latter had spotted his talents as an organizer and journalist almost at once, and although Goebbels had allowed him to take part in some of the fighting in Russia with the SS he had called him back to Berlin to make him Germany's youngest Secretary of State at the ripe old age of thirty-three. As a result of his position in the Third Reich, Dr. Naumann knew that he would come under the category of "automatic arrest" if any one of the four victorious Allies discovered his true identity.

But how could he conceal this identity and still stay alive? He needed to report to the police in order to get a ration card, and once he reported to them, the game would be up. Finally he did what many other wanted men were doing that year; he became a farm labourer on a remote farm where few questions were asked and where there was plenty to eat, even without ration cards. And to make doubly sure he wouldn't be discovered, he moved on after a few months, repeating the procedure from farm to farm, and then moving into the vast anonymity of the gangs of construction workers who were roaming the country eager to be hired for the rebuilding of Germany's shattered industrial plants.

In 1950, when the new West German government announced an amnesty, he settled in Dusseldorf and took on his old identity. There he looked up an old prewar friend, Herbert Lucht, who was running an import-export firm with his wife Lea van Dievoet, nicknamed "Slissy," who was a cousin of the Belgian SS man and right-wing renegade Leon Degrelle, also on the run from the Allies.

Herbert Lucht welcomed Naumann with open arms. He took a job with the firm and made a success of it, as he did with virtually everything he tackled, save politics. When Herbert died he was buried in the grounds of his big villa in a Dusseldorf suburb; Werner Naumann now took over the running of the firm, side by side with "Slissy."

By 1953, he was a prosperous, well-established businessman, but he had not lost his taste for radical politics. Three years before, he had written: "One cannot betray an ideal in which one has believed since his early days as I have done. Maybe the ruins of the Reich Chancellery hold for us greater values than are dreamed of by rash critics." The statement was an indication of the way his mind was turning even then.

That same summer he talked to Arno Breker, the Dusseldorf sculptor who specialized in naked "aryan" men and women of heroic proportions (and who, incidentally, did a highly publicised bust of Bormann's wife, Gerda). According to Naumann's diary: "Breker [says] I shouldn't let things drift. He says of all the people he knew, only one was really able to master the situation and that was me. According to him, I was able to put forward ideas that would adopt the good things of the past and add what the new times require. I should withdraw to lonely places and work it all out."

Naumann had no time to withdraw to "lonely places" but he did attempt to work it out. Over the next two years he worked feverishly in his off-duty time trying to establish old and new contacts, not only within Germany but elsewhere in Europe. Using the cover of his business trips for his firm, he got in touch with Nazis not only in Germany, but also in France, Italy, Belgium, and Spain, as well as with Sir Oswald Mosley, the chief of the prewar British blackshirts, who was living in Paris at that time. But his main efforts were directed, naturally, at his fellow countrymen. However, unlike other neo-Nazis who surfaced in the early fifties and tried to get into politics, he realized that a new style was needed. As he wrote at the time: "One of the mistakes of Dorls, Romer and the SRP[1] was that they slavishly copied the style of the NSDAP. We need a new style, new watchwords, new concepts and a new language, if we are again to shape our people politically and win through."

For the exceedingly clever ex-journalist, the way to success was through a democratically elected party which needed votes and was not too particular where they came from. Such a party was the FDP. Naumann was shrewd, taking care not to alarm the Liberals. After two of his associates, ex-generals, had spoken too openly before public audiences, he warned them: "It is dangerous to tell the world that though they may think we are dead, we are actually already there again."

On the night of January 14/15, 1953, Sir Ivone Kirkpatrick decided that, come what may, it was time to tell the world exactly that.

In the small hours of that cold, foggy morning, with the little suburb of Buderich lying muffled in silence, save for the periodic solemn chimes of the church clock, the impassive-faced British MPs – the "redcaps" – and the intelligence agents in civilian clothes began to seal off the house. A lone German policeman turned the corner, but swiftly ducked back when he saw the long line of army trucks and jeeps parked in the side road; he probably guessed what was going to happen and wanted no part of it.

Satisfied with their dispositions, the civilian in charge gave the wordless signal to commence the "operation." Swiftly two burly MPs applied their shoulders to the gate labelled "*Import und Export – firma H.S. Lucht.*" It gave and they were in. Suddenly everyone was galvanized into action. There were surprised shouts. Angry bellows of rage. A woman screamed. Lights started to go on everywhere. A window was flung open on the second floor and something fell heavily to the frozen ground.

The first, red-faced agent, his breath fogging in the icy night air, came out escorting a struggling, angry German. He was

---

[1] Neo-Nazi leaders of that time and the name of their party.

the first of several. The engines of the waiting trucks and jeeps burst throatily into life. They began to drive up to the door. MPs came out, bearing huge cases of papers and documents. In the garden another group of them were busily trying to find out how to open the vault in which lay the rotting corpse of "Slissy's" husband Herbert, in case the neo-Nazis had been smart enough to hide incriminating documents there. They hadn't.

And so it went on, throughout the night, until in the end Naumann and his seven most important fellow conspirators had been arrested, a ton of papers and documents had been removed from the villa in the Lorrickesstrasse, and thirty crates, each four by two feet, filled with similar "incriminating evidence" (as the British authorities would call it later), had been seized from other sources.

By dawn it was all over and the British were ready to hold their first press conference for a shocked and alarmed German press at the surprisingly early hour (for diplomats) of 7 A.M., while in the nearby jail of Werl, Werner Naumann found himself associating with an assorted bunch of "war criminals," at last being confronted with the fate he had successfully escaped eight years before. Destiny had finally caught up with the "man who had come back from the dead," as the German press called him that January.

At the first press conference of his whole career in Germany, Sir Ivone Kirkpatrick explained his dramatic action by maintaining that Naumann and his group "were like a Chinese pirate gang that intends to seize the ship by gaining control of the bridge, [and] then boards other ships and collects a nice little navy."

But when the aggressive German and British reporters asked him to give proof of his allegations, he backed off, retreating into that cold, formal, diplomatic posture that Foreign Office members seem to imbibe with their mothers' milk, saying he had nothing specific; his people needed time to check through the captured documents and prepare charges. "We really don't know what Herr Naumann and his friends are up to. We've arrested them to find out."

His explanation did not satisfy the press in either Germany or the United Kingdom. British Foreign Secretary Anthony Eden's similar vague declaration in Parliament was equally ineffective. The newspapers on both sides of the Channel fell on the two diplomats. The British maintained that the Foreign Office was trying to sabotage the new German state of West Germany for some strange reason of its own; whereas the German papers stated baldly that the British were afraid of the growing economic power of the new state and that this was one of a number of attempts to discredit honest German businessmen. The more popular papers made fun of Kirkpatrick's "*Nau-Nau.*"[2]

Adenauer, the wily, ancient German Chancellor, took up the case. He had not liked the British ever since they had removed him from his office of Chief Burgomaster of Cologne at the end of the war for "incompetence." (The Americans had given him the job in March, 1945, because he was a well-known anti-Nazi when they had captured the Rhenish city.) He forced Kirkpatrick's hand. The discomfited and embarrassed High Commissioner, unable to produce evidence of Naumann's guilt, handed him over to the German authorities after Naumann had been questioned by British intelligence officers for over ten weeks and there were still no charges preferred against him.

The then Minister of Justice, FDP man Thomas Dehler, conceded now that "Naumann was trying to fill key positions in the rightist parties and the FDP with his supporters. . . . The final goal was the restoration of the Nazi dictatorship with the emphasis on the leadership role of the German race. . . . The plot to destroy the democratic system in Germany had considerable support here and abroad."

But the damage had been done to Kirkpatrick's case. On July 20, Naumann's lawyer pleaded to the High Court in Karlsruhe that "Naumann is a man who says yes to the state, who knows that this state is our state; that he does not wish to destroy it. He wishes to improve [it]. He wants to bring former National Socialists closer to today's state and he urges moderation and understanding."

The court withdrew and when it reappeared toward evening, its spokesman announced its decision: "The accused [are] to be released. Reason: The present status of the

---

[3] A pun on the African underground organization the Mau-Mau, which was giving the British trouble at that time.

preliminary investigation indicates that, in the view of the court, there is no longer any justifiable suspicion that a genuine conspiracy existed. The arrest warrant must thus be withdrawn."

Werner Naumann and the rest had won. The dapper little British diplomat had failed. On that warm sunny evening the smart ex-Propaganda Ministry man stepped out of the Karlsruhe court a free man.

But the story did not end there. The reappearance of Werner Naumann in such a dramatic manner – and one which seriously injured Anglo-German relations at a crucial stage in the young republic's life – shocked certain authorities into having another look at the case of the man who had fled with Dr. Naumann on that May night of 1945.

For during his long weeks of cross-examination by the persistent British counter-intelligence agents, Naumann had not confined himself to the present; he had also wandered about in the mental past: his days as a student; his career as a foreign journalist; the days at Goebbels's HQ during the war; the situation in the bunker. Indeed, he stated, he had lost his entire enthusiasm for the Nazi cause in those last months of the war when he and other members of Goebbels's intimate circle had made an earth-shaking discovery: Hitler's most loyal servant, "his eyes and ears," his "well-trusted Secretary," was a Soviet spy. *Martin Bormann had worked for the Reds all the time!* And as if that were not enough, the suspected neo-Nazi Naumann went on to explain almost casually, "Bormann was rescued by the Russians. He was a Soviet spy and he must have arranged beforehand where to meet the Russian Army's advance units. . . . We had to run for our lives. One of us, Dr. Stumpfegger, was killed by shrapnel." And then Naumann added, *"Martin Bormann now lives in Moscow."*[3]

---

[3] When in 1953 Naumann was questioned for the first time by the German authorities on this subject, he did not repeat the above statement. Indeed, ever since his arrest in 1953, he has been very smart in his attempts not to let himself be pinned down one way or another on the subject of Bormann's fate.

15

Naumann's arrest, coupled with the renewed interest in Martin Bormann in that spring of 1953, did not pass unnoticed at the newly founded United States Central Intelligence Agency; in particular, its Berlin headquarters located in the woody suburb of Dahlem, not far from the university residences.

The British arrest of Dr. Naumann and his associates had come as a surprise as well as a welcome change from dull routine to the CIA's Berlin office chief, a man whose true name has never been revealed, but who is usually spoken of as "Dr. John Broderick." It also intrigued him. After the first storm following the arrests had calmed down, he began to occupy himself with two questions: 1) Had Bormann been able to escape from Berlin as Naumann had? 2) Was he the man behind the Naumann plot to return the Nazis to power?

In spite of the Nuremberg decision of 1946 and subsequent events, there still was no real proof, the spymaster told himself, that Martin Bormann was dead. In addition, the "last" hours of the two men – Naumann and Bormann – had been spent together; Bormann had even asked Naumann specifically for permission to join his particular escape group from the bunker. If Naumann had been able to escape, why not Bormann? The more Dr. John Broderick thought about the Naumann affair and the questions it raised, the more he felt that the CIA should take a hand in a search for Bormann. In the end he wired his superiors in Washington, D. C., for permission to undertake an investigation. Some time later he received the go-ahead.

Although Broderick retained overall supervision of the case, he turned over its day-to-day running to a young

New Yorker named James McGovern. McGovern was a dark-haired, pugnacious-chinned civilian who had served during World War II in the Philippines and New Guinea as an Army Signal Corps cryptographer. At war's end he entered Harvard, graduated in 1948 and then went to the Sorbonne to study literature. One year later he took a job with the Office of Scientific Intelligence at the Office of the U. S. High Commissioner in Frankfurt, a post which he left in 1951 to join the CIA. There he could use his Army training as well as his knowledge of German and French.

After two years with the CIA, McGovern had already learned that his original belief that intelligence would be exciting, with glamorous blond countesses named Olga and lots of backstreet skullduggery, was misleading. Intelligence, he had discovered, was a routine job, as different from the cloak-and-dagger stuff of the Hollywood movies as the sun is from the moon. He wrote later: "Like most espionage work, this was not glamorous or exciting, but instead required the drudgery of checking out evidence and coordinating the work of different individuals and organizations."

He set about his task, therefore, logically and realistically. He alerted CIA offices throughout the three continents, Europe, Asia and South America, where Martin Bormann had been "sighted" at one time or another, and asked them to check out the authenticity of these reports. He then approached Reinhard Gehlen's "Org" in Pullach near Munich, where Bormann himself had once lived as a young aide to Rudolf Hess, and requested their help in the search.

The Gehlen Org (a short form of "Organization") was a spy outfit named after its boss General Reinhard Gehlen, a thin-faced, dome-headed German spymaster who had been in charge of the entire German Army's espionage and intelligence network in the East during World War II. After Germany lost the war, Gehlen had with amazing audacity done a *volte-face*, and transferred the group to the service of the U.S. Army – and later to the CIA. By 1953, for an annual fee of some five million dollars, he supplied the CIA and, indirectly, NATO, with some eighty percent of its intelligence about what was happening behind the Iron Curtain.

Satisfied that he had gotten the investigation started, McGovern now turned his attention to the "psychological" side of his quest, using the new techniques that the CIA had developed since its inception in 1947. He called upon the Berlin HQ's psychiatrist-in-residence and his principal "scenario writer." The former's task was to review the known details of the life of the "man in the shadows" and then to compose a psychological profile of him. This would be then handed to the "scenario writer" who would use it to combine the details of his life with the events of the last days in the bunker for the purpose of writing a "scenario" of what a man of his type and temperament might conceivably have done in the circumstances. McGovern wrote later: "This was a recent and sophisticated technique designed to stimulate the thinking of case officers who might find themselves 'locked in' or inhibited by conventional thinking and a mass of information."

Then the young case officer sat back and awaited developments.

Gradually, as the Naumann Affair blew over and Naumann was turned free, the reports started to come in from the various overseas CIA offices. One by one they reported that there was no substance to the statements made by over a dozen individuals: those of British soldiers who swore to having mown Bormann down with a greasegun in 1945; of Danish doctors who claimed to have spotted him landing in a submarine on the Baltic coast; of informants who reported him hidden away in the more remote mountain regions of Albania; or of the many South American eyewitnesses across the Atlantic. As James McGovern recorded later in the account he wrote of his mission (*Martin Bormann*, Arthur Barker, 1968): "There were different speculations on the eyewitnesses' motives; they were honestly mistaken, or publicity seekers, or the kind of persons who see flying saucers."

Grimly he stuck to his task. The Gehlen Org came through with a negative, too. They had been unable to find out what had happened to Bormann after he had fled the bunker, but, in the opinion of the cool-eyed, medium-sized General Gehlen (who always carried a loaded pistol and disguised himself with assumed names and dark glasses for fear of Soviet assassins – it was rumoured that there was a Russian reward of a million marks on his head, dead or alive), Martin Bormann was neither alive nor in Russian hands. (This was the first time the elusive general, who has been called "the spy of the century," made mention of Bormann's fate; we shall return to his statement later.)

However, the Gehlen Org had turned up one new item. It made mention of photographs seen by one of Gehlen's "V-men"[1] which Russian soldiers had made of a journal found on the corpse of an unknown German in May, 1945, in Berlin. This journal turned out to be that of Martin Bormann and contained two entries which indicated that the corpse on which it was found was that of Martin Bormann himself. In other words, Gehlen had good reason to assume that Bormann had been killed by the Russians and buried in some mass grave at an unknown spot in Berlin.

McGovern does not say what he thought of the Gehlen report. He left the CIA that same year and makes it quite clear that he has had "no connection with the agency since then."[2]

However, we do know the results of the scenario writer's labours.

As he saw it, there were four possibilities. Bormann's whole career suggested that he was a born opportunist. His entry into the Nazi Party after his release from jail; his marriage to Gerda Buch; his building up of the NSDAP *Hilfskasse*; his gradual takeover of power behind Hess's back; and his long-term attempts to eradicate any rivals at Hitler's HQ during the war all indicated that he was primarily out for Number One, turning any and every situation to his own advantage.

Consequently, when he became aware in 1942 that the Nazi cause was lost, he offered his services (by means which we shall discuss later) to the hated Russian enemy. For three years he radioed them top-secret information, so that when in the last moments of the battle for Berlin General Krebs went to negotiate the surrender of the bunker to the Russians, he unwittingly carried with him a message from Bormann fixing a time and place for the latter's own personal meeting with his hitherto unknown masters. When this was done, Bormann

---

[1] Literally "man of trust." i.e., undercover man.
[2] In a letter to author Whiting, 1972.

broke out with the rest, but managed to become separated from them as soon as it was possible. The easiest means was by feigning death; an apparent death which satisfied the excited Axmann who was concerned with his own escape. Soon afterward Bormann was picked up by a Russian patrol sent out to find him and carried off to Soviet Russia, where he was still alive and well, working as a leading expert on German affairs. If and when the occasion arose, he could be returned to Germany in any capacity his Russian masters thought suitable.

Thus Psychogram Number One.

Number Two was even more fantastic; yet there was sufficient substance behind it to make it almost believable. The scenario writer could not quite believe that Bormann had known nothing of the intended flight of his chief Rudolf Hess to Scotland in 1941. Bormann had his eyes and ears everywhere; and there were at least four people who knew for some months that Hess had intended to go to Great Britain and attempt to arrange a peace. As the scenario writer saw it, perhaps it was Bormann himself who had been the mastermind behind the flight. He had shown his boss Hess that his power was waning rapidly and suggested that the only way he could regain the Führer's favour was to do something dramatic, such as ensuring Britain's withdrawal from the war at a time when Hitler wanted his hands free for an all-out attack on Soviet Russia. Although Hess's mission had failed, he had got in touch with his former aide Bormann and convinced him to work for the British. Thus, when the Third Reich had gone down in flames, Bormann had made his way westward – hence his determination to reach Dönitz – to meet British undercover agents somewhere in north Germany. They had then spirited him away to some remote part of the island kingdom. Here he was still living, working as an adviser for the British government against the time it would be appropriate for him to return to his fatherland where he could live out his days in peace.

In spite of the seeming impossibility of this "scenario," there were certain elements of it which rang true: Bormann's determination to get to Dönitz; the fact that two people reported spotting him in north Germany in May, 1945; and the Britishers' highly sophisticated habit of using enemies and even known war criminals for their own purposes as long as they needed them.[3]

The third scenario was based on the conclusion that the testimony of Kempka, Baur, Axmann, and the rest who claimed Bormann was dead was false, motivated by an effort to protect a still-living Reichsleiter. According to the scenario writer, Bormann had escaped from Berlin and slipped aboard a submarine somewhere on the Baltic or North Sea coast. From here he had shipped to Argentina living there on the many millions he had already salted away before the end of the war, and protected by the heavy hand of the country's Fascist dictator Peron. Later he had moved, safeguarded by a band of tough ex-SS and SD men; he had gone to a more remote part of the great unexplored continent. From there he aimed at trying to re-establish the European Fascist parties. Once this was done and he had a chance of success, he would reappear like some long-awaited saviour.

Young CIA deskman McGovern was just not excited by the first three scenarios. They didn't "seem very promising" to him. They were supposed to stimulate thinking, but the stimulus had to be based on facts.

It was, therefore, with relief that he turned to the fourth and last scenario, which appeared to him to have merit. It was based on the assumption that Bormann's world went to pieces when Hitler died. As a result, Bormann had had no real escape plan but had blindly followed the others, as evidenced by his plea to Naumann to take him along. The scenario writer accepted the whole story of the events of that night as told by the participants and came to the conclusion that when Stumpfegger and Bormann found themselves trapped, with the Russians to their front and rear, they realized there was no longer any way out save suicide; and Bormann, who knew what to expect if the hated "Reds" caught him, did not hesitate to swallow his cyanide pill. In a final irony, the Russians did not even recognize the Secretary of the Führer. They had

---

[3] When Churchill was told in May, 1945, that Dönitz himself was regarded as a "war criminal," Churchill told his informant that he didn't give a damn as long as the German admiral, who was accused of having started unrestricted sea warfare, was of use to him.

him buried, along with scores of other bodies lying in the area, in an unmarked mass grave.

When, finally, James McGovern presented his report to the mysterious Dr. John Broderick, the latter did not appear disappointed by its inconclusive nature. He personally agreed with the fourth scenario that Bormann had taken poison when he had found there was no other way out. But, unlike McGovern, Broderick believed the Russians had discovered Bormann's identity; according to his sources of information at Karlshorst, the Soviet Army HQ, the discovery of the Bormann Journal had occasioned Moscow to order the exhumation of the body. A group of Russian officers had dug it up in secret and, taking it to an isolated spot deep in their Zone, had reburied it in an unmarked grave[4] to make sure that no "Bormann legend" would arise in years to come.

This seemed pretty pointless to McGovern, but the older operative lectured him on the devious nature of the Soviet mind. He told him that Stalin wanted it to be thought that the Secretary of the Führer was still alive. This would be a powerful propaganda tool. As long as it could be thought that the leading Nazi was alive in some western country, the West could be accused of sheltering a Nazi revival. Thus, for the Russians, Martin Bormann would remain "alive" as long as it suited their purpose to let him do so.

And in the end, if from somewhat different motives, this was the same attitude taken by the CIA chief Dr. John Broderick. Although he thought he now knew the truth about Bormann's fate, he decided not to make the story public.

He had three reasons for doing so. During the course of the inquiry, Stalin had died, and the U.S. government did not want to do anything which might endanger the delicate new baby called "coexistence" which had just been born to the superpowers. Secondly, it would be highly embarrassing to let it be known publicly that the Nuremberg Trial had spent so much time, effort, and money trying a man already dead for nearly a year; the Allies would be the laughing stock of the new Germany, a country which was already beginning to have

---

[4] This is what the Russians, who discovered them, did with the bodies of Hitler and Eva Braun and Goebbels.

serious doubts about the legality and purpose of the trial. And finally, as McGovern put it later: "Stalin's curious idea was not really such a bad one. Let the suspicion linger that the second most powerful Nazi leader was still alive as a reminder not to forget the horrors of the Third Reich."[5]

---

[5] In a letter to the author in 1972, Mr. McGovern, now a writer as well as a public relations man in his native New York, wrote: "Fortunately he's (Bormann) been dead for 26 years. Or perhaps unfortunately, for a more melodramatic fate would surely sell more books." Mr. McGovern had obviously become a cynic in the intervening years.

16

There were obvious flaws in the CIA argument, especially in Scenario Four which concluded that Bormann was dead, killed during his escape from the bunker. If, as the scenario writer maintained, ". . . Hitler was dead. Bormann's life work had turned out to be worthless. Psychologically, he was completely disoriented. There was no way out," why did the Reichsleiter even attempt to break out of the bunker? Why did he not take his own life as the remaining key figures, Goebbels and General Krebs, did? After all, as the scenario writer maintained in Psychogram Number Four, "within minutes, he was going to fall into the hands of the Russians, whom he always despised and whose vengeance he had good reason to fear."

Instead, if we are to believe the CIA's staff psychiatrist, Bormann committed suicide in the middle of an open street with lead flying about and Russian patrols only some hundred yards away (according, that is, to Axmann).

But does this ring true? Even in death human beings like their comfort, their ease, their accustomed milieu – their time. How often when someone commits suicide by means of gassing himself, we find the victim's head cradled in a pillow or neatly deposited against the back seat of a car with the appropriate note of explanation at his side. Or if the job has been done by the more direct and classical method of slashing the wrists, the suicide is more often than not found in a bath of his own blood, for he has wanted to enjoy – for the last time – the sybaritic pleasure of hot comforting water while watching, with no doubt fascinated horror, his life fluid ebbing away. That particular method of ending one's life was naturally not available in the bunker; but even if Bormann had been forced to kill himself by the direct brutality of a bullet through his brain, surely he would first have drunk himself into a state of almost complete mindlessness and immunity to pain. This was the way that Krebs took before he finally reached drunkenly for his service revolver. Why, then, the hazardous venture outside and the hours of fear if he knew the game was up even before he left the bunker?

And what about the Bormann diary? "According to Dr. Broderick's Soviet source, whose accuracy he did not question, Russian officers identified Bormann. He was carrying his *Tagebuch*, or daily log, in his pocket," to quote McGovern. Where was it found (if it ever was) and by whom? Apparently it was discovered by the troops of the Fifth Assault Army of the Russian forces. But the troops of the Fifth were not employed in that sector of the front during the fighting in Berlin; that is, around the station area where the Bormann corpse conceivably could have been found. *The Soviet troops which attacked in that area were those of the Eighth Guards Army.* How, then, did men of the Fifth come by a log book taken off a corpse immediately after or during the fighting in a sector a long way off? And who has ever seen the journal in the West? Even those in the East who maintain they have seen it (a copy of it is supposed to be kept in the safes of the East Berlin district attorney's offices) report that it looks to them like a translation. And it is obvious from which language it is translated — *Russian*.

Does this mean that the reputed East German journal is the copy of a Russian version of the original Bormann journal? *Or does this mean that there was no original?*

According to Dr. Broderick's statement to young James McGovern in 1953, "They [the Russian officers who had identified Bormann] had him buried by the employees of the Lehrter Post Office." After notifying Moscow of their discovery the officers were then ordered to exhume him and reinter him in the lonely spot in their own Zone already mentioned. So far so good, but what happened to those post office officials from the Lehrter Post Office? They should have been easy to find. Would they not have confirmed the fact that Martin Bormann was dead?

As I write this, I have in front of me a yellowing photostat of a letter dated 14th August 1945. It is addressed to Frau Gertrud Stumpfegger, 2 Hohenlychen, Heilanstalt[1] and reads:

Dear Mrs. Stumpfegger:

On the 8th of May this year a soldier was found by the officials of the post office on the railway bridge in the Invalidenstrasse. It was the body of a soldier who had been killed in the fighting for Berlin. According to the pass found on the body the man was Ludwig Stumpfegger. As one must assume the dead man was your husband. I am forwarding you this sad news and at the same time may I convey my deep sympathy to you.

Your husband was interred, with the bodies of several other dead soldiers in the grounds of the Alpendorf [the former exhibition park[2]] in Berlin NW 40, Invalidenstrasse 63. I am sending you the photos found on the body. His pass was destroyed.

[Signed] Berndt
Chief of the Office.

Naturally the dead man was Dr. Stumpfegger, who was reported as dead also by Axmann as Stumpfegger lay side by side with Bormann. So here we have convincing proof of Bormann's comrade's death. But there is no mention of the Reichsleiter himself, which is perhaps understandable in the circumstances. Nonetheless, we have the clue to a key witness, for the address on the letterhead of that sad communication is *Postamt 40 (Lehrter Bahnhof).*[3] Berndt was one of those men who may well have helped to inter Bormann's body (if we believe the CIA story) under Russian supervision. *But where was the mysterious Berndt, who confirmed the death of the unimportant doctor, yet did nothing about notifying the world of the death of the key Nazi Party official presumably lying at his side (according to Axmann)?*

Indeed, many questions, and few satisfactory answers. In that summer of 1953, when the CIA inquiry was ended, the people in the know were not so much concerned with the Americans' answers as those the Russians might give, now that

---

[1] German for "mental home."
[2] Already mentioned in the first part of the book.
[3] "Post Office 40, Lehrter Station."

the dictatorial power of the longtime Soviet ruler Josef Stalin had been broken and the country seemed to be ready for a new and more enlightened form of government. Would the Russians now finally break their reticence, not only about the fate of Nazi Leader Adolf Hitler and his mistress Eva Braun, but also about Martin Bormann? Would they finally come out with a definitive statement about the fate of the man who by this time had become one of the most wanted figures in history?

However, the Russians remained silent year in, year out. Indeed, they never mentioned the subject and did not encourage foreign journalists wanting to do research on it in Moscow's archives. This continued for just over a decade. Then, in 1964, a little book appeared in Moscow entitled *In the Footsteps of Martin Bormann*. Its author was a forty-four-year-old journalist and German expert named Lev Bezymenski. For the first time, a Russian writer had occupied himself in detail with the problem of Martin Bormann; and if we bear in mind that everything which was published in Soviet Russia in book form was printed in government publishing houses, then we may assume that Lev Bezymenski's book represented the official Soviet attitude to the almost twenty-year-old hunt for the Reichsführer.

But who was Lev Bezymenski?

In 1941, he had been a third-year student of classical German philosophy at the country's foremost university, the University of Moscow.

On June 22 of that hot, dry summer, he had been listening to music on the radio when the broadcast was interrupted to bring an excited speech by Russian Foreign Minister Molotov. The bespectacled, lantern-jawed politician (whose name meant "hammer" and had been adopted by him in his early revolutionary days) announced that Germany had launched a surprise attack on the "peace-loving" Soviet Fatherland. As a result, Russia was beginning to take "defensive measures."

Young Lev sat there on the sunny sofa, "stunned" (as he said afterward), until his father, of whom it was rumoured that he knew the Soviet dictator Stalin well, came in and said simply, "Son, it's war."

Thereafter things moved quickly for the young student. He was drafted into the Army; was promoted to the rank of lieutenant; saw action on the River Don; was present when Field Marshal Paulus surrendered the German Sixth Army at Stalingrad, the turning point of the war; took part in the Battle of Kursk; and ended the war as a captain on the staff of Marshal Zhukov in Berlin. Thereafter he became a journalist, first of all in Moscow and later in Bonn as the German correspondent of the *Novoe Vremya*.

But was that all? Did Lev Bezymenski have any other function? His father reputedly was, as I have already said, an intimate of Stalin's. He himself spoke fluent German and was allowed the unusual privilege even for a journalist of travelling extensively and for long periods throughout West Germany. There are those, in Germany at least, who suspect that he was more than a journalist. At all events, two books he published in Germany after the war on the subject of Bormann and later of Hitler seemed to be propaganda works directed at American-German "Imperialism" and "neo-Nazism" more than the explorations of the subjects with which they were supposedly concerned.

In 1965, in the German version of his book, *Auf den Spuren von Martin Bormann*, he wrote: "Martin Bormann perhaps doesn't deserve to be the subject of historical research. After all, the personality of Martin Bormann is unimportant. But nonetheless, his fate represents the dangerous political process of Nazi regeneration which is taking place in different forms and in different countries throughout the world. As a person, Bormann is nothing, but in union with the Nazi regime he has grown to be a significant figure."

It is against the background of his declared intention to see Bormann in the framework of a revived Nazism in the postwar Western world that we must evaluate Lev Bezymenski's personal search for the missing Martin Bormann: that of a man who is perhaps something more than he purports to be.

In Bezymenski's evaluation of the question of whether Martin Bormann were dead or alive, he noted the following:

1. The first statements made to the effect that Bormann was dead were given immediately after 1945 by people like Axmann and Kempka, with "the apparent aim of convincing the world that the Reichsleiter had been killed."

2. But as soon as the authorities began to concern themselves with the Bormann problem, it became clear that the first statements were invalid and the "whole building which they [the first witnesses] had so carefully constructed was starting to collapse."

3. It was exactly at this period that "Axmann tried to convince the world that he had seen Bormann lying dead. In addition, one must bear in mind that the statements made by the people in the second stage were given during their period of imprisonment when they could not communicate with each other. Bernd Ruland, the author of the *Bunte Illustrierte* article,[4] was of the opinion that Bormann pretended to be dead in order to deceive Axmann. It is more probable, however, that Axmann and Naumann agreed upon their statements in order to fool us."

4. Finally, Axmann's statements "give rise to a lot of doubt, especially when one considers that he changed his explanations at least three times in the postwar years."

On this basis the Russian journalist started to look for survivors of the Red Army's battle for the German capital in 1945. Seemingly, he succeeded right away; he found Lieutenant General Konstantin Fyodorovich Telegin, who told him: "During the night of 2nd May we were told that a large group of enemy, with about 12 tanks and self-propelled vehicles had tried to break through the lines of the Fifth Assault Army[5]. The group consisted mainly of SS men. A large number of them were scattered by our fire and many were taken prisoner."

"Was it known that Martin Bormann was in this group?" Lev Bezymenski asked eagerly.

"Yes," the elderly general replied. "That was known. A lot of prisoners revealed this in their statements. I remember especially the statement of a cook who had sheltered behind a tank with Bormann. He said that the tank had come under heavy

---

[4] An article which appeared in the magazine, *Bunte Illustrierte*, in 1963, which maintained that Bormann was alive.
[5] Note again the wrong Army.

artillery fire. The group was literally torn to bits. He was badly wounded. He never saw Bormann again."

The listening journalist realized that he had arrived at what he called "Stage One": the explosion within the Tiger, probably due – as the German witnesses maintained – to the effect of a Russian bazooka. But he did not interrupt the general. Instead, he prompted him with a further question:

"What did you do?"

"Naturally we sent a recon group to the bridge, who searched the site of the breakthrough attempt. All they found were a few civilians. *Bormann was not found.*"

Lev Bezymenski thanked the general, but did not accept the old soldier's statement that Bormann was not found. After all, he might have been among the civilians. The question now was whether Bormann had been wearing civilian clothes or uniform when he left the bunker. Most of the eyewitnesses known to the Russian journalist had maintained that Bormann had been wearing a uniform at the time – usually it was described as a Waffen SS uniform covered with an ankle-length leather coat (a favourite of the Reichsleiter). Naumann, Baur, and Kempka all stated very definitely that Bormann was clothed in this uniform. Yet this very certainty made Bezymenski suspect something. ". . . One could only draw a negative conclusion. If they maintain that he was wearing a uniform, then he must have worn civilian clothes."

In other words, Bormann might well have been among the civilian dead found by the Russian reconnaissance patrol.

But Lev did not give up his search for evidence. And then he had a stroke of luck. After the "same old question a hundred times over," he met a Soviet Army veteran, Colonel Alexander Smyslov, who surprised him with the statement: "But then you've got to take the notebook business into account. Don't you remember it?"

The journalist shook his head. He didn't. But General Telegin did.

"Naturally," he replied eagerly. "I saw Bormann's diary. It was brought in immediately after the fighting had ended. As far as I remember, it was found on the road when they were cleaning up the battle area."

Lev Bezymenski, puzzled yet intrigued, decided to set about

what appeared to be an almost impossible task: to find the man who discovered the notebook.

He failed to do so, and returned a little chastened to ex-Colonel Smyslov, who had given him the original story. Lev related to him what he had heard from General Telegin. But when he came to the latter's statement about the book being picked up on the road, Colonel Smyslov interrupted him hastily.

"What do you mean, on the road! As far as I know the book was discovered in the bunker of the Reich Chancellery. It looked completely everyday and was undamaged. The last entry read: '*Der Ausbruchsversuch* ...' "[6]

The Russian journalist felt his head reel. He knew what the colonel's statement meant. By this time he was aware that the finding of Bormann's journal on the street near a body (or, in some descriptions, on it) meant that the corpse was more than likely that of Martin Bormann. But if the document had been found in the bunker – and it was well established that Bormann had left the bunker on the night of May 1/2 – then that particular corpse could not have been that of the Reichsleiter. The hunt for Martin Bormann was becoming "curiouser and curiouser."

---

[6] The breakout attempt.

17

During this stage of Lev Bezymenski's investigation he had been concerned with two major problems: 1) the question of whether the missing man had been wearing civilian clothes or uniform;[1] 2) where exactly the Bormann journal had been found.

But suddenly a third problem presented itself.

Talking over the subject of his hunt with the Russian writer Sergei Smirnov, he was startled when the latter remarked almost casually, "It's all very interesting. But do you know the story about Bormann's journal being found in a tank?"

The journalist could hardly believe his ears. *"In a tank!"* he stuttered.

The writer chuckled, satisfied with the effect he had created. "Yes, in a tank. Fyodor Schemyakin can tell you about it."

Schemyakin had been a "political instructor" with the Red Army investing Berlin, but now he was a professor of psychology. He was eager to relate what he knew.

"On one of the first days after the fighting had ended," he explained, "an officer from one of the divisions at the front came into the Political Administration [HQ] which had its staff in Spandau on the western boundary of the city. He gave me a trophy – a small notebook. As far as I can remember, it was found in the following circumstances. A group of German

---

[1] Naturally, Lev Bezymenski realized that Bormann could have been wearing *both* a uniform and civilian clothes. Indeed, there is one participant in the fighting that night who maintains he saw Bormann changing into civilian clothes in a doorway at one stage. And most successful escapers managed it by changing into mufti.

tanks had tried to break out westwards. After the fighting, this notebook was found. Bormann has not been found to this day. There is no sure proof that he is dead."

Bezymenski decided thereupon to write to several international figures who had been connected – directly or indirectly – with the search for Martin Bormann. Some, like Trevor-Roper, thought he was still alive; others, like William Shirer, had no evidence to offer one way or the other. But one man, who in 1965 was in a better position to know than any of them, replied with a positive statement about the Reichsleiter's fate. This was Dr. Fritz Bauer, state attorney for the West German Federal state of Hesse.

Dr. Bauer, who had had one Jewish parent, had been imprisoned in a concentration camp, but had escaped. He had overall responsibility for the official German government's search for Martin Bormann, which had begun in 1964, the year before, and had been instrumental in convincing the authorities that they should offer one hundred thousand marks[2] for information leading to the apprehension of the missing Nazi leader.

Dr. Bauer wrote he was of the opinion that "Bormann succeeded in escaping from the Reich Chancellery . . . Thereafter he probably lived for some time in Schleswig-Holstein. There he attempted to make contact with Grand Admiral Dönitz. We can suppose that he did this and Dönitz helped him to cross the border into Denmark. We believe that Bormann stayed for some time in the Danish Royal Castle at Grästen, which is not far from the town of Sønderborg. The castle was at that time an SS military hospital and it became known later that many high-ranking Nazi leaders hid there. The man who hid them and Bormann from the public eye was a man named Heyde."

The wheel had come full circle. The search was back where it had started in 1945: in the little enclave at Flensburg where Admiral Dönitz had had his HQ at the end of war, which was not occupied by the British forces until May 23, 1945, when the "Dönitz Government" was finally arrested.

---

[2] At that time equivalent to $25,000.

The eighty-year-old Grand Admiral, who in the winter of 1942 nearly brought Great Britain to her knees with the success of his U-boat attacks, lived in a little village not far from the great port city of Hamburg. He lived alone in the first storey of a white-painted, nineteenth-century villa that was slightly run down and a little shabby. He welcomed me at the door, fit and slim, dressed in a smart dark suit, his hand cupped to his ear to get my name. "Nothing wrong with me save that my hearing has gone and my brain has gotten smaller," he snapped and then added, as if he was back on the quarterdeck, *"Speak louder!"*

Admiral Dönitz lost all his possessions in Berlin during the war. (He also lost both his sons at sea.) Now his large room was decorated with a few antiques, a shabby carpet, and books – books everywhere.

"When I was released from Spandau in 1956,[3] I didn't even have a piece of paper to write on," he commented, noting my eyes searching the many books, most of them decorated with bookmarks to aid him in his prolific writing. As I sat down, he explained that he lived alone and cooked for himself; he didn't want a woman in the house. "Then when you've been married to one woman for forty-two years, you can't get used to another one." But the interested looks the eighty-year-old ex-Admiral cast at my female companion with those dark, lively eyes of his belied his supposed lack of interest in the opposite sex.

The old sailor, who had been captured by the British as a young U-boat captain in World War I and who had subscribed to the Nazi cause earlier than most regular naval officers (who had looked down on that "upstart Hitler"), had worked himself up to be the only high-ranking sailor that the Führer trusted. Dönitz was not one for idle chatter or small talk. A few glances at his watch convinced me that he was a busy man who wanted to get back to his voluminous writing and his justification of his actions in World War II.

I brought the conversation around to the subject of Bormann. How long had the Admiral known him?

He thought three years – perhaps from 1942 on.

---

[3] He was sentenced at Nuremberg at the same time as the missing Bormann. He received ten years which he spent in Spandau Jail, Berlin.

What did he think of him?

"Bormann played no role in my scale of values – neither up nor down," he snapped, as if he were giving an order, those keen eyes searching my face for a reaction.

I waited for a qualification, a further explanation, but none came. Dönitz had obviously said his last word on the subject.

In the end I posed the question that I had come so far to ask: "Did Bormann get through to you – is he still alive?"

He did not even hesitate. "If he had, I would have had him arrested at once. *Bormann alive – absolute nonsense!*"

And with that, the man the German Navy once called "the big lion" rose to his feet. The interview was over. But I believed him.

But in 1964, Lev Bezymenski, the Russian hunting for Martin Bormann, did not. In that year he decided to get in touch with the man whom he thought had somehow smuggled Bormann across the German frontier into Italy, Dr. Helmut von Hummel, Bormann's aide. He telephoned him at his villa in Munich. After asking the German if he was Bormann's adjutant, he was told, "No, I wasn't his adjutant. I was his economics adviser."

"But you knew him?"

"Naturally. But I have never seen him again since the spring of 1945. But I don't want to talk about this subject . . . ."

The conversation went on for a little while longer until finally Dr. von Hummel snapped, "No, I don't want to speak with a Soviet journalist. Look, I never talked badly about Herr Bormann while he was alive. It would be incorrect on my part to do it now."

Thus the conversation was broken off, but as Lev Bezymenski noted afterward: "Helmut von Hummel probably knows the answer to the 'Bormann puzzle.' I was strengthened in this point of view by a document I found later in the archives of the Reich Chancellery. It is a telegram which Bormann addressed to Hummel. It was sent to Obersalzberg[4] on the 22nd April 1945 and reads as follows: *'Agree with the proposed transfer overseas.'*"

---

[4] Bormann's home on the Austrian-German border.

This was the last communication Hummel ever received from Bormann (at least officially), and for Lev Bezymenski it could mean only one thing. Martin Bormann had flown to South America.

18

Two years after Lev Bezymenski's statement that Martin Bormann was alive and probably residing in South America, a reputable correspondent of one of the world's most reputable newspapers, Anthony Terry of the London *Sunday Times*, came up with some evidence that seemed to indicate his Russian colleague was right. After the world had been hunting the missing Reichsleiter for twenty-two years, with at least five different intelligence services participating at one time or another in the search, an ex-corporal in the German Waffen SS came forward in 1967 to offer convincing proof that Bormann was alive and living where Bezymenski had said he was – in South America.

The corporal was dark-haired, pudgy-faced Erich Karl Wiedwald, and the man he told his story to, former British intelligence agent Anthony Terry, was Bonn correspondent of the well-respected London Sunday newspaper.[1] Martin Bormann, according to Wiedwald, was living in the southernmost tip of the Brazil-Paraguay border area, one kilometre west of the western bank of the River Paraná and twenty-four kilometres north of the border with Paraguay – in a colony of his own creation called "Waldner 555."

Kolonie Waldner 555, as Wiedwald described it, was a collection of thatched huts, ideally located in what Terry later in his article called "one of the world's greatest natural fortresses." The estate, which was about forty by a hundred miles, was protected on one side by the River Paraná (ten miles

---

[1] Terry "found" Wiedwald ". . . by his walking into my Bonn office one day after being recommended to see me by another [German] journalist. . . . It was as simple as that." Letter to author Whiting, 1972.

wide in places) and on the other by almost impenetrable jungle, filled with ferocious Indians who were on Bormann's payroll. In addition, Bormann employed forty to sixty Central Europeans as guards, who were supported by the members of the fourteen other German colonies in the area. The latter were prepared to protect Waldner 555 from prying eyes, and even if the newcomer tried to approach the colony from the sea by means of the river, all the pilots who could negotiate the treacherous currents and sandbanks were Germans from the River Elbe, who were also in Bormann's employ. The thatched huts which housed the guards were arranged with military precision around a central courtyard, with Bormann's own house – the only stone construction in the place – to the far left of this courtyard, close to the colony's landing strip and two Piper Cubs, which were always at the ready to whisk the fugitive away in case of danger.

As Wiedwald remembered it, the hangar for these planes was "an open arched shed," and running down its centre was the "colony's pride," an American bowling alley. The ex-corporal did not know where it came from, but he did recall that polishing the alley and keeping it repaired was "the colony's most vital maintenance job." Otherwise there was little work done at the colony. There was much celebrating, with Hitler's birthday (April 20th) the main holiday of the year; at that time the group of fugitives solemnly sang the *Horst Wessel Song*[2] with raised arms and followed it with a wild orgy of drinking. Otherwise Bormann and the rest spent much time in making wild plans for returning to Europe. Once, according to Terry's informant, they attempted to enlist the European Red Cross by means of a well-known German princess, called sardonically by others "the Florence Nightingale of the SS." The idea was to get an international commission to visit the colony and pronounce the place harmless. Nothing came of the idea. Thereafter Bormann gave way to the group's demand for women. At first he had refused to have them on the grounds of their being a "security risk," contending that any attempt to set up an SS stud farm would be "irreverent to Hitler's memory." But in the end he gave in,

---

[2] The Nazi marching song.

and Wiedwald remembered that thereafter Waldner 555 started importing "the Pill."

Anthony Terry, the man who had once worked as a British War Office interrogator of German POWs and later of Nazi war criminals, naturally did not accept the ex-SS man's story on its immediate face value. First he asked himself what motives Wiedwald had in telling him, a British correspondent, the story. Did he want to make money out of it? But the German refused any payment for it.

Was he then one of those "slightly touched" people, familiar to every journalist, who want notoriety and public attention? But that motive did not seem applicable either, for Wiedwald said he did not care in the least whether his name was mentioned or not.

What then *were* the forty-one-year-old German's motives?

Terry wondered whether he was being taken for a ride. Was the tall man opposite him perhaps working for Bormann still, as he claimed he had once done nearly ten years before in South America? Was it his aim to try to convince the world that Bormann was now a harmless old man buried in the heart of the South American jungle, a danger to no one?

But after a while the British correspondent dismissed that possibility. Bormann would not have dared to take such a risk.

Perhaps Wiedwald was really working for the German intelligence service – perhaps General Gehlen's old "Org." which had now become the official Federal Intelligence Service, was using this oblique method of putting pressure on the Brazilian government so that they would extradite Bormann to face a German court?

But the manner in which Terry had come across the Wiedwald story led him to discount this possibility along with the others. Finally he decided that Wiedwald's motive was revenge. The German was suffering from cancer of the throat. Indeed, he had returned from South America because he had found he was afflicted by the killing disease – or so he had told Terry. But he had arrived in his *Heimat* (homeland) penniless; Bormann had refused to give him money even to set up the little cigar store he wished to open in Bonn and thus earn his keep. Because of this, he told the Englishman with the sharp eyes, he had decided to let the world know of the existence of Waldner 555.

It was a plausible enough motive. But Terry wasn't satisfied. For eleven days he continued to question Wiedwald. How did Bormann live? What were his sources of money? What did he look like? And so on and so on.

And the German answered readily and convincingly. As Germany's most sophisticated and skeptical magazine, *Der Spiegel*, was to comment later: "Although the story is not yet proved, it is the most detailed and the most easily verifiable." Bormann, according to Wiedwald, had an income of some fifteen thousand pounds a month.[3] It came from two sources: Nazi Party funds, which he had administered,[4] of about thirty-five million pounds; and the SS funds of about thirteen million. As a result, Bormann could perfectly easily buy himself all the protection in the world from the highest to the lowest level.

As to Bormann himself, the renegade said there were two crucial facts: he was dying and he was unrecognizable. Due to a poorly-executed job of plastic surgery carried out in Buenos Aires in 1947, Bormann's face was puffed up, blotchy, and badly scarred around the forehead. To hide these scars, Bormann always wore a floppy straw Panama and dark glasses. These, plus his habitual dress of wide breeches and high riding boots gave him the appearance of "a typical prosperous landowner."

One thing, Wiedwald noted, was strange about his dress: he invariably wore *brown* riding boots, which were spurned by the SS men (who wore black) as a sign of "the decadent upper classes." Terry thought that "the apparent reason for Bormann's eccentricity may perhaps indicate one factor in his seeming immunity from arrest: the Paraguayan President Stroessner favours brown boots and Bormann admires Stroessner extravagantly. . . . According to Wiedwald, a framed photograph of Stroessner – inscribed 'To my friend' –

---

[3] About $75,000 in those days.
[4] In October 1944, a mysterious meeting took place in a hotel in occupied Strasbourg (France) where prominent German industrialists gathered to discuss how they could save some of Germany's wealth by owning cover firms or accounts abroad. It is often said that this money was used to finance ODESSA. It is conceivable that Bormann might have attended this meeting.

has pride of place in Bormann's bedroom with portraits of Hitler and Goebbels."

Unknown to Terry, he had hit on a significant detail but given it the wrong interpretation. As related to me by Bormann's brother-in-law, Hermann Buch, Martin Bormann had a weakness for brown riding boots. Indeed, one day when Bormann was walking in Munich before the Nazi takeover his boots had been sprayed with red ink and ruined by a Communist "thug." Instead of trying to remove the ink, Bormann had simply thrown the boots away and had shown the amazed Hermann fifteen other pairs he had in reserve – they were all brown.[5]

But what about Bormann dying, Terry persisted.

Unhesitatingly Wiedwald explained that Bormann was dying of stomach cancer, caused ironically enough by "his first hero, Hitler." Because Hitler did not like him to smoke, the *"Bratwurstvegetarier"* had been forced to "furtive drags in the lavatory." The strong tobacco and "his anxiety neurosis" had given him cancer, or so Bormann thought.

This made sense. Terry knew that Bormann had been forced to this kind of evasion, because Hitler hated tobacco as much as he did meat. Wiedwald's story was taking shape and everything he related seemed to ring true. But the proof of the pudding, Terry told himself, was in the eating. He prepared himself for the $64,000 question: *How did Martin Bormann escape from Berlin?*

On the morning of May 3, 1945, as the fighting was finally dying down in embattled Berlin, Erich Karl Wiedwald found himself a prisoner in a Russian emergency field hospital in Koenigswusterhausen on the southern boundary of Berlin.

Up to the day before, he had been a member of the SS Frundsberg Division, defending the Hotel Adlon, a few yards from Hitler's bunker. A mortar fragment had knocked him out; now the nineteen-year-old corporal was a prisoner of war. Wiedwald knew what would happen once the Russians discovered the SS blood group mark tatooed under his arm. If they didn't shoot him outright, he would spend most of his remaining life in some miserable Soviet camp in the Siberian

---

[5] According to the brother-in-law, he bought them *en gros.*

wilderness. In spite of his weakened state – he had lost a lot of blood – he decided to chance a getaway to his uncle who lived in the suburb of Dahlem, where, eight years later, CIA agent McGovern would begin his search for Martin Bormann.

Looking around for someone among the "walking wounded" who would have the guts to make a break with him, Wiedwald eventually found another man in the same mess as himself, but their conversation was overheard by a group of five men on the hospital veranda. They joined in, asking if they could go along, too. One of them, a short, stocky, middle-aged man dressed in the uniform of the Berlin Flak Regiment, which had been pressed into service as infantry in the last days of the battle, and who was wounded in the left foot, did some of the talking. But most of it was done by a tall, blond man in an SS camouflaged smock, whom Wiedwald guessed was a member of the Waffen SS like himself. His name, he said, was Rolf Schwent.

In the end the latter convinced the young corporal that the journey would be less hazardous for a group. So one day later – May 4 – they set off and after some adventures reached their target, an ivy-covered semi-detached house in Dahlem. Wiedwald could still remember the street and the number: *Number Nine, Fontanestrasse.* There they hid out for ten days until Schwent thought "the air was clear." Then they set off for an estate that the middle-aged flak soldier said was an ideal hiding place. It was located in Mecklenburg.[6] But they never made it. The Russians turned them back at Neuruppin.

Back at the house in Dahlem, Schwent and the middle-aged flak soldier decided to abandon the attempt to break through the Russian lines; instead, they planned to move north and join Admiral Dönitz, who was still holding out in the Schleswig-Holstein peninsula. Their plan was simple and daring. They would walk right down the autobahn, heading westward and thus cross the Russian-British lines.

There was no hitch in their plan. Perhaps its very boldness and unconventionality ensured its success: who would expect Germans to attempt to escape along the dead-straight nakedness of the great superhighway? At all events, according to the

---

[6] Could this have been the farm where Bormann had worked as a young man? It is an interesting possibility.

ex-corporal, the party crossed the British paratroopers' lines on the Elbe without incident, thereafter heading for Denmark – for the little border town of Glücksburg. But before they reached their destination Erich Karl Wiedwald left them, preferring to take his chances in the warmer south.

One year later, when Erich Wiedwald had long forgotten about the strange little group with whom he had escaped from beleaguered Berlin and was now working for the U.S. Military Police (of all people) in Munich, he bumped into the tall, blond Schwent once again. Schwent, now grey and pinched with lack of food in that *Hungerwinter*, as the Germans were already calling that terrible winter of 1946 told him bitterly he had had enough of Germany; he had "a nose full." He was going to get out – go to South America.

Erich Wiedwald, who was equally sick of the *Amis* with their big cars, lavish supply of cigarettes, and nubile blonde Fräuleins, shared his feelings, but he could not figure how Schwent was going to get out of occupied Germany. One needed money, a pass, permission – a hundred and one documents which were virtually impossible to come by.

Schwent had laughed cynically and, flipping away the carefully hoarded butt of an American cigarette which some GI had thrown away and forgotten to grind to pulp under his heel as many of them did in their hatred of the Germans, he had said, "There is, of course, the ODESSA Line."

Wiedwald had pleaded ignorance and Schwent had carefully explained the details of the SS escape line. According to him, it would be easy for him – and Wiedwald too, if he so desired – to make their way along the Bremen–Bari route to the Italian port where they could "hop a freighter" sailing for South America. The younger man did not take long to make up his mind. He had had enough of occupied Bavaria and his bosses, the casual, lean, gum-chewing MPs. "More from a sense of adventure than anything else," he decided to accompany Schwent in his attempt to make a new life for himself in far-off South America.

The escape succeeded just as the other one over a year before from Berlin had. Crossing the Brenner Pass into Italy that winter, the two of them made their way to a monastery in Rome and from thence to Genoa, where after some time they "found" their boat, "a terrible tub," as Wiedwald, who was continually seasick on the long voyage to South America, explained ruefully much later.

But three days after they had left the Italian port, the younger man's seasickness vanished as abruptly as it had come when Schwent broke the news to him about where they were really going. He informed a deathly pale, hollow-eyed Wiedwald that the little flak soldier they had helped in Berlin that May had really been a very important man. He, too, had escaped along the ODESSA Line, very much in the same way they had done, save that he had taken a fishing boat from Genoa to a port in Spain, from where he had sailed to Argentina. They were now on their way to join this very important man.

At this stage of his story, Schwent paused and seemed to be weighing his words exceedingly carefully before he actually uttered them. Wiedwald watched his face, nervously, intently, his seasickness completely forgotten, despite the old tub's continual heaving in the green-grey winter sea.

Then the older man spoke. "You should know now," he said solemnly, *"that the man you helped to escape from Berlin was Reichsleiter Martin Bormann."*

19

In those circles still concerned directly or indirectly with the hunt for Martin Bormann, Anthony Terry's report as it appeared in the London *Sunday Times* under the supremely confident title, "The Hiding Place of Martin Bormann," created a minor sensation.

Simon Wiesenthal, the man who had been instrumental in finding Eichmann seven years before, was first off the mark. He met with the dying ex-SS man, but Wiedwald refused to give the *Menschenjäger* (the "hunter of men," as he was commonly called in Germany) any further information. All the same, Wiesenthal was inclined to believe what he had heard from Terry. He told *Der Spiegel* in the same week he met with Wiedwald: "There is no doubt now that Bormann is still alive."

Other authorities pointed out that Eichmann had constantly talked about Bormann as if he had been alive, both before and after his arrest.[1] As Dr. Fritz Bauer, the Hessian lawyer responsible for the German hunt for Bormann said: "He talked about Bormann all the time as if he were speaking about a living person," a statement which was confirmed by Eichmann's son.

The *Spiegel* also reported some new evidence occasioned by the *Sunday Times*'s disclosure. According to *Der Spiegel*, Walter Buch's second wife said that in 1949 her new husband

---

[1] One of the most attractive scoops any journalist would like to bring off is to gain access to the tapes allegedly made by Eichmann before his arrest, which were supposed to be in the possession of Dutch ex-SS officer Willem Sassen (he lived in Argentina). Although the latter refused categorically to give any information about these tapes (if indeed they do exist), in which Eichmann relates his life story, they are reputed to give details of both Eichmann's and Bormann's means of escape.

had been visited in Bavaria by two strange men late one night. She had not heard what their discussion was about because her husband had sent her to bed, but when Bormann's father-in-law had finally joined her, he had muttered, *"Nun lebt das Schwein doch!"* (So the swine lives after all!) He was referring to the missing husband of his dead daughter.

But there was no means of proving that Walter Buch, the former Chief Nazi Party Judge, had really made the statement, for he committed suicide that same year, walking into the lake near his house in despair.[2] Nonetheless, these and similar statements occasioned Dr. Fritz Bauer to comment on Terry's article: "We've had a lot of disappointments [in our hunt for Bormann], but I have a quiet feeling that all our work has not been for nothing. We are pursuing our inquiries."

But what of Erich Wiedwald?

In spite of Bauer's confident feeling that Bormann was still alive, one of his staff, middle-aged, bespectacled Frankfurt lawyer Dr. von Glasenapp, was not so sure. He took the train to Bad Godesberg, the high-class suburb outside Bonn where the diplomats accredited to the West German federal capital reside, and arranged a meeting with the ex-SS man. He did not attempt to bully or frighten the cancer-stricken veteran. Instead, he said simply, "Tell me your story – once again, please."

Wiedwald did so, adding such details as that Bormann had been to Montevideo in 1965, that "Gestapo Müller" was also alive and hiding in South America, running a small provision store with an Italian girl in the suburb of Natal in the north-east of Brazil, and that Schwent, Bormann's lieutenant, had been in Holland in 1967, where he, Wiedwald, had visited him.

Von Glasenapp listened carefully, nodding his head every now and again in apparent agreement and asking a soft little question from time to time. Then when Erich was finished, he sent him away with a murmured *"vielen Dank,"* but no further comment. Two days later he once more summoned the forty-one-year-old ex-soldier. He repeated his original demand.

---

[2] Walter Buch had broken with Bormann early, both for professional and personal reasons. He knew about Bormann's many affairs and, in fact, never met his son-in-law again after 1942. After the war Buch married a dentist's widow who had come to visit him in his internment camp, but he had not been happy with the much younger woman.

"Tell me your story once again please;" then he paused. *"But this time under oath!"*

Erich Karl Wiedwald swallowed hard. The sweat pearled under the dark line of his thick hair. Then he broke down. He couldn't – just couldn't swear to it on oath.

"Why?" snapped van Glasenapp, hard and incisive.

"Because – because, I've –" The other man seemed to find it difficult to get his breath. Perhaps it was due to his cancer – or fear. Then he pulled himself together. *"Because I have lied."*

Yet another promising lead in the now twenty-two-year-old hunt for the missing Martin Bormann had ended in confusion, bewilderment, doubt, and bitter disappointment.[3]

---

[3] Thereafter Anthony Terry washed has hands of the case. But Wiedwald went on to collaborate on a book on Bormann published in Holland, of which Terry remarks (in a letter to the author): "Official German authorities claim his information is not entirely correct." Perhaps somewhat of an understatement.

V

Enter "The Spy of the Century"

At this point I want to break my silence about a secret – well protected by the Soviets – the key to one of the most puzzling cases of our century.

—GENERAL REINHARD GEHLEN, 1971

20

On September 8, 1971, a sunny, pleasant day in that part of central Europe, a grey Mercedes diesel halted at the autobahn crossing-point into Austria. The bored official in his blue uniform checked the passports of the elderly, middle-class couple in the car: Reinhard and Herta Gehlen. Then, touching his peaked cap politely, he waved them on. There was nothing suspicious about the thin, balding man in his late sixties with the narrow pencil line of a mustache adorning his upper lip and his plump, somewhat homely wife seated beside him. Nothing save the man's eyes – they were cold and hard. But the bored official did not see those eyes.

Slowly the somewhat ancient Mercedes picked up speed. The characteristic blue cloud of diesel smoke poured from its exhaust as it reached fifty miles an hour and disappeared over the Austrian border in the direction of the ancient tourist centre of Salzburg. General Reinhard Gehlen, up to one year before head of West Germany's espionage organization, the BND, had slipped across the frontier unnoticed.

As the bored official bent to examine the next group of passports, little did he realize that he had missed a man whose name would soon be on everybody's lips; a man who Horst von Glasenapp, then head of the Bormann enquiry, would soon proclaim in an emergency telecast on West German TV was "sought for questioning" in the Bormann case.

That weekend Gehlen celebrated his fortieth wedding anniversary. He went swimming in a lake near the house of an acquaintance of his old wartime years at "Foreign Armies East."[1] (Swimming had been his habit for years, "Come rain

[1] The Wehrmacht's intelligence organization, which Gehlen headed from 1942 to 1945.

or shine," as a friend commented.) All in all it was the typical holiday weekend of a European of his class and age; a little stiff and formal, but at the same time relaxed.

Yet as the man who has been called "the spy of the century" took his ease that September weekend, he knew that by now his last great operation was under way. Soon the world would know that he was ready to "tell all," as West Germany's largest conservative newspaper[2] chortled. Reinhard Gehlen was going to break his silence of nearly three decades and publish his memoirs.

The news was broken by the *New York Times*.[3] Under the headline "Memoirs Tie Bormann to Soviet," it reported that "A manuscript described as the memoirs of General Reinhard Gehlen, former head of the West German Intelligence Service, asserts that Martin Bormann, Hitler's top lieutenant, was a Soviet agent during World War II."

The article went on to say that the "alleged Gehlen book" stated that after the war Bormann became an adviser on German policy in the Soviet Union and that he had died there "less than three years ago." Martin P. Levin, chairman of the board of World Publishing, which had bought the manuscript for a reported million dollars,[4] the largest sum ever paid for a book up to that time, was quoted as saying, "We are totally convinced that the memoirs are authentic. We are equally convinced that they will create an international sensation."

He was right. The news hit the front pages in magazines and newspapers ranging from *Time* to *Pravda*. All the old Nazi Party members and those once close to Bormann who might know something – anything – were inundated with telephone calls from reporters for the least snippet of news. "London – Paris – Munich – my phone was going all day! The calls were

---

[2] The Hamburg *Die Welt*, which bought the prepublication rights to Gehlen's autobiography.
[3] The *Times* had been offered the "Bormann chapter" of the memoirs. However, the newspaper had not been satisfied with it and sent its vice-president Sidney Gruson to Mainz to see the Gehlen publishers. Here he had demanded more information. He was refused. He told the German publishers "No deal unless we see the rest of the manuscript." Soon thereafter the N.Y. *Times* received a letter from Gehlen stating he didn't want his memoirs appearing in the paper.
[4] The actual figure was $400,000.

coming from everywhere," commented former SS Colonel Otto Skorzeny.[5] Donitz told reporters, just as he had told me a few days earlier, that it ". . . was all nonsense. Bormann was dead." Albert Bormann, who lives incognito in Munich, agreed. Of all the prominent Nazis still alive, only Albert Speer, the publication of whose memoirs had reportedly inspired General Gehlen to write his own, felt that there might be something in Gehlen's story. "One can be surprised by people," he told an inquiring reporter from the London *Times*. "I could not say it was absolutely impossible." Speer, who had hated Bormann violently throughout their work together, continued: "Bormann was a very shrewd intriguer – he made some surprisingly intelligent moves. If he was so good at this, he could have been good at other things."

In Bonn, the West German capital, and in Frankfurt, where von Glasenapp's office was located, the official machinery went into action. Bespectacled Frankfurt lawyer Horst von Glasenapp went on TV at prime viewing time to tell his audience that as soon as "the Gehlen book" was published, its author would receive a summons to appear before von Glasenapp's court and make a statement about his Bormann "disclosure."

Also in Bonn, Professor Ehmke, the minister in charge of the office of the chancellor, who had been Gehlen's boss up to two years before, was asked whether Gehlen had broken his oath of loyalty by revealing what he knew about Bormann now and not previously while he had still been the head of the secret service. The shock-haired, thick-lipped young minister, who was reportedly at loggerheads with Gehlen, gave a brusque "No comment." But it was an open secret at the federal capital that the government was considering whether or not Gehlen should or could be arrested when – *and if* – he returned to West Germany; and whether the government could risk the scandal that would be occasioned by the headlines in the morning papers: *Ex Secret Service Chief Arrested*.

One month later Gehlen's book *Der Dienst*[6] started to appear in excerpt form in the West German daily *Die Welt*. For the most part it was pretty boring stuff – the figures of

<hr>

[5] In a letter to the author.
[6] "The Service" – i.e., the intelligence service.

Russian coal production in 1942, and such sensational tidbits of information as, "We estimated that in the summer of 1942, the following Anglo-American tank types had appeared in thirty tank brigades," etc. But tucked into its pages were five hundred enlightening words about the man everyone was talking about again – Martin Bormann.

Under the alarmist headline: "Bormann Was Stalin's Agent," the sixty-nine-year-old spymaster gave a very dry and unexciting account of how both he and Admiral Canaris, head of the German *Abwehr*,[7] had come to the conclusion that the Soviet Russians were receiving information from a source "close to the top." Independently of each other they had come to this conclusion, upon discovering that the Russians were receiving top-level, detailed information about decisions almost as soon as they were made at Hitler's HQ.

Announcing rather pompously, "At this point I will break my long silence about a secret which the Soviets have kept guarded most carefully," Gehlen went on to comment about Martin Bormann that "as the most prominent adviser and informer, he started working for the enemy at the beginning of the Russian campaign"; i.e., in the summer of 1941.

According to the ex-general, Bormann was in possession of the only radio transmission station within Nazi Germany which was not checked by the Gestapo and the Luftwaffe antisubversive squad.[8]

Naturally the question which flashed immediately into everyone's mind here was, why hadn't Gehlen done anything about the top-level spy?

But Gehlen was prepared for that one. As he saw it, Bormann was too powerful a man to be tackled just like that. ". . . One false move would have meant the end of our researches and our lives too."

Canaris felt that Bormann was being blackmailed into working for the Russians. Gehlen, for his part, felt Bormann was engaged in the nasty business of espionage (which Gehlen had once stated was fit only for gentlemen; they could afford to get their hands dirty) because of his immense ambition and

---

[7] Abwehr was the Nazi civilian intelligence (counter-espionage) organization
[8] In Nazi Germany a special Luftwaffe group was responsible for checking the air waves for illegal radio transmissions.

frustration at the knowledge that he could not succeed Hitler. So Gehlen had done nothing during the war, but afterward when he had first started to look seriously into the case of Martin Bormann in 1946, he discovered two "reliable sources" who assured him that "Bormann was living ... in the Soviet Union," where he died in 1967.

The world had its sensation. Reinhard Gehlen had successfully executed his last grand coup. Now it was up to the journalists, historians, secret servicemen, politicians, and police to put the pieces together and try to make some sense of them. Martin Bormann, Hitler's "eyes and ears," his "most loyal paladin," had been a Soviet spy for over three years, supplying the Russians with top-secret information which undoubtedly played an important role in Nazi Germany's defeat in World War II.

Naturally, all those concerned with the hunt for Martin Bormann over the last quarter of a century knew that the rumours about the latter's work for the Russians went right back to the very start of the chase. Indeed, in most German newspaper archives one could find a dusty yellowing bundle of cuttings on poor quality, postwar newsprint labelled something on the lines of "M. Bormann, the Red Gauleiter."

In 1947, SS Gruppenführer Otto Ohlendorf, who was later executed by the Americans, stated that Bormann was a Russian agent and that he was "voluntarily in the hands of the Russians." Shortly before the capitulation in Berlin he had made contact with the enemy.

One year later (1948) another high-ranking SS officer, Gottlob Berger, had told a court that, in "the opinion of the SS," Bormann had been a Russian agent. Bormann had used his important position to send information to the Russians. Just before he fled to the Russian lines he had ordered (at the request of the Russians) that "all Western European POWs should be shot in Germany so that an atmosphere of enmity be created between Germany and the Western Allies. This would prevent any peace treaty being signed."

Berger was asked by one of the judges why the plan wasn't carried out. Berger did not reply, but his lawyers stated later that their client believed that "Bormann was in Russia and would turn up again one day as 'General Commissar for Germany' as soon as Russia took over."[9]

In the years that saw the start of the Cold War, Berger's and Ohlendorf's testimonies proved useful for a man named Walter Rupp, who was on the staff of U.S. General Maxwell D. Taylor. Rupp told the French newspaper *France Dimanche* on October 3, 1948, that their statements had been proved by evidence given by the head of the SS Secret Service, smart young General Walter Schellenberg, who believed that "Gestapo Müller" was really a Red agent and that he had convinced Bormann to turn traitor. According to information Rupp had from the CIA, Bormann had been behind "organizing some kind of propaganda organization within American-run German POW cages," and that "one day he would return as Reich Commissar in the Russian service."

In 1949, Albert Bormann, "Alberti," who had so hated his elder brother Martin, suddenly turned up in rural Bavaria. (He had been working as a gardener under an assumed name since 1945.) He said that he hadn't heard anything from his brother since the war but believed nonetheless that he was in Russia. The Russians, in his opinion, were looking for everyone save Martin Bormann. *Wasn't that a significant fact?*

This was the same argument used by a renegade Soviet officer who had fled to the West in 1949. The man, ex-Captain Vassily Vassilevski, who had been on Marshal Zhukov's staff in Berlin, maintained he had seen Bormann in Potsdam on April 30, 1945.

As we have already seen, Werner Naumann also stated that Bormann was working for the Russians after his arrest in 1953.

To sum things up, there had been a lot of unsupported assertions but very few concrete answers. How, for instance, had SS General Berger gotten to know of the Soviet order to shoot British and American prisoners? Why hadn't Walter Rupp's statement been confirmed by former German POWs? How had the Russian renegade Vassilevski managed to see Bormann in the Russian HQ two days before he left the Berlin bunker? And above all, a question that none of the informants were

---

[9] Naturally it doesn't take a clairvoyant to see what Berger's intentions were.

prepared to answer: How had Martin Bormann escaped from the bunker?

But now, for the first time in the quarter-of-a-century-old search for the missing Nazi leader, one of the world's greatest spies, a man who had made espionage a modern science, who had had thousands of agents in his employ in the Soviet Union and knew its deepest secrets, was asserting that Bormann had been the Reds' top agent. Did this mean Bormann was the missing link in the chain that led from a cover firm called the Simex Import Company, "manufacturers of the excellent foreign raincoat," located at Number 78 on the Champs Elysees in 1942, to the innermost circle around Adolf Hitler in Berlin? *In other words, had Martin Bormann been the key member of the "Red Orchestra"?*

21

Shortly before 3 A.M. on the morning of June 30, 1942, Franz Fortner,[1] a short, stumpy figure with large, outstanding ears and a huge nose, who was in charge of operations against the Red Orchestra in German-occupied Brussels, was at last ready to strike. It had taken him nearly two years to prepare for this moment. But now he was ready, with twenty-five secret police and a company of eager young Luftwaffe soldiers under his command.

The night was perfect: cool, clear and bright with moonlight. Carefully he positioned his young soldiers in doorways and yards sealing off the whole street in which the spies had their radio station. Then he and his secret police started to converge on the tall, three-storey house, cold and silent in the moonlight. All life was dead in the Belgian capital, stilled by the strict German curfew regulations. Fortner suddenly discovered his heart was beating more rapidly and the hand gripping his revolver was damp with sweat. He was very excited. At long last he would solve the puzzle.

Then it was exactly 3:00. He gave the signal. The door flew open. He and his police galloped up the rickety stairs. Abruptly there was an urgent shout from the attic: *"Hurry . . . Hurry! It's up here!"* Someone had found the transmitter.

The transmitter was still warm. Nearby lay piles of documents in German. Strewn about the floor were dozens of picture postcards, mailed from Germany. But the attic was empty. Fortner cursed angrily. They'd gotten away again!

Suddenly there was a single shot. It startled the three panting men in the room. Fortner jumped to the window and poked

---

[1] A cover name given by Gilles Perrault, author of *The Red Orchestra*.

his head out. "Look out!" one of the soldiers shouted from the cobbled street below. "He's crouching by the chimney!"

The man in the shadows now started to fire back. Ducking for cover, Fortner shouted desperately, "Whatever you do, don't shoot. *Don't shoot!* I want him alive!"

While Fortner clattered back down the stairs, the man on the roof broke a window and fled through the house. Now and again there were angry shouts. Then silence. It looked as if the operator had got away. Then there were more cries of rage from the cellar. Fortner ran down. A group of red-faced, angry young soldiers were beating up a scared, middle-aged man with their rifle butts. It was the man Fortner was looking for; he had been hiding under an overturned tin bathtub.

Roughly Fortner ordered the soldiers to stop. Then he turned to the prisoner. Almost as soon as he advised him he was to be questioned, the prisoner said, "I warn you here and now, I'm not the kind of man who makes bargains. You needn't expect any disclosures or betrayals from me."

He spoke fluent German![2]

Fortner had made his big breakthrough. He had captured his first member of the Red Orchestra.

The Red Orchestra, a major part of the international espionage network which Soviet Russia had thrown around Germany in the late thirties, had been founded by a Polish Communist, Leopold Trepper, in Brussels in the spring of 1938. As soon as the Russians went to war, the organization started to operate in top gear. Trepper and his partner Leo Grossvogel were joined by two Soviet officers, Mikhail Makarov, Molotov's nephew, and Viktor Sukulov; plus a number of German refugees such as Wenzel; hardcore Communists; and one American, the blond Georgie de Winter.

In the year that followed, the organization spread its tentacles to France and probably Holland, too, on the theory that a network is more effective if it does not have its HQ in the country against which it is operating. But by this time the Red Orchestra's illegal radio transmissions, carried out by Wenzel, who was nicknamed "the professor" because of his ability

---

[2] In fact, he was a native-born German Communist named Johann Wenzel.

with the Morse key, had not gone unnoticed. A German Abwehr man, Captain Harry Piepe, had been sent to Brussels to discover the whereabouts of the transmitter; by an amazing coincidence he had set up his HQ (he was disguised as a Dutch businessman) in the same house as that used by the Red Orchestra members for their own cover firm "Simexco." Thus, in Number 192 Rue Royale, the two opposing organizations worked side by side, separated solely by a glass door, with the two heads of the rival intelligence services occasionally bumping into each other in the corridor, to the accompaniment of a polite *"Bonjour,"* and a *"Comment allez-vous?"*

But not for long. In December, 1941, Hauptmann Harry Piepe had his first major break. At Number 101 Rue des Atrebates, he raided an apartment in which he found not only a forger's workshop (complete with German identity cards and Wehrmacht passes) and a radio transmitter, but also the transmitter operator who carried an Uruguayan passport bearing the name Carlos Alamo.

The "South American" soon talked under Gestapo pressure. He was in reality Captain Makarov, Molotov's nephew!

The next day Captain Piepe reported his astonishing capture to his chief at the HQ of his organization in Brussels. The Abwehr boss thought the news important enough to be transmitted to Berlin at once. Looking up at Piepe, he asked him what this *"Orchester,"* as the Abwehr jargon termed all illegal radio transmitters, should be called. Piepe thought for a moment, then he said, *"The Red Orchestra."*

When Fortner returned to his billet on the morning of June 31, he was dog tired, but he did have a chance at last to look at the documents he had captured. One of them stated that the addresses it contained should be hidden from the Germans at all costs. Another and the ones below it ". . . were enough to drive all thought of sleep from my mind. It was unbelievable!" Fortner held in his hands messages giving exact details not only of German aircraft and tank production, but also of a German offensive planned for the Caucasus!

"Obviously Berlin had to be warned," he remembered later. "We telephoned them, but they refused to believe us." As a result, Fortner ordered a car and drove all the way to the Tirpitzstrasse in Berlin, where the Abwehr had its HQ. At the main entrance, the officer in charge of the guard asked him to open his briefcase with the vital documents. Fortner refused and when the former insisted, drew his service revolver and, pointing it at him, said, "If you try to take this briefcase from me, I'll shoot!" That produced the desired effect.

Two hours later he was ushered into the presence of Field Marshal Keitel, Chief of the German High Command, himself. The wooden-faced, stiff-necked general was flushed and angry. He could believe anything, but not this, he told the intelligence man. The messages contained the exact details of the year's major anti-Russian offensive. As Fortner recalls: "As for the hush-hush Berlin address which the Germans must never be allowed to discover, it proved to belong to a high-ranking personage in the Luftwaffe who had many connections in ruling circles. A great scandal was in prospect."

It was. In that same summer, "Arvid" and "Coro," two of Russia's major agents in Berlin, were arrested and "liquidated." They were First Lieutenant Harro Schulze-Boysen, grand-nephew of Admiral von Tirpitz, and Arvid Harnack, nephew of the distinguished theologian of the same name. With them died their wives Libertas and Mildred, one of them an American, who, according to the Gestapo, were both bisexuals who gave their bodies to both men and women in order to recruit them as agents. In all, the Gestapo arrested 116 persons engaged in every aspect of Berlin military and civilian administration. Hitler was beside himself with rage. He told a crony that the only thing the Russians were superior to the Germans in was espionage. Angrily he ordered: *This cancer must be burned out!*"

A few months later, Trepper himself – *le grand chef* – was arrested and by the end of 1943 most of his organization was destroyed or driven underground, although the German *Kommando Rote Kapelle* still operated in Paris until the Allies arrived in August, 1944. Yet in spite of the destruction of this major Soviet spy ring, there is ample evidence that there was still a source of information right at the top in Berlin supplying the Russians with military and top-secret news right up to the end. For instance, the "Lucie Network," run by German refugee Rudolf Roessler and the mysterious Englishman Alexander Foote, continued to send information to Moscow until the end of 1943, when the Swiss intelligence arrested the group; and Roessler's chief source of information was someone very high up in Berlin.[3]

Even when the "three R's," as the Abwehr had named Roessler's three transmitters, had been silenced and the Luftwaffe counter-espionage radio troops could report that there were no more "illegal stations" operating within Germany, the Russians continued to receive the information they wanted. Where did it come from?

General Franz Halder, who was responsible for German operations in Russia in the middle forties, and was, incidentally, the man who gave Gehlen his chance as head of Foreign Armies East,[4] once commented that "nearly all the plans of the High Command were revealed to the Russians as soon as they were drawn up – even before they got to my desk. They were betrayed by someone in the High Command. No one succeeded in blocking this source right up to the end of the war." (In 1969, Halder said further that this statement ". . . wasn't based on documents but on personal observation.")

In 1966, Cornelius Ryan, best-selling author of *The Last Battle* (an account of the fighting in Berlin), said that a German general "told me he once had a secret meeting with Hitler, with Bormann the only other man present. Hitler gave orders about a change in command on the Eastern Front. Within two hours the Russian radio broadcast the names of the generals who would be replaced, who would take over and specific details on new strategy." The implication is obvious.

Obviously Canaris thought that Bormann was the top-level leak, if we are to believe General Gehlen's 1971 statement. But how would Canaris know?

The link seems to be provided by *Oberregierungsrat* Wilhelm Flicke, who had worked in counter-radio espionage for thirty years before his somewhat mysterious death in 1957 in Lauff, near Nuremberg. According to Flicke, he had been employed in 1942–1943 listening for illegal messages between Berlin, Switzerland, and Moscow. After nearly two years'

---

[3] Foote might have been an agent of British intelligence, too. As soon as he had a chance to after the war (he had been "repatriated" to Russia), he fled the country and made his way to England; there he lived modestly as an official in one of the ministries until his death in the late fifties.

[4] He appointed him to the job on April 1, 1942.

work he had traced their source to Berlin's central ministry district. Localizing the place they had come from, he decided that there was only one ministry which came into question: Bormann's Party Ministry, which had its own transmitter, used to send messages to the various branches of the Party. (Behind his back Bormann was often called "General of the Teleprinters" because of the torrent of messages which flowed from his office through the airways.) Although Flicke, a naturally careful man, did not point his finger directly at Bormann, he did name his ministry to Canaris and told the latter the code name used to sign all the treacherous messages. It was *"Pabko."*

In 1943–44, Canaris made some progress in his search for the top-level leak. The Swiss expert Marc Payot arrested a female member of the Lucie Organization in the autumn of that year. In Payot's own words, "After we had arrested Miss Bolli . . . we searched her flat – and found on the desk near her typewriter, in which there were several sheets of paper, a book.

"Apparently Miss Bolli had just been copying a page from the book for other agents – and not, as she maintained during her cross-examination, in order to practice typing because she had now given her job as waitress up and was looking for a post as a typist. At all events, we had the book. Its title was *Es Begann in September (It Began in September)* and it was [the organization's] code book."

The book enabled the Swiss to break the Communists' code, find "Pabko" and put an end to "Lucie's" operation. But the coup didn't end there. Some of the Swiss must have been in German pay (not an uncommon thing in that country in which, as Graham Greene has remarked cynically, "they've had five hundred years of democracy and produced nothing save the cuckoo clock"); for the search (and probably the solution to the code too) passed on to Germany. But then suddenly in 1944 it was ordered to be stopped. The Gestapo gave the order.

After the war and just before he died, Flicke revealed his interpretation of the letters which went to make up the mysterious "Pabko" to a noted military historian, Dr. Wilhelm von Schramm. According to the latter, Flicke said that "Pabko" was a cover name; it stood for Bormann's own abbreviation of his organization, *"Parteikanzlei Bormann,"* i.e., "Bormann's Party Office."

It all seemed too easy to be true. Yet in October, 1971, serious and none-too-serious newspapers all over Europe seemed to be prepared to accept the monstrous supposition that the fanatical Nazi and, in Professor Trevor-Roper's words, "the most powerful man in Germany after Hitler" and, as a result, the most powerful man in continental Western Europe at least up to 1944, Martin Bormann had been a soviet agent all along. "Was Bormann Blackmailed by Stalin?" read the headline in Germany's most popular tabloid *Welt am Sonntag*, while the American *Stars and Stripes* entitled its story "Journalist Backs Claim Bormann Was Russ Spy" (and after all, the "Stripes" was sponsored by the U.S. Army in Europe). Even the august London *Times* seemed to be beginning to believe the amazing story. It headlined its story: "Bormann-As-Spy Theory Gains Support."

Was it possible then that Gehlen's theory was right after all? Twice he had told the CIA that Bormann was dead – in 1953 and 1964. He had not told his various civilian bosses of his suspicions even at the height of the great hunt for the missing Nazi boss. And all he had to base his theory on was the testimony of two sources, dating back to the fifties, who could not be named. *Was it possible?*

22

In the days that followed Gehlen's sensational disclosures, there were a surprising number of people who reported to the authorities or the newspapers that they had evidence which supported the views of the still missing ex-spymaster.

In Berlin an aristocratic lady named Getrud von Heimerdinger, who had been in Soviet custody in Moabit Prison in that fateful May, reported that her Soviet interrogator had told her: "We've taken Bormann to Russia now." Indeed, she had (as she swore on oath before a public notary), "seen through the open door the Secretary of the Führer ringed about by a great number of Soviet soldiers."

Asked if she had ever seen Bormann before this time, she replied that she hadn't, but swore she was sure it was he. She had remained silent up to now because she was afraid of "being put on a Russian black list."

She was supported by "witnesses" from all over the world who, in essence, said roughly the same. But the first big breakthrough came when an exiled Czech journalist gave an interview with a Swedish paper explaining how Bormann came to be associated with the Russians. According to Dr. Rudolf Stroebinger, a deputy editor of Prague's *Lidova Demokracie* until he had fled in 1969, Stalin himself had confirmed Bormann's role as a spy to Czech President Eduard Beneš in 1946.

Stroebinger had his information from General Josef Bartik, who had been head of Czech wartime military counterespionage and a close friend of Beneš.

In 1968, he had repeated Beneš's words to Stroebinger: "If Bormann is living today, he will never be hanged because he was an agent of the Soviet Union." According to the Czech journalist, Stalin told Beneš that Bormann had been captured by the Soviet authorities sometime in 1920 as a member of a German free corps[1] in the Baltic area. He had won his freedom by promising to spy for Moscow.

"This signed statement was completely forgotten until the Russians rediscovered it in 1941," Stroebinger maintained. "Then they blackmailed him into spying for them."

The Czech revealed that the intelligence chief had given him the information during the course of an interview Bartik gave him for a book that he, Stroebinger, was writing on the history of the Czech intelligence service. However, Bartik had asked him not to publish the story because he wanted to use it in his own memoirs.

"Bartik died in June or July, 1968," Stroebinger said. "No one would have believed me until Gehlen came with the same kind of information."

A few days later, *Das Bild am Sonntag* "revealed" that Bormann had been forced to betray Germany because of "his numerous love affairs which often ended with abortions and suicide attempts, as well as his greed for money which he deposited in Swiss accounts and his boundless ambition to take over Germany after Hitler's death."

In Bonn, the West German capital, Minister Ehmke took a decidedly less aggressive attitude than formerly as soon as the Gehlen disclosure had been revealed. He stated that he "could not confirm" Gehlen's statement; but then again he could not *deny* it, either.

Attorney von Glasenapp also took up a less confident posture. It was not possible to question Gehlen at the moment . . . perhaps when his book was published . . . yes, there might be something in it after all . . . .

The world seemed about to believe Reinhard Gehlen.

It is probable that the suspicion that Martin Bormann might have been a Soviet agent is caused by two things. The first is the perennial German belief that they were not beaten in either World War I or World War II by their enemies in battle but by traitors within their own ranks: in World War I it was the Jews and the Socialists who gave Germany "the stab in the back,"

---

[1] This could refer to the Rossbach Free Corps, which as we have seen Bormann belonged to and which fought in the Baltic.

and in World War II it was a man close to Hitler who had betrayed them to the Russians – a man like Martin Bormann. The second support for Gehlen's theory can be pinpointed exactly to an interview which that smart ex-lawyer, SS General Schellenberg, the "on-the-make" head of the SS Secret Service, maintains he had with "Gestapo Müller" in the last months of the war.

"He began to talk about the *Rote Kapelle*," Schellenberg relates in his postwar memoirs. "He had occupied himself a great deal with the motives for these treason cases and with the intellectual background from which they stemmed."

"National Socialism," he told the watchful, slightly bemused young SS general, "is nothing more than a sort of dung on this spiritual desert [he meant Germany of that time]. In contrast to this, one sees that in Russia a unified and really uncompromising spiritual and biological force is developing. The Communists' global aim of spiritual and material world revolution offers a sort of positive electrical charge to Western negativism."

Schellenberg relates: "I sat opposite Müller that night deep in thought. Here was the man who had conducted the most ruthless and brutal struggle against Communism in all its various forms, the man who, in his investigation of *Rote Kapelle*, had left no stone unturned to uncover the last ramifications of that conspiracy."

Müller did not seem to notice his visitor's unease; perhaps he was too drunk. For he launched into a diatribe against the intellectuals in the Red Orchestra ring and how he had never had any advantages, being born of poor parents, concluding with the statement: "With us everything is only half attempted and half done, and if we are not careful, it'll finish us. Himmler is only tough when he knows that the Führer is standing behind him. Otherwise he wouldn't make up his mind one way or another. Heydrich was far superior to him in that way; the Führer was right when he called him 'the man with the iron heart.' Bormann is a man who knows what he wants, but he's much too small to think in a statesmanlike way."

Schellenberg was amazed to hear Müller express such opinions. "He had always said that Bormann was nothing but a criminal, and now suddenly there was a change in his attitude." Schellenberg ended the strange conversation (Müller was normally a very taciturn man) with an attempt at humour. "All right, Comrade Müller," he joked, "let's all start saying 'Heil Stalin!' right now – and our little father Müller will become head of the NKVD."

Müller was not amused. "That would be fine," he said threateningly in his thick Bavarian accent, "and you'd really be for the high jump, you and your die-hard bourgeois friends."

A little while later the SS general left in a state of bewilderment. "I still could not work out," he comments, "what Müller was driving at – but I was enlightened a few months later."

At the time that this strange conversation between the two secret policemen took place, attempts within Germany were being made to convince Himmler, at that time still regarded as Hitler's number two man, to enter into negotiations for peace with the Western Allies. The negotiations came to an abrupt end when one of the messages which passed between Berlin and Switzerland (the seat of Allen Dulles's OSS which was trying to make the contact) was intercepted – by what branch of German intelligence is still unknown – and passed on to the authorities.

Himmler dropped the peace overtures like a hot potato, and it would take all Schellenberg's smooth-tongued efforts to convince him that he should make another attempt; but by then it was too late.

The two men who played a major role in discovering this "treacherous attempt" at a separate peace and a persecution of the "criminals" were Müller – and Bormann. The question is now raised – Why? Out of loyalty to the cause and Adolf Hitler? Or because they were acting on orders from Moscow, where Stalin had an almost pathological fear that the Western Allies would conclude a separate peace with the Germans and allow them to turn their undivided attention on Communist Russia?

Seemingly, (if we are to believe those close to Admiral Canaris, head of the Abwehr), the latter was the case; Peter Leverkuehn, one of the Admiral's assistants who respected him not for his pro-Western attitude but for his obstinate anti-Communism, reports: "He was extremely worried about the situation revealed by the discovery of the Red Orchestra, being convinced that the network stretched into Hitler's own HQ and possibly to his deputy Martin Bormann." According to Leverkuehn, Canaris called Bormann "the brown Bolshevik."[2]

Schellenberg, who in spite of his rivalry with the older-established Abwehr organization, kept close relations with Admiral Canaris, riding with him daily every morning until finally the older man was arrested as a traitor,[3] shared the same point of view. As Schellenberg wrote after the war in his memoirs, he finally found out the reason for that strange drunken conversation with Müller. He wrote: "I discovered toward the end of 1943 that he had established contact with the Russian Secret Service . . . [then] in 1945 he joined the Communists and in 1950 a German officer who had been a prisoner of war in Russia told me that he had seen Müller in Moscow in 1948 and that he had died shortly afterward."

The conclusion we must draw from this is that the reason for Müller's sudden "change of attitude" during his drunken conversation in 1943 was that Bormann had gone over to the Russians, just as he (Muller) is believed by many to have done (though in his memoirs Schellenberg makes no explicit statement). If it were possible for Müller to escape from Berlin to Russia, then Bormann could have done so too.[4]

In short, three of Germany's top intelligence chiefs – Schellenberg, Canaris, and Gehlen – have made an accusation, never made about any of the leading Nazis other than Bormann (and heaven knows the whole lot of them were not without their vices, temptations, and weaknesses!), *that a high-ranking member of the Party was a creature of the Russians – in deed nothing better than a spy!*

Having now established the source of the Gehlen "disclosure," let us look at the facts.

The first point which must be made is that Bormann was almost universally hated at all levels of the Party. The SS hated

---

[2] Peter Leverkuehn, *German Military Intelligence.*

[3] He died an atrocious death in 1945, being strung up naked on a meathook. It is said that Hitler had moving pictures of the death made so he could gloat over them.

[4] As we have seen, the bones of three other skeletons were found in "Müller's grave" in Berlin, and Simon Wiesenthal reports him disappearing eastward in the early summer of 1945.

him because he had eased out Himmler; the Luftwaffe for his doing the same to Goering; and the main civilian minister, Speer, his most formidable rival, claimed that "no one in the party was so hated as Bormann"; in the end, Gauleiter Kaufmann was claiming the privilege of personally killing "the Führer's Mephistopheles."

To the Army, engaged in a life-and-death struggle in Russia, it seemed that Bormann was deliberately frustrating all their efforts to build up an anti-Soviet army recruited from Russian POWs and renegades[5] with which they hoped finally to beat the Communists and which, toward the end of the war when they were clutching at straws, became their *only* hope.

Later, after Germany was defeated, many of these high officials and officers, rationalizing about the reasons for their defeat, came to the conclusion that it was not Hitler who was at fault, nor the soldiers and workers who had fought and worked to the bitter end for a German victory. The man who was responsible was Bormann, who had insisted on treating the occupied population in the East like animals; had refused permission for a Russian anti-Communist army to be set up until it was too late; had frustrated any attempt to make peace overtures to the West in the middle years of the war; who had insisted on scorched-earth tactics in 1945 and a "war fought to the bitter end." And why had he done so? The answer was obvious – or so Canaris, Leverkuehn, Schellenberg, Ohlendorf, Berger, and all the rest who were to follow them, thought; because Bormann wanted to ruin Germany and make a desert ready for the delicate red rose of Communism. In other words, he was a Communist agent, who had deliberately and premeditatedly led Germany to her overwhelming defeat at the command of Comrade Josef Stalin, the Russian dictator.

But why and how had Bormann become a Soviet agent? According to the Stroebinger version, he had been captured with the Rossbach Free Corps in the Baltic countries in 1920. But according to "Alberti," Bormann's younger brother, Bormann had never really joined the Corps, and he certainly had not taken part in the fighting in the Baltic states. And even if he had, why had he allowed himself to be blackmailed on

---

[5] An attempt which had as its motivating force no other than – *General Gehlen!*

the basis of an undertaking he had given as a twenty-year-old so many years before?[6] As former Nazi editor *Direktor* Schwaebe, who had known Bormann from 1929 on and had sat with him for years in the German Reichstag as a deputy for the Nazi Party, told me: "If the Russians had approached him, all he would have needed to have done would have been to go to Hitler and tell him. Indeed it would have added to his reputation. Not only had he been imprisoned for his political beliefs [the Parchim murder], but he had also been a prisoner of the Reds. His stock within the Party would have gone up considerably!"

What other means of blackmail could the Russians have used? According to the German newspaper already quoted, *Das Bild am Sonntag*, the Russians pressured him into spying for them on account of his many love affairs and their outcome. Yet it is well known that although the Nazi Party was outwardly very puritanical, in reality it allowed a great deal of sexual freedom and even license. Heydrich, Himmler's number two man, seems to have had a stable of mistresses and actually ran a brothel, *Salon Kitty*, which was purportedly established for spying purposes (on foreign diplomats) but which also serviced Heydrich and his cronies. Himmler himself had a long-term mistress who bore him two children; and even the Führer had his Eva Braun. Naturally, Bormann had his mistresses (this author managed to find two of them without too much difficulty), and probably indulged in a series of casual liaisons in the late thirties and early forties. According to those close to him, he would visit his girlfriends on those evenings when Hitler sent his "shadow" away so that he, the Führer, could dally with Eva Braun. Bormann also indulged in his taste for pornographic pictures (as did Schellenberg, incidentally), according to information given me by the son of Hoffmann, Hitler's photographer, who probably supplied him with the pictures.

These affairs were widely known among the Nazi leaders (and as we have seen from their correspondence, Bormann's long-suffering wife knew of them too). As Speer, that intimate

---

[6] Communicated indirectly to the author by A. Bormann. All the official Nazi yearbooks state that Bormann was in the *Freikorps Rossbach*; perhaps Bormann deliberately lied to show that he had been an active fighter for Germany's rights.

observer of the Hitler scene, has noted: "There were certainly a good many love affairs in Hitler's entourage and he tolerated them. Thus Bormann with a crudeness that might be expected from this unfeeling and amoral man, had his movie actress mistress visit him at Obersalzberg and actually stay in his house in the midst of his family."[7]

Why, then, should such a man allow himself to be blackmailed or frightened into working for the Russians?

But let us assume that for some reason or other – ambition, greed for power and wealth, both of which he had in abundance after 1941 – Martin Bormann had been a Russian spy. Now we must ask ourselves (a) How did he transmit his information to the Russians, and (b) How did he obtain *military* information, when his job was essentially a *civilian* one?

In an interview with the Munich magazine *Quick*, whose editors had intimate connections with General Gehlen, Frankfurt lawyer Horst von Glasenapp reported on October 13, 1971, that he had talked now with Gehlen. ("I find the General's statement is of great importance.")[8] Like Gehlen, von Glasenapp believed that Bormann had the opportunity of establishing contact with the Russians; ". . . Interviews with former members of the High Command" had revealed that ". . . even after the Red Orchestra died, information from the Führer's HQ had been sent to Moscow with amazing rapidity, via Switzerland." Indeed, sometimes it had arrived in the enemy capital quicker than in the various German headquarters for which it was intended.

As a result, the "Abwehr had thrown a ring of listening posts around the Führer's HQ for six weeks in order to try to find a secret transmitter. They found nothing." However, one detail was singularly strange: Borman ". . . *was successful in being able to maintain the only unchecked radio frequency.*"[9] As von Glasenapp pointed out, a certain General Praun, who had been

---

[7] Frau Schwaebe, wife of the journalist already mentioned, told author Whiting that while "Goebbels exuded sexual charm [he blackmailed many a young actress into going to bed with him], Bormann had no attraction for women at all – at least not for me."
[8] Later van Glasenapp reported that the "General had almost pleaded with him to believe the Bormann Story."
[9] See over

in the High Command, had stated very mysteriously just after the war (by 1971, he was long since dead) that he hoped Bormann ". . . was happy with the frequency he had chosen . . ." and continued, ". . . perhaps the future will show." Did this mean, the lawyer queried, that the elderly general had known that Bormann had had radio contact with the Russians?

At this juncture it is not important for our case whether the general knew or not. What is important is whether Bormann was in a position to deliver military information via this radio.

Bormann was Hitler's intimate and naturally knew most of the top-level secrets of the Third Reich. But with his activities confined chiefly to the civilian sphere, what access did he have to the day-to-day high-level military planning, which was decisive for the conduct of Germany's war?

Of course, he had an adjutant attached to the military, Standartenführer Wilhelm Zander. But Zander would learn of major military decisions in the area of upper-level strategy only when they were in process of being carried out; much too late to help the Russians to plan counter-measures.

Bormann was also very close to Keitel, who with Jodl was Hitler's main military planner. The two men often got drunk together (in private of course, and away from Hitler's puritanical eye). Yet it would be hardly likely that the Field Marshal would discuss high-level strategy with the Party Secretary. The proud, somewhat stupid yet exceedingly *korrekt* soldier would have undoubtedly found it very strange if Bormann had started asking him questions about this highly technical and top-secret sphere. Even his wooden brain would have queried, "What's this got to do with Bormann?"

In the end, a magazine reader's letter came to the aid of those who supported the Gehlen thesis, and explained how Bormann had been in a position to obtain top-level military information. Writing to the German *Stern* that October, a Dr. Gunter Ostermeyer from Bonn explained: "It was Bormann who was in the position to check and evaluate the stenographic records made during Hitler's military conferences. From reports made

---

[9] By very roundabout means Bormann managed to keep control of a radio transmitter right to the very end even in the last days in the Führerbunker. A little-known fact is that he had a small Navy radio transmitting team in his charge.

to me[10] I know that Bormann was very concerned with providing the best possible working conditions for the stenographers attached to the Führer HQ."

Dr. Ostermeyer went on to say: "It is very strange that when it was discovered that there were not enough stenographers available who were loyal Nazis and at the same time had the requisite speeds, Bormann decided personally that stenographers were attached to Hitler's HQ *who had been refused entry to the National Socialist Party!* (Author's italics.) " The retired official ended his letter with the remark that Bormann read through all the stenographic record daily with great energy and "devotion to duty".

One wonders to what purpose? To transmit top-secret military information to his Red masters in Moscow?

As October, 1971, came to an end, it seemed as if even the German authorities, in the person of the official *Bormann-jäger* (Bormann hunter), Horst von Glasenapp, believed Gehlen. In the *Quick* interview already mentioned, the lawyer stated that Gehlen had made an "energetic and open impression" and that he had been very impressed by the general's lively manner. Naturally the latter could not reveal who had informed him of the Bormann contacts with the Russians, whether the two informants in question were Germans or Russians and whether they had been agents of the Federal Intelligence Service. As the little, balding, bespectacled lawyer then hinted darkly, "These days people die very suddenly *of a heart attack or in a traffic accident.*"

Quick reporter Arne Boyer, who was taking down the lawyer's remarks, nodded sagely, but said nothing. He knew well what von Glasenapp meant.

At all events (as von Glasenapp stated): "When a man of this rank insists so strongly on the credibility of his informants and has taken so much care to check his sources, then you can't just forget it like that."

---

[10] Dr. Ostermeyer had been employed in the West German Parliament as an official and had come into contact with many of the stenographers who after the war had taken jobs with the Bundestag as official recorders.

23

As Christmas, 1971, approached, the information came to light that after the Brussels arrests of the Red Orchestra spies in 1942, Admiral Canaris, head of the Abwehr, which had been responsible for the arrests, received a report stating: "The address [i.e., in Berlin] must not fall into German hands," because it would reveal the names of the "four persons in the highest German circles" who knew about the forthcoming "Stalingrad-Caucasus offensive plans."

Admiral Canaris, the cunning, long-nosed sailor of Greek descent, had soon worked out who these "four persons" were: "Chief of the General Staff Halder, Head of the Army Jodl, Adolf Hitler naturally – and Martin Bormann."[1]

At almost the same time that this information saw the light of day, a former Communist spy, long thought dead, finally opened his mouth about the whole affair. He was the man who in 1941 had revealed to the alarmed Soviet High Command the date of the German attack on Russia (they didn't believe him), one year later he had been the first to report in a single laconic message: "To Director. In September, a large-scale organization was discovered in Berlin which was supplying information to the Soviet Union. A lot of arrests have already taken place and others are planned. Gestapo hopes to capture the whole organization. Head of organization and radio

---

[1] When one considers Admiral Canaris's role in the '44 conspiracy against Hitler, the opportunities he had through his thousands of agents and access to top-priority information and his hatred for the Nazis (for both political and personal reasons), one wonders whether or not he was the "mysterious leak at the top." Were his accusations levered at Bormann intended to deflect suspicion from himself?

operator captured." (He meant naturally the "Red Orchestra.") This man decided to tell what he knew about the "Bormann story." The ex-spy, now an old man living in semi-retirement in faraway Switzerland, contacted the reputable Swiss newspaper *Die Weltwoche*. For the excited journalists he was Herr Otto Pünter. But for the Swiss Secret Service agents who had failed to arrest him twenty-seven years before, he was simply: *Pabko!*

When Marc Payot had made his first arrest in 1943 which led to the rounding up of the Lucie Organization, only Otto Pünter, a journalist attached to the Swiss Parliament, and Alexander Rado, a professional spy with the network, had managed to escape the Swiss secret police at the time by going underground.

Then, toward the end of the war, the Swiss had repatriated the Red spies (interestingly enough, via American machines supplied to the Soviet Military Mission in Paris by General Eisenhower) to Moscow. Rado was arrested and sentenced to twenty-five years' imprisonment (he was thought to have betrayed Russia), as was *le grand chef* Trepper of the Red Orchestra.[2]

Roessler, who had first built up the Lucie Organization, returned to his old activity (which makes one wonder if the two organizations, Lucie and the Red Orchestra, were not still functioning in Western Europe): spying for Soviet Russia, this time on NATO.

In November, 1953, he was again arrested by the Swiss police and sentenced to one year's imprisonment. The bespectacled, lantern-jawed former German citizen who had worked so long for the Russians emerged a broken man. Four years later, in 1958, he died and was buried in the Kriens Cemetery near Lucerne. He carried to the grave in the lonely little leaf-bedecked Swiss cemetery the name of his top informant in Berlin. As one of the writers on the Lucie Organization has

---

[2] After Stalin's death Rado was pardoned and became a respected professor of geology at the University of Budapest under the name of Alexander Radolfi, perhaps his real one. Trepper was also released and when this book was written his three sons were trying to get the Polish Communist authorities to allow him to emigrate to Israel. One wonders if the authorities are scared that Trepper might begin to sing if he is allowed out.

stated: "The riddle of his German source during the war has remained unsolved. The question of how he, Roessler, was in a position to know within hours what the decisions of the German High Command were, was answered by Roessler himself with the statement that he had a radio link there." No more, no less.[3]

Of the original outfit, the only man still left alive in the West was Pünter, and he stated categorically to the *Weltwoche* that "Pabko cannot make any contribution to the Bormann rumors. The interpretation of this word as meaning *'Parteikanzlei Bormann'* is too clumsy." He went on to explain that "since 1936, Patko had been the cover name for the most important bases and meeting points [of the Lucie Organization] at Pontresina/Poschiavo, Arth-Goldau, Bern-Basel, Kreuzlinger, and Orselina." In short – PABKO.

The Punter statement seemed the turning point in the public and official attitude to the Gehlen "disclosure." Several continental publishers withdrew their offers for *Der Dienst*, Gehlen's book, and even its eventual publishers had to order extensive rewriting. One of the chief figures involved in its purchase for a major American publishing house was fired and another stated that when a man of this kind starts talking (i.e., Gehlen): "You can't stop him."

The implication was clear.

Gehlen began to lose in credibility. It was asserted convincingly that he had certain ulterior motives for publishing his book with its startling revelation about Bormann.

The first was that in it he was trying to answer the accusations levelled at his former Organization and himself by two German journalists from *Der Spiegel* in their book, *Pullach Intern*. Heinz Höhne, the casual, bespectacled, cardigan-clad journalist mainly responsible for it, had launched a devastating attack on the Gehlen Organization on account of its general corruption, nepotism, sloppiness, and downright inefficiency. Now General Gehlen had decided to counterattack via his book, *Der Dienst*. But perhaps the ferocity of the official Soviet news agency *Tass*'s attack on the book indicated the real

---

[3] Janus Piekalkiewicz, *Spione, Agenten und Soldaten* (Sudwest Verlag, Munich).

reason for its publication. First of all the Soviet spokesman dismissed *Der Dienst* as "a meaningless forgery," aimed at "undermining the European *détente*." Then he went on to state that the release of the "Gehlen papers" had "a specific purpose.... At present there is a clear-cut breakthrough in the direction of the *détente*. Certain quarters in the West would like to block it at any price," and, the writer for *Tass* concluded: "Any method is permissible as far as these quarters are concerned, including outright lies and testimony from Nazi criminals."

The remarkable sharpness of the Soviet attack on Gehlen's Bormann story is understandable only if one remembers that Bormann formulated Nazi policy for treatment of civilians both in Germany and the occupied territories for most of the war. His harsh policies toward the "Slavs" are well known. If Bormann now could be proved to have been a Russian spy all along, not only would the Nazi Party be whitewashed, but the dreadful measures taken against so many occupied territories would be shown to be the work, not of a Nazi German, but of a renegade turncoat working for Russian gold.

In addition, the question would spring to any honest man's mind: *"What kind of people are these Russians who could utilise the services of such monsters as Martin Bormann?"* Surely the proverbial man in the street would also reflect that if the Russians could achieve the almost impossible coup of placing an agent next to Hitler himself, then they could accomplish a similar "plant" once again in 1971. Did they have a second Bormann – a kind of super spy – close to the top in the Federal capital at Bonn? Was there a Soviet spy in Willy Brandt's own intimate circle of acquaintances and advisers?

The major right-wing and nationalistic newspapers in West Germany seemed to follow this line of thought as well. The Munich *Deutsche National Zeitung*, which decorates its front page with a black iron cross as an indication of its ultrapatriotism, thought there was such a man. In its issue of September 24, 1971, it headlined its whole front page, devoted to Gehlen's book, with the alarmist words, underlined in red ink: "Bormann Was Stalin's Spy with Hitler. Who Is Brezhnev's Agent in Bonn?" They featured a picture of Brandt and Brezhnev at their Crimean meeting of that month below a caption which read: "Conspiracy Against Germany."

After praising Gehlen for breaking his habitual silence "in the service of his country," because the future of the Fatherland "must cause the patriot the greatest of concern," the right-wing paper left the question of Russia's spy in Bonn open. But in its next issue,[4] it laid it right on the line, this time in violent red print. "Bormann and Wehner – Stalin's Agents (*see page 10*)".

The alarmed reader, assuming that the paper had finally proved that one of its *bêtes noires*, the ex-Communist Herbert Wehner, a member of Brandt's inner circle and Socialist Party ideologist, was a second Bormann and, turning to the page in question, found that the supposed link between the "two traitors" was not the work of the newspaper's editors, but of one Larisch, who wrote in a reader's letter: "It was highly piquant that both Bormann and Wehner served the same boss."

The nationalist newspaper's approach pointed up the real reason for Reinhard Gehlen's memoirs appearing at the time they did. "The grand old man of espionage," as the German nationalists called him; the "dyed-in-the-wool Cold War warrior," in the opinion of his opponents, evidently had hoped that his disclosures would contribute to sabotaging the West German Chancellor's attempts at a rapprochement with Soviet Russia – attempts which gained him the Nobel Peace Prize in 1971.

The aging Gehlen, whose rabid anti-Communism had been awakened as a boy when he and his terrified mother had been trapped in a Breslau theater by a howling Red mob and who believed in his later years that "there are thousands of Communist agents in the Federal Republic," felt that the publication of his memoirs would be generally regarded not only as an answer to *Der Spiegel*'s accusations but also as a warning to the gullible German electorate of what might happen if they supported the treacherous policies being advocated by people like Willy Brandt.[5]

---

[4] October 1, 1971.

[5] At this point in time it was not uncommon for right-wing papers to remind their readers that Brandt had returned to Germany after the war in the uniform of a captain of the Norwegian Army. To visualize what kind of a red rag (waved in front of a bull) this was for the typical right-wing German reader, we must postulate a situation in which Benedict Arnold might have become first President of the United States.

In East Berlin, the alarmed authorities secretly dug up a grave-yard plot in the hope of finding Bormann's body and thus easing the tension which had been built up between East and West by Gehlen's "disclosure." No body was found and the midnight exhumation was hushed up by the all-powerful State Security Service.

But in West Germany, a harassed Horst von Glasenapp, who had been so impressed by Gehlen's statements a few weeks before, was forced, probably on orders from above, to call a hurried press conference on December 13, 1971. Almost immediately, he announced that he was handing back his brief in the case against Martin Bormann to the authorities. After travelling thousands of miles searching for the missing Reichsleiter and questioning hundreds of witnesses (to the tune of thirty packed files), he had decided to relinquish the case.

Asked about the Gehlen theory, von Glasenapp, visibly nervous and very probably acting on orders, stated that the general had "almost pleaded with him" to accept the story that Bormann had fled to the East. But in his opinion, although Bormann's body had never been found, "there was no proof that he was still alive." As for his having gone over to the Russians, "there is no proof, no reason, and no knowledge of this."

The assembled pressmen looked at each other; they knew what that meant. Although some of the right-wing papers would headline the story one day later, "General's Theory Not Proved Wrong," it was clear to even the most chauvinistic of them that Gehlen was no longer of any importance in the "Bormann case."

Indeed, as von Glasenapp said, though he had met a lot of people who had known Bormann prior to May 2, 1945, and a lot who had reported seeing him after that date, "I have not yet met anyone who knew him before and after that date." It was always either the one or the other.

In other words, the lawyer, who explained now for the first time that he, too, had *"just happened"* to be in Berlin on that May 2, 1945, when Bormann was seen for the last time, was dropping the case. After being occupied with it for three years and eight months, he was finished with it;[6] there "was no possibility of finding evidence any more that Martin Bormann was alive or dead."

Thus it was that after a hunt that had been going on for twenty-six years – one that had covered the globe and cost thousands of dollars – the last official search for the missing Reichsleiter was declared ended on Monday, December 13, 1971.

At last Martin Bormann was dead. *Or was he?*

---

[6] The German authorities had been officially searching for Bormann since 1964. After Bauer's death, von Glasenapp took over the case.

VI

The Man from Stern

Bormann was a born survivor. If anyone got out, it would be he.

—ALBERT SPEER, 1971

24

Great men cannot die.

Whether they are famous, or just infamous, the men whom the public adores or detests do not simply die to be transported away in a wooden box, buried and forgotten in the due course of time, as is the fate of most of us. They live on, mostly in people's minds, but often even in physical form; some people simply will not believe that they are dead. John F. Kennedy, President of the United States, died at the hands of a murderer in full public view. Yet two years after his death, serious writers and serious magazines gave expression to the whispered rumor that he was still alive, completely paralyzed, in a Dallas hospital. And the situation had been no different over a hundred years before when the actor Booth assassinated the great American President Abraham Lincoln.

Ever since there has been a popular press, great men have not been allowed to die in peace. Hitler, Czar Nicholas, Field Marshal Kitchener, Napoleon, Ney – they have all been reported as having escaped death by "some miracle" and to be still alive in a suitably remote part of the globe. And before the time of the popular press, the great man "who could not die" entered folk mythology to live on for centuries; as, for instance, the German hero-king Barbarossa, waiting in his remote cave, sword in hand, grey beard grown through the stone table, ready to answer the call to rescue his threatened people once again.[1]

There is something buried deep in the public mind which cannot accept the loss, the emptiness left behind by the death

---

[1] It is interesting to note in this context that Hitler called the plan to invade Russia in 1941 "Operation Barbarossa."

of the great man. Thus there were those whose world crashed around them when they heard of the death of their beloved Adolf Hitler in 1945. They couldn't take it. They committed suicide. There were others, however, who felt in their hearts that the report was an Allied trick or a cleverly executed scheme on the part of the German authorities to fool the victors. They went on believing that *"unser Führer"* was still alive.

It is not surprising, therefore, that when von Glasenapp, representative of the only government still officially looking for Martin Bormann (as far as we know), laid down his brief, there were still those who persisted in believing that, "Martin's fooled them again. He's still alive, believe you me. . . . Somewhere or other, he's having a good laugh at all this!" Even von Glasenapp seemingly did not quite believe his own conclusions; at that December 13 conference when he announced his decision, he admitted that the investigation was not altogether closed. There were still two lines of inquiry being followed by his office: (a) an official request to the Soviet Government for a copy of the "Bormann journal," and (b) an application to the East German authorities for permission to have a certain spot in the Invaliden *Friedhof* (graveyard) close to the Lehrter Station dug up to check whether it contained Bormann's body.[2]

Thus the twenty-seven-year-old hunt for Martin Bormann was in essence back where it had started, in the German capital, the battered, bombed, burning Berlin of May, 1945.

Most of those who had investigated the "Bormann case" over the last twenty-seven years had accepted the fact that if Naumann, Axmann, Zander, and the rest could get out of the besieged capital, Bormann could have too. As a result, they had started their search somewhere or other along the "B–B escape route"; or, if they had an ample expense account, in the more exotic regions of South America.

Few had attempted to reconstruct the Bormann escape route from the bunker to the spot where Axmann reportedly had last seen him. This would have been what the conventional plodding policeman would have done. But most of the men who

---

[2] As far as I can discover, neither of his two requests has been granted.

had looked for Bormann were of a different breed; they belonged to the nefarious exotic world of espionage or were gifted and somewhat slightly cracked amateurs. Mostly they argued that one couldn't trust Axmann's testimony. After all, he had a vested interest in fooling the Allies. Why should he tell the truth about what had really happened that May night? In addition, any search for Bormann's "remains" in the area in question had been made exceedingly difficult by the construction of the Berlin Wall, another example of man's age-long inhumanity to man.

Fifteen years after Bormann had last been seen, the East German authorities had erected the infamous grey concrete wall to prevent the citizens of the "Peasants and Workers' Republic" from voting with their feet; i.e., going westward. Now the "Bormann area" was within the death zone; and indeed, the first East German to be shot while attempting to "escape" had died in slow agony only a matter of yards from where Bormann had disappeared.

But in the mid-sixties, when the Wall had made the search difficult and dangerous too, a few people did attempt to cover the ground once again, this time with a difference. Now they would try to do the job like good, average, trained policemen; they would look for witnesses.

One of these was tall, exceedingly thin Jochen von Lang, a then forty-year-old staff editor of the Continent's largest illustrated magazine, *Stern*, located in Hamburg.

Then van Lang was a sick man (three-quarters of his stomach has been removed in a life-and-death operation), but his dark eyes behind the black horn-rimmed spectacles gleamed with animation when I mentioned Bormann to him.

"You see, I was in Berlin at the same time as he made the breakout," he explained, eagerly puffing at his cigarette. "I was a young soldier badly wounded in the East and I had been attached to Goebbels's Propaganda Ministry. Yes, I knew Fritzsche and Naumann, naturally. I worked for them.

"I got away successfully, roughly at the same time. But afterward, when I entered journalism, I was always interested in what kind of people the big bosses really were, especially Bormann."

As proof of his interest, he put down his gin and tonic and

showed me the numerous files he has on Bormann, neatly labelled with that meticulous German *gründlichkeit*.

"I spent my twentieth birthday trying to get across a bridge out of Berlin and to freedom. There was shit from the Russians flying all over the place and at the back of the mind I had the warning given me in the bunker by a naval officer that if you get caught with them [he meant high-ranking Nazi officials who were trying to escape with him], you're for the chop. But I did, yet I could never forget the big wheels. In 1949, I had my paper send me to Rome to interview Bishop Hudal about the B-B escape route. He threw me out on my ear. Lauterbach,[3] who was flogging vegetables in Rome at that time, dodged every question I asked him, too. No, as far as he knew, there was no escape route for war criminals out of Germany."

Von Lang stubbed out one cigarette and lit yet another almost immediately. "Since then, I've seen them all. I'm an educated democrat. I know what it was all about – the Third Reich. Yet I could never find out enough about Bormann." The painfully thin editor licked his dry lips and wriggled once again on his chair. Outside a heavy truck went by and shook the dilapidated nineteenth-century villa in which he lived with his pretty blond wife. "What worried me was that the normal civilian police force hadn't tackled the job on the spot to try to find witnesses who knew something about the last place where Bormann had been seen. I went to see Axmann – he lives in Berlin these days. He told me, 'I'm no damn doctor. I couldn't say he was dead or not. He *looked* dead to me – *but I couldn't swear he was dead!*'"

Jochen von Lang looked at me across his second drink. It was nearly twelve now and the traffic was beginning to thicken. The echoing white-painted villa in the street which had once housed the port city's *Prominenz* shook constantly, as if it were about to fall around us at any moment. "It was then that I started to look for Martin Bormann myself."

That had been in 1965, and the German journalist was lucky right from the start. On May 3, 1965, exactly twenty years after Bormann disappeared, a Berliner named Herbert Seidel

---

[3] An escaped gauleiter who was supposed by some (in particular, by Simon Wiesenthal) to have played an important role in the escape route.

wrote to *Stern*. The then thirty-five-year-old worker's letter was clear and to the point. It read:

On the afternoon of May 4 or 5, 1945 (I can't remember the exact day), I was walking down the Invalidenstrasse in Berlin-Moabit, toward the Lehrter Station. According to rumours, there were supposed to be freight trains there, filled with food. At that time I was living in Moabit and was nearly fifteen. As nobody in my family dared go out on the street (my foster father was a member of the Party) I and a friend decided to look for food. . . . We went along the right side of the Invalidenstrasse. The streets were full of Russians. Often they stopped us and said: "You Hitler Youth – We shoot you!" But fortunately they let us go on.

The numerous dead that we saw everywhere no longer worried me. On the left side of the railway bridge (Invalidenstrasse) we suddenly made out two dead bodies. They struck me because of their grotesque appearance. They wore (as I established once again on the way back) officers' tunics without insignia and possessed neither pants nor boots. The bodies – due probably to warmth and deterioration – were swollen up so that their white underpants looked as if they were hanging on a line and had been filled with wind. Their feet were covered with army socks. The special thing about these bodies was that they didn't have any signs of wounds. They lay on their backs and you could think they were asleep. One was, according to my way of thinking today, about 1.65 metres[4] and the other about 1.75 metres. Here I'd like to say that the dead men were of different heights. At that time Martin Bormann was not known to the public . . . so that I can't say whether one of the dead bodies was that of Martin Bormann.

Yours faithfully
Herbert Seidel[5]

An excited Jochen van Lang knew that he was on to something. *For the very first time in twenty-odd years, someone had come forward to confirm Axmann's statement!*

---

[4] Bormann was roughly 1.66 meters tall.
[5] From the original kindly supplied by *Stern* (author's translation).

The statement made by the short, slim, dark-haired Seidel seemed to start the ball rolling.

Soon the German had another "witness," in the person of the retired postman Albert Krumnow. Krumnow now walked with difficulty by means of a stick, but his mind wasn't slow. He was a typical fast-talking Berliner. He remembered the time well when he had been employed at the Lehrter Station Post Office.

"On about the eighth of May – I can't recall the exact day – we were ordered by the Russians to recover and bury the bodies lying about on the railway bridge in the Invalidenstrasse. I went to the bridge personally and found two male corpses there. They were a member of the Wehrmacht and another man, dressed solely in an undershirt and pants. I can remember there was some talk of a paybook, from which I concluded that the man dressed in his underclothes was an SS doctor. But I didn't see any parts of an SS uniform in the area.

"My colleagues Wagenpfohl and Loose were ordered with me to bury the two bodies. We did so in the Alpendorf. . . . Wagenpfohl took the paybook with him.

"If anyone should ask me today whether I saw any other bodies of soldiers or SS men on the bridge apart from the two corpses, then I would have to answer no."

Without any knowledge of Seidel's testimony, Krumnow had confirmed the presence of the two bodies on the bridge. Both men had also indicated that the bodies had probably been looted, and in a conversation with von Lang, the old pensioner had stated, "It seemed strange to me and my pals that there were no external wounds or injuries on the bodies." Again a confirmation of what the fifteen-year-old boy, looking for food in May, 1945, had seen.

Comparing the two statements, the *Stern* journalist von Lang concluded that "when Krumnow interred the bodies, one of them had a jacket on. This must have been Martin Bormann, for the man dressed only in his underwear possessed a paybook. The looters had left it on his body for identification purposes. *But what had happened to that paybook?*" Searching through his files back in Hamburg, Jochen von Lang came across that long-forgotten letter to Frau Stumpfegger written by the head of the Lehrter Station Post Office, Berndt, on August 24, 1945, which we have mentioned earlier. In it Berndt had said: "According to the pass found on the dead man, the corpse is that of Ludwig Stumpfegger." Although the "pass was destroyed" (as the letter went), it was clear, at least to von Lang, that in reality "the pass" was Stumpfegger's paybook.

Hardly able to contain his excitement, Jochen von Lang wrote a dry note to himself in an attempt to dampen his mood of triumph: "But these are all suppositions. Up to now all we have done is to establish that Dr. Stumpfegger is dead. Where is Bormann? *Was he the other soldier?*"

For a time this apparently fruitful avenue of search came to a dead end. Jochen von Lang began to despair. Perhaps he thought that his hunt for the missing Reichsleiter was going to end as all the others before it had – in failure. But then he had another "stroke of luck," as he called it much later. The news of the fresh search for Bormann had gotten about in a Berlin isolated from the rest of the West and hence a city which had become a kind of urban village where gossip travelled fast; and a fresh "witness" made his appearance.

He was Willy Stelze, a fifty-nine-year-old toolmaker who went to the police that summer to report that in May, 1945, "I was working in the Solex Factory[6] in the Heidestrasse. On the way there in the first days of May, I saw two bodies on the bridge in the Invalidenstrasse. They were both clad solely in their underwear. It was perfectly white and fresh. It might even have been completely new – at any rate it was of a new style."

As Jochen von Lang read the testimony, his sharp dark eyes flying from line to line, he could not help telling himself that this might be just one more nut (and already his experiences in Berlin had taught him that the former German capital was full of them) trying to cash in on the Bormann hunt. But he persevered.

"I was of the opinion," the testimony went on, "that the two dead men were important people or at least they were well off. I was able to look at them a little more closely. I couldn't make out any signs of external wounds."

Again the same as before, von Lang mused. Then his eyes hit the next words and he almost stopped breathing

---

[6] A firm which manufactured carburettors.

"On the day that followed," Stelze wrote, "a workmate told that he had found a book in the neighbourhood of the place where I had seen the two dead bodies. It was the journal of the former Reichsleiter Martin Bormann."

Von Lang had found the first reference to the finding of the mysterious "Bormann journal" mentioned by Lev Bezymenski! *Was this the real clue he had been looking for all the time?*

25

Things began to move fast after that. The West German office concerned with the hunt for Martin Bormann, which had already begun a tentative "dig" for the missing man in Berlin, now ordered the working squad of the Berlin police to intensify its efforts. Von Lang now began to follow up the "missing link in the chain of evidence," as he called the elderly toolmaker's statement.

He checked up on the entries in the copy of the "journal," which was lodged in the East Berlin District Attorney's office, and discovered the identity of the missing "MB,"[1] Bormann's mistress of 1943. But he could get no further with Manja Behrens; for the ex-movie star, with whom Bormann broke when neither she nor her brother turned out to be "patriotically inclined," was now a celebrated stage actress in East Germany. Indeed, she had become a "state actress" and often appeared in "anti-Fascist plays." But the "MB" noted in the copy of the journal which von Lang saw seemed to indicate that it was a genuine possession of the missing man.

Now he turned his attention to finding other men and women who had been employed at the Solex Factory in 1945 in order to confirm Stelze's statement. Again he was lucky. Balding, bespectacled Bruno Fechtmeier, a machinist, was discovered. *Yes*, he had been in the factory in May, 1945; *yes*, he knew something about the Bormann diary; *yes*, he could add something to the Willy Stelze story. It was like this.

While von Lang listened with bated breath, the elderly Berlin worker told his part of the tale in his clipped, rapid

---

[1] Is it just a coincidence that both Bormann and his mistress had the same initials, "MB"?

Berlin dialect, interrupted now and again by a loud chuckle and a slap of his thighs.

"At Solex there was a Frenchman working for us at the end of the war. In the first days of May he came in with a dark leather coat and said he'd found it on the Invalidenstrasse. As he was searching through the pockets, he pulled a book out of one of them. My pal Ernst Ott established that it was the journal of the Reichsleiter Bormann. *Ott kept the book*."

Von Lang could again hardly contain his excitement. He was getting closer and closer to *the* piece of evidence which would prove that the other man was Bormann. Where was Ott?

His hopes were dashed when he discovered, shortly thereafter, that Ott had left his wife and gone westward soon after the war. The *Stern* organization sprang into action. After all, the powerfully built, cleft-chinned publisher Henri Nannen himself was interested in a search which could result in a worldwide scoop for the Hamburg-based magazine.

And it didn't take them long to find the whereabouts of the missing factory foreman whose wife in Berlin had not seen him for over twenty years. He was discovered in the little town of Löbberich on the Germany-Netherlands border, in the Rhineland. *In the local cemetery*. His Volkswagen had been involved in a head-on crash with another vehicle a few weeks before. Ernst Ott, the vital link, was dead, and he bore with him to the grave the knowledge of how the all-important journal had found its way to the Russians.

Von Lang almost gave up in despair. He had been so close to success! But again his extraordinary luck, and the *Stern* organization, did not desert him.

One of the *Stern* reporters, Herr Markwort, found the woman with whom Ernst Ott had lived for the last twenty years – forty-eight-year-old Inge Schwandt.

"She is," he wrote to von Lang from the little Rhineland village of Löbberich, "an excitable, rundown woman who talks without any logic. Apparently she is still suffering from the shock." (She had been in the Volkswagen with Ott and had only just been released from hospital.)

But in spite of her confused state, Markwort managed to get Inge Schwandt to talk and tell him her story. She had been drafted to work in the office of the Solex factory during the war. There she had met Ernst Ott, who was a foreman and chief air raid warden. She fell in love with the then forty-two-year-old man, but they couldn't marry each other because at the time both of them were already married.

"In July, 1945, we were walking over the Weidendamm Bridge," she related, when she had stumbled over a black note-book. She lifted it up and read on the first page the name "Martin Bormann" written in black ink. It "contained a lot of numbers and addresses."

The patient reporter here asked politely if she could remember any further details.

The greying woman with the dirty, uncared-for clothes, who did not yet know that she was dying, shook her head. All she remembered was that the book lay near "a body lying on its belly upon a bright leather coat."

Markwort allowed her to continue. "We decided to take it to my father. He is called Kurt Kolander and he is an old-guard Communist. For that reason the Red Army had made him deputy mayor in a district of Berlin. He said to us: 'I'll bet the Russians will give you a big fat parcel of grub for this.'

"My father gave the book to the Russian commandant and about ten days later Ernst Ott and I were called for by a Russian officer in a car and driven off to Karlshorst [the Russian HQ]. We were interrogated for two days and two nights. We were asked about our past and how we came to the book. Then we were released and a few days later we got the parcel of food . . . ."

Inge Schwandt's rambling, often incoherent story was a shock for Jochen von Lang. Naturally it helped to substantiate that there had been a Bormann journal and that Ott had had it in his possession. That was the positive side of the Schwandt statement: she was the fifth witness to testify directly or indirectly to the corpses and the journal.

But her story differed radically from the others. First, she maintained that it had been in July when she and Ott had stumbled over the bodies, whereas the (already quoted) letter to Frau Stumpfegger from the post office had stated that Stumpfegger's body and several others had been interred in May. And second, there was no talk in her statement of the corpses being clad in their underclothing; in fact, she recollected one of them still possessing a leather coat and lying on his belly (not on his back as Axmann and the rest had reported).

Could the body near which she had found the journal have been Bormann's at all?

In his original confidential report to von Lang, Markwort had written: "Possibly she wants to hide something. She certainly could remember no further details. But she swore: 'It was definitely July, then it was terribly hot.'" With this statement in mind, von Lang decided in the end to send another man, Klaus Buchholz, to interview the woman once again.

On November 15, 1965, Buchholz saw her and tried to get her to change her story. She refused. Even the usual methods often applied by experienced journalists, who have seen and done everything and become cynical about human motives, failed to move her. In the end he gave up, writing to von Lang: "Her different version of the place, time and manner of finding the journal is doubtlessly intended to veil the inglorious method with which she got rid of it [i.e., to the Russians] and possibly to protect her reputation too."

However, Jochen von Lang's luck continued to hold. Just when he thought he had arrived at an impasse, another witness turned up completely out of the blue: a woman whom he had thought long dead. On the morning of November 20, he received a letter from sixty-three-year-old Frau Ott, who had learned of the *Stern*'s search from the Berlin papers. "My husband brought it – the journal – home and we leafed through it," she wrote. "Then we decided that I should copy it out. . . . But one day my husband took it with him to Kurt Kolander, the father of Frau Schwandt [about whom Frau Ott knew nothing at that time]. Thereafter I never saw the book again."

Six years later, facing me across the antique table in the high, echoing room of his Hamburg villa, Jochen van Lang expressed himself convinced that the Ott letter was the final link in the chain of evidence. "Bormann's dead," he said excitedly, stabbing a nicotine-stained finger at me, "and he has been since 1945."

I pointed out the strangeness of his theory of suicide. Why commit it on the open street when he could have done it in the bunker?

"But Bormann was psychologically ready for suicide. He

had failed to make a deal with the Russians. He had stopped the Werewolf operation, which indicated that he had no hope of continuing the fight after an Allied victory. Now, after the tank breakout had failed at the anti-tank barrier, he pulled off his badges of rank. For the first time he saw himself for what he was – an insignificant little nobody. It was the end of the road for Martin Bormann."

"But why there – why not in the shelter of a building?" I persisted.

Von Lang shrugged his thin shoulders expressively. "Who can tell what goes on in the human mind? We're animals after all, you know. We don't act rationally in moments of great stress. And after all, in his journal he wrote, 'Attempt at escape' (*Ausbruchsversuch*) and not, 'We are going to escape.' Isn't that an indication of his frame of mind in those last moments before he left the bunker for good? Physically he was prepared to make an attempt, but psychologically he had already given up."

If that "attempt at escape" written on the last page of the journal is genuine, I told myself; and I muttered to Jochen von Lang; "Assuming there is a Bormann journal."

But the man from the *Stern* did not seem to hear. Perhaps he did not want to . . . .

In the summer of 1965, the Berlin police made determined efforts to find Bormann's body under the direction of the witnesses discovered by von Lang, the enterprising *Stern* man.

Neal Acheson, a British journalist, who was present at the dig, wrote about the attempt with cynical detachment:

On the wasteland beside the railway arches on a rainy Berlin afternoon, a blue police bulldozer rolls slowly back and forth. It roars and groans and after each little charge brings up another hundredweight of yellow Prussian sand. Six or seven policemen in overalls shelter from the rain under two trees and lean on shovels. They are looking for the bones of Martin Bormann.

Nothing has been found. Under a layer of ash the sand seems firm and undisturbed . . . the police turn up a piece of iron which might be part of a stretcher . . . An archaeologist who had worked in Jericho is called in to give professional advice.

In the end the police gave up. The area covered several thousand square metres and had changed radically since the time when Albert Krumnow had buried the two bodies on Russian orders. As he confessed to them, he could not remember it exactly any more; after all, it was twenty years ago.

And even if a body had been found, how could one have identified it?

As Jochen von Lang wrote later: "Even if the bones had been discovered, it would have been exceedingly difficult to identify them as those of Martin Bormann . . . normally in such cases one uses the dead man's teeth as a means of identification. But in Bormann's case, his dentist reports that Bormann's teeth were healthy and did not exhibit any special characteristics. There was only one means of identification open to the law. If they had found the skeleton, they might have looked for tiny glass particles from the cyanide bottle (with which he presumably killed himself) in the skull. But if they had discovered these particles after so many years, it would border almost on the miraculous."

But now Jochen von Lang's amazing streak of luck ran out. No body was found, and the police broke off their costly search at the orders of Dr. Fritz Bauer. In vain the journalist applied to his boss for money to continue the search. But Nannen, who had been so enthusiastic at the start, had lost interest. He refused to grant von Lang the five thousand marks he had requested to hire a bulldozer. The great *Stern* hunt for the missing Reichsleiter fizzled out ignominiously. Von Lang's personal hunt for Martin Bormann, which had started so long ago in those desperate days in May, 1945, was over.

26

In those three months of the summer of 1965, the tall, bespectacled editor of *Stern* had done more for the "Bormann case" than had many a professional investigator in three years. He had discovered new witnesses who had supported Axmann's until then unconfirmed statement that he had seen two corpses on the road that night.[1] As he wrote to his boss Nannen in the first excitement of his discovery: "I believe Albert Krumnow, Herbert Seidel and Willy Stelze. They made statements independently of each other . . . Not one of them has any interest in being dragged into the light of publicity."

In addition to the location of the bodies, Stelze had reported that on the following day a workmate had told him that a diary "wrapped up in wax cloth" had also been discovered. It belonged to Martin Bormann. This, Jochen von Lang felt, was the vital piece of evidence which linked the corpses to Martin Bormann.

Yet it must be remembered that *Stelze himself had not seen the journal*; he had only heard of it secondhand. Bruno Fechtmeier had seen the journal – or the book, whatever it may have been – *but he had not looked inside it himself*. He had taken Ott's word for it that it belonged to the Reichsleiter.

Who then was still available who had actually looked into the book? Kurt Kolander was still alive, but he was in East Berlin and as an old Communist might take the official Party line. Any statement coming from that source would have to be taken with a grain of salt. Frau Ott was still alive, yet she had written to von Lang *after* the details of the story had become

---

[1] This does not mean, however, that the corpses were necessarily those of Bormann and Stumpfegger.

public and, as her letter to the *Stern* man shows, she seemed to have an amazing memory about not only the items contained in the book, but also the actual phrasing. Almost too good to be true, one might surmise. Ott himself was dead. The only other witness who had actually looked inside the book (if we are in truth to believe that she found it) was Frau Inge Schwandt.

Looking back at Jochen von Lang's fascinating inquiry from the perspective of 1971, it seemed to me that his whole case rested in fact on the testimony of two women: Inge Schwandt for the Bormann journal; and the last person to see him before he left the bunker, a woman who had worked in close proximity to him for three years and could make a reliable estimate of his frame of mind at that moment in time; whether or not he was in a state in which he might conceivably commit suicide. That second woman was Fräulein Else Krüger – "Krügerchen," or "Little Krüger," as the Bormann staff called her.

Thus, at the end of my own personal six-month-long hunt for Martin Bormann, which had taken me to six countries and two continents, I set off to look for the two missing women.

Inge Schwandt, I told myself, would probably still be in Germany and as I knew her last address, I should have little difficulty in finding her. Else Krüger was a different story. All I knew of her was that she had been born in Hamburg-Altona in 1915 and had entered Bormann's service in 1942. Her last address known to me had been the one in Hamburg which she gave when she swore her affidavit on Bormann for the Nuremberg Trial. But that had been in 1946, twenty-five years ago, and a lot of water had flowed under the bridge since then. She might even be dead.

While I was pondering this apparently insurmountable problem, the ever-resourceful Jochen von Lang came to my aid. From those overflowing files of his, he produced – with the superior grin and grandiose gesture of a conjuror – a green marriage certificate. It was dated 1947 and recorded the marriage of one Else Krüger to a Mr. X,[2] who had been born in Liverpool and whose profession was recorded as that of

---

[2] Mr. X has requested that his name not be mentioned.

lecturer. *In 1947, Else Krüger had gone to – of all places – England!*

But England is large and there is no efficient police registration system for British citizens (and in 1947 Else Krüger had automatically become British by virtue of her marriage to Mr. X). Where would I start my search for a middle-aged German woman who had married a teacher twenty-five years before? The task looked hopeless.

Then I remembered a telephone call which one of my informants on Bormann had carried out in my presence with Hitler's secretary, Fräulein Wolff. At that time I had not paid much attention. Now I recollected that "Krügerchen" had been mentioned and the name of a street. *What had it been?*

Halfway through a sleepless night, I had a moment of total recall. *It was James Street.*[3]

One day later I was on a plane bound for England.

After that, things went easily. A search through the *University Year Book* gave me a list of various teachers with the same last name as Mr. X. Thereafter it was not too difficult to work through the university cities where my Mr. Xs were employed as lecturers, checking with the help of the local telephone directories to see if one of them lived in James Street. All in all, it took half a day. Then I had him! Dr. X, residing at Number One James Street – in that fine old, Gothic university town of Cambridge. I caught the night train northward from London.

Cambridge was beautiful in the winter sun. The thin, brittle rays shone hazily through the aged grey buildings as I drove out to the suburbs where the former Else Krüger lived. I found the house almost immediately; a large detached building in a quiet middle-class cul-de-sac. But no one was at home.

The neighbouring housewives were informative, though. In that foolish fashion of the bored suburban wife left at home with the dishes, the kids, and "coffee afternoons" while hubby goes to the office, they were easily drawn. Yes, Mrs. X was a foreigner. She had not lost her accent. Her husband was a lecturer at the University. No, they rarely had visitors from abroad. In most years though, they went abroad themselves. At the moment they were in North Africa. Thus my immediate

---

[3] This is not the real name of the street in which Else Krüger lived.

attempt to interview the ex-secretary of Martin Bormann ended.

Two weeks later tried I the formal approach by means of letter. The results were exceedingly depressing. My first answer to a request for an interview ran to exactly seventeen words. It read: "Mrs. X is not available on December 30, or at any other time, to answer your queries." It was signed in a barely decipherable academic scrawl with the name of her husband.

My next letter was answered with a few more words but in the same negative manner: "I am sorry that you had come all the way to England to see me, but I had no previous knowledge of your intention. . . . As a matter of principle I have over the years refused all enquiries and offers and I am convinced that my attitude has been right."

This one was supposedly signed by Else Krüger herself, but strangely enough, both signatures were almost identical. Who was protecting whom? And what was meant by "enquiries and offers"? Why was Else X scared to talk? She had been the first person connected directly or indirectly with Bormann to refuse me an interview.[4] Has she something to hide? Did she smuggle out of the bunker a copy of Hitler's will, as the son of Hitler's personal photographer Hoffmann, who knew her well, maintains?[5] *Or did the former Else Krüger know something more? Was the answer to the riddle of Martin Bormann to be found in that quiet middle-class English suburb with its pleasant little pretensions and academic airs?*

A lot of questions with no answers. But I had no further time to spend on Else Krüger; I turned my attentions to Frau Inge Schwandt.

---

[4] Save Martin Bormann's brother Albert who, as mentioned earlier, told me that his brother had had no time for him during his lifetime and as a result he felt "I shouldn't talk about him now. When the right time comes, then I'll talk about him." His attitude was perfectly understandable.

[5] As we have seen, there are three of these known to be in existence. A fourth, that I have suggested earlier I suspect exists, would probably be worth a fortune.

Löbberich is a complete contrast to Cambridge; it is a working-class town, all red-brick and medium-sized factories. But if the environment was different, my results were similar. The fat police official in the town's little registration office was helpful enough. After putting down his sandwich of black bread and sausage – it was that holy quarter of an hour devoted in Germany to what is called the "second breakfast" – he soon found the address I was looking for.

But while I stood at the counter, pencil eagerly poised to take it down, he stared at the red card for a long time. Then he shook his shaven head and scratched his jowl with a thick fore-finger of the kind the Germans call *Wurstfinger* – -sausage finger. "It's no good," he grunted at last. "No good at all."

"What do you mean?" I queried, puzzled.

He grinned, showing a mouthful of gold teeth, once the pride of the German lower-class official. "Your Frau Schwandt, she's gone!" he said.

"Gone where?" I asked stupidly.

For answer, he pointed downward to the earth. "There – she's dead. *She died six weeks ago.*"

After the first shock of finding out that my second key witness was no longer available – she had died a miserable death of leukemia – I decided it would not hurt to go and have a look at the place where she had once lived.

It was not far from the town square where the police station was located; a working-class street, lined with three-storey apartment blocks indistinguishable from the hundreds of such buildings which the German authorities busily erect all over the country to keep their workers satisfied and believing that the shoddy little apartments make them participants in the "economic miracle" of which they are so inordinately proud.

The name of the dead woman was still on the tag above the bell. But when I rang it, no one answered. I rang again; still no reply. Finally I went around the back of the building where I found two people digging in the garden there. The one was a woman with a shock of white hair and a purple face that indi-cated high blood pressure or worse. The other was an older man dressed in the faded blue overalls of the German farmer. I had struck luck; they were the landlords of the apartment in which the dead woman lived for the last ten years.

Like all small-town folk, they were hesitant. "No, we don't

want to speak bad of the dead. Poor woman, she was in such a bad way in the end that I had to wheel her to the police station in a baby carriage for questioning."

"*For questioning?*" I queried.

"Yes, just before she died. The police wanted to talk to her about that business with Bormann—" The man stopped suddenly, as if he had just uttered a dirty word.

I told myself, von Glasenapp must have been so alarmed by the Gehlen disclosure that he had even requestioned the dying woman.

"Did she ever talk about Bormann?" I asked them.

The shock-haired woman with the purple face shook her head. "Never! We only found out when *Stern* published the story. Then the whole place knew. Why, you couldn't buy a *Stern* for love or money!"

"Was she a reliable witness?" I asked.

The odd couple – they were father and daughter, I later found out, although there seemed no difference in their ages – looked puzzled; I repeated my question.

The woman finally shook her white head. "We can't say anything bad of the dead," she said with that working-class solemnity reserved for such statements, although I strongly suspected that streets like the one in which they lived bred gossip, back-biting, and worse.

I tried a different approach. "How was she off for money?" I made that German gesture of rubbing thumb and forefinger together, as if counting coins to make my intention clear.

The odd man grinned, his eyes almost disappearing in a sea of wrinkles. "Money! She was always broke. We were keeping her for most of the time before she died. She was always down here borrowing, borrowing, borrowing." The grin disappeared from his face as he remembered the cups of sugar, the slices of bread, the odd bits of sausage that had disappeared from his own table to the disorderly, poverty-stricken room of the dying woman. "*Pumpen. Die war immer am Pumpen,*"[6] he grumbled.

"Would she have been prepared to make up the whole thing – the Bormann thing – for money?" I asked, trying to get the old man away from the subject of borrowing.

---

[6] Slang for "Borrowing. She was always borrowing."

For a moment neither of them reacted. I thought again that they had not understood my question. *"Money!"* the woman echoed, then abruptly she threw back her head with its brilliant white hair, and started to laugh.

The old man stared at her momentarily. Then, imitating her gesture, he revealed a mouth full of ancient black and yellow stumps and began to giggle. It seemed a strange sound to be coming from such an old man. It rose to a thick, throaty chuckle that threatened for a moment to choke him and reached a crescendo which shook his whole frail body. *"Money,"* he gurgled. *"Money, that's rich! Money . . ."*

I could still seem to hear them laughing at my question as I got into my car and started the engine. But perhaps their very laughter was an unspoken answer to my query about the dead woman's credibility. As I drove out of the little town and its smoky red-brick factories, heading for the sickly yellow sun of the south, I knew that I, personally, had come to the end of the trail. My hunt for Martin Bormann was over.

In 1972, twenty-seven years after he first disappeared, Martin Bormann was finally regarded as officially dead. But there are those who do not believe the official pronouncement and probably never will. Simon Wiesenthal is one. He still thinks that Bormann is hiding out in some remote part of South America. There are others, too, who believed that Bormann went eastward, as General Gehlen said, but they believe Bormann did not die a few years ago as the cold-eyed spymaster maintains.

If he was really dead (and the decisive link between the two corpses on the bridge and Martin Bormann is the journal – the "Bormann diary"), then his bones must be mouldering somewhere in the Lehrter Station area.[7] But where exactly?

The area is full of cemeteries and mass graves dating from the last days of the war. For some of the hunters there is, however, only one place where the missing Reichsleiter could

---

[7] In his December 13 announcement, van Glasenapp stated that the death thesis received a certain confirmation, by the finding of the diary on the part of a Frenchman employed at the Solex factory. This French POW, usually called "Maurice," has never been found in spite of tremendous exertions on the part of *Stern* in France, aided by French POW organizations. No "Maurice" has ever been found, regardless of what van Glasenapp says.

be buried – in the same mass grave that houses the bones of Professor Klaus Haushofer, ordered shot by no less a person than "Gestapo" Müller himself.[8]

Strangely enough, Professor Haushofer was no less a person than the man who in 1941 advised Rudolf Hess to fly to England to try to convince Churchill to make peace with Nazi Germany. Thus he indirectly ensured that the obscure secretary to Rudolf Hess became Hitler's number two man. So – by some obscene coincidence – it could be that the bones of Martin Bormann are mingled with those of the learned professor whose advice so long ago brought Bormann to power. An odd coincidence in a twenty-seven-year-old hunt that is rich indeed in odd coincidences.

---

[8] He was arrested for the second time (the first time was after Hess's flight) for his role in the July, 1944, plot against Hitler's life.

The Final Solution

"The bad jokes of Fortune. Village pierrots yesterday, arbiters of life and death today, tomorrow keepers of the public latrines."

—JUVENAL

Berlin, 1972, still a divided city, was not a very happy place. The one-time capital of the Third Reich was isolated and divided into four sectors, split by the infamous "Berlin Wall". In essence it was a dying, backward-looking metropolis, full of old men and women who got drunk in the street-corner pubs on beer and gin before 9 o'clock in the morning. The vibrant life which had once animated the great city appeared to have vanished.

But there were attempts to keep the former capital going, although no one wanted to invest much money in a place that was isolated in the heart of the communist German Democratic Republic, one that the Red Army could take in thirty mintues if it wished. One such building project was an exhibition park being built just opposite the site of the Lehrter railway station from which the *Prominenz* had started the second stage of their escape back in May, 1945. There, on one snowy morning that winter of 1972, workmen excavating the foundations for the future exhibition park swiftly stopped their excavator when its shovel uncovered something white in the disturbed soil. They had been in the war and knew what it was – a skeleton, in fact two skeletons.

The police were soon called. The detectives saw that one of the skeletons belonged to an extremely tall man, at least 1.90 metres in height. The other was much smaller, just 1.70 metres. And both had glass cyanide-tube splinters, such as those used by suicides, in their jawbones. The two skeletons and a piece of jawbone, broken off presumably by the excavator, were removed to a laboratory in Berlin-Tempelhof for possible identification.

The forensic scientists realized that the skeletons had been under the earth for a long time. They concluded too that, as they could find no other sign of injuries, the two men had taken poison. It was then that someone told them that, seven years earlier, a retired postal worker, Albert Krumnow, had claimed that he had buried the bodies of Martin Bormann and Dr Ludwig Stumpfegger in this very area, indeed only twelve metres away from where the skeletons had been unearthed.

Immediately attempts were made to match the skeletons with what was known of Bormann's and Stumpfegger's medical and dental records. The heights were exact. Two of Bormann's sons told the investigating officials that their father had broken his collarbone whilst out riding in 1939 when he had fallen off his horse. The skeleton of the smaller man showed that he, too, had broken his collarbone at some time.

Did this mean that this was Bormann's skeleton? Had the long hunt ended at last? The researchers needed Bormann's dental records as a clincher. They knew that Hitler's and Bormann's dentist, Dr Blaschke, had made a chart of Bormann's teeth for the Americans immediately after the war. They knew, too, that the dental laboratory technician, Fritz Echtmann, was still alive and could identify the teeth from the chart, for he had carried out the work on bridges for Dr Blaschke. But where was the chart?

In the end that well known British revisionist historian (some would say infamous) David Irving took a hand in the investigation. With that talent of his for finding missing documents, he discovered those charts in the USA. A comparison was made and Fritz Echtmann stated categorically that Bormann's chart matched the teeth of the skeleton.

Still the authorities were not completely satisfied. The German examining judge wanted to be absolutely certain. The hunt for the missing *Reichsleiter* had been going on for too long. He asked for a photomontage to be made on a face, based on the skull. It was done. It looked remarkably like surviving photos of Bormann's face back in 1945. The examining judge took it one step further. He ordered a plastic reconstruction of the head to be made from the skull. This was slow, painstaking work that only few experts can undertake. But when it was completed even the most sceptical couldn't deny that the bust looked remarkably like Bormann. There was that balding, receding forehead, the long nose, the pugnacious jaw. There was no doubt about it. The examining judge knew the investigation was at an end. The skeleton belonged to Bormann. Knowing there was no way out of a dying Berlin, knowing there was no future for him in a post-war world, he had done what others of the Nazi *Prominenz* had done; he had taken cyanide.

In September, 1973, ironically enough at the same time that a spokesman for Paramount Studios announced that the film makers had bought the rights of American–Hungarian author Ladislas Farago's account of how he, personally, had met Bormann in the jungles of Paraguay, the examining judge made an announcement of his own. It was couched in that dry official prose of German officialdom. Dated 24 September, 1973, it read:

"*Certificate*

The burial of the skeleton of Reichsleiter Bormann, found on 7/8th December in Berlin(West) on the terrain of the Ulap site in the Invalidenstrasse is authorized. Cremation will not be allowed.

(signed) Richter."

The running man had stopped running at last.

Bibliography

Lev Bezymenski, *Auf den Spuren von Martin Bormann*. Zurich, Aurora Verlag, 1965.

E. Cookridge, *Gehlen: Spy of the Century*. London, Hodder & Stoughton, 1972.

Reinhard Gehlen, *The Service: The Memoirs of General Reinhard Gehlen*, David Irving, tr. New York, World, 1972.

Hoehne & Zolling, *The General Was a Spy*. London, Secker & Warburg, 1972.

Erich Kuby, *Die Russen In Berlin, 1945*. Munich, Schersverlag, 1965.

W. Ludde-Neurath, *Regierung Dönitz*. Göttingen, Musterschmidt-Verlag, 1964.

James McGovern, *Martin Bormann*. London, Arthur Barker, 1968.

Gilles Perrault, *The Red Orchestra*. London, Mayflower, 1968.

Walter Schellenberg, *The Labyrinth*. London, Harper, 1956.

Albert Speer, *Inside the Third Reich*. New York, Macmillan, 1970.

John Toland, *The Last 100 Days*. New York, Random House, 1965.

Hugh R. Trevor-Roper, The Last Days of Hitler. London, Macmillan, 1947.

Hugh R. Trevor-Roper, ed., *The Bormann Letters*. London, Weidenfeld & Nicholson, 1954.

Andrew Tully, *The Central Intelligence Agency: The Inside Story*. N. Y., Morrow, 1962.

K. Wahl, *Es ist das deutsche Herz*. Published by the author, 1954.

Charles Whiting, *Gehlen: Germany's Master Spy*. New York, Ballantine Books, 1972.

Charles Whiting, *Hitler's Werewolves*. New York, Stein & Day, 1972.

Josef Wulf, *Martin Bormann: Hitlers Schatten*. Gütersloh, Bertelsmann, 1963.